University of Limerick

This book is based on the second phase of a research project commissioned by the Department of Enterprise and Employment and conducted by Faculty at the Department of Personnel and Employment Relations, College of Business, University of Limerick. Phase I of this project was published under the title *Continuity and Change in Irish Employee Relations* (Oak Tree Press, 1994).

Irish Studies in Management

Editors:

W.K. Roche
Graduate School of Business
University College Dublin

David Givens
Oak Tree Press

Irish Studies in Management is a new series of texts and research-based monographs covering management and business studies. Published by Oak Tree Press in association with the Graduate School of Business at University College Dublin, the series aims to publish significant contributions to the study of management and business in Ireland, especially where they address issues of major relevance to Irish management in the context of international developments, particularly within the European Union. Mindful that most texts and studies in current use in Irish business education take little direct account of Irish or European conditions, the series seeks to make available to the specialist and general reader works of high quality which comprehend issues and concerns arising from the practice of management and business in Ireland. The series aims to cover subjects ranging from accountancy to marketing, industrial relations/human resource management, international business, business ethics and economics. Studies of public policy and public affairs of relevance to business and economic life will also be published in the series.

Industrial Relations and the New Order

Case Studies in Conflict and Co-operation

Thomas Turner

Michael Morley

with

Juliet MacMahon

Kieran Foley

Patrick Gunnigle

Oak Tree Press

Dublin

in association with

Graduate School of Business

University College Dublin

Oak Tree Press
Merrion Building
Lower Merrion Street
Dublin 2, Ireland

A catalogue record of this book is
available from the British Library.

ISBN 1-86076-016-3

Printed in Ireland by Colour Books Ltd.

CONTENTS

LIST OF CONTRIBUTORS

THOMAS TURNER lectures in industrial relations and organisational behaviour at the Department of Personnel and Employment Relations, University of Limerick. His research interests include the impact of market deregulation on human resource management strategies and employee behaviour, and the economic and social effect of trade unions at the firm level.

MICHAEL MORLEY lectures in personnel management and industrial relations at the Department of Personnel and Employment Relations, University of Limerick, where he is also Institute of Personnel and Development Course Tutor. His research interests include industrial relations in the Irish food industry, high-performance work design and expatriate adjustment.

KIERAN FOLEY is former research assistant and graduate of the Master of Business Studies Degree of the University of Limerick. Currently employed as a personnel specialist in a leading multi-national company, his research interests include the nature and role of the personnel function, labour market flexibility and reward systems.

PATRICK GUNNIGLE is Senior Lecturer in industrial relations and personnel management at the University of Limerick where he is also Head of the Department of Personnel and Employment Relations. He has written five major textbooks on aspects of personnel management and industrial relations in Ireland. Among his current research interests are employee relations in greenfield sites and the individualisation of the employment relationship.

JULIET MacMAHON lectures in personnel management and industrial relations at the University of Limerick. Her main research interests include industrial relations and human resource management in small firms, and quality and continuous improvement in small/medium enterprises.

LIST OF TABLES

LIST OF FIGURES

ACKNOWLEDGEMENTS

This book represents the culmination of the second phase of a research project funded by the Department of Enterprise and Employment. Many individuals assisted in bringing this research to fruition, in particular the overall project advisors, Patrick Gunnigle and Patrick Flood.

The authors would like to acknowledge the contribution of the companies involved in the research and the individuals who participated in the study. In particular, we would like to thank the personnel managers, shop stewards and union officials interviewed during the course of the research, and also the many employees who completed the survey questionnaire which provided much of the material for the book.

A number of colleagues from the Department of Personnel and Employment Relations — Daryl D'Art, Patrick Flood, Patrick Gunnigle, Noreen Heraty and Joe Wallace — provided valuable comments on an earlier draft of the manuscript, while Deirdre O'Dwyer and Geraldine Flanagan provided the administrative and data-processing skills.

We would like to thank staff at the Department of Enterprise and Employment and the Labour Relations Commission for initiating and co-ordinating the research. Especially helpful were Damien White, Martin Territt, Padraig Cullinane, Cathal O'Gorman, Kieran Mulvey, Sean Healy and Jim Palmer.

Finally, we would like the thank the editors of the series "Irish Studies in Management", Professor W.K. Roche, University College Dublin, and David Givens of Oak Tree Press.

Thomas Turner
Michael Morley
Department of Personnel
& Employment Relations
University of Limerick

Chapter 1

INTRODUCTION

There are, as Salamon (1987) notes, as many definitions of the subject area of industrial relations as there are writers on industrial relations. Traditional definitions of industrial relations stress the rules governing the employment relationship in the workplace as the core focus of the subject. Dunlop (1958), for example, defines industrial relations as the study of employment rules and their variation over time. This definition set a broad and integrated agenda for the study of industrial relations which dominated industrial relations research for almost three decades. According to Dunlop, management, unions and government agencies establish a network of rules to govern the workplace and the work community. This network of rules consists of procedures for establishing rules and the procedures for deciding their application to particular situations. In a unionised company, collective bargaining between union and management is a recognised procedure for establishing rules governing the employment relationship, and the resulting collective agreement establishes the application of the rules to particular situations. Substantive rules are the output from the collective bargaining process and Dunlop divided these into three categories:

1. The rules governing compensation in all its forms

2. The duties and performance expected from workers

3. The rules defining the rights and duties of workers regarding promotions, lay-offs and the deployment of workers to particular positions or jobs.

Since substantive rules are viewed as a function of the procedural process, Dunlop (1958: 13) argues that the establishment of procedures and rules is the "centre of attention in an industrial relations system". The central task of industrial relations scholars, therefore, was to explain why a particular set of rules was established and how those rules were administered. The actual content of these rules varies across firms and industries as a consequence chiefly of their market and technological contexts.

Over time, the rules alter as a result of changes in the external environment in areas such as: the business cycle, technology, the distribution of power in the wider society, employer labour strategies, and government agencies. In short, the study of industrial relations is concerned with who makes the rules governing worker–management relations in the workplace, the nature of those rules, and how they are administered and regulated. Variation in how the rules are made — who makes them and the content of the rules — is deemed to be a central concern to industrial relations scholars in distinguishing different approaches between firms, industries and national industrial relations systems. This emphasis on rule-making as the central feature of industrial relations represents one of the most distinctive and enduring features of industrial relations research and debate. It is reflected in Flanders' (1965: 4) definition of industrial relations "as a study of the institutions of job regulation". While various criticisms have been levelled at Flanders' definition of industrial relations (Bain and Clegg, 1974; Woods et al., 1975), the essential focus remains the making and administering of the rules which regulate employment relationships (see Salamon, 1987). The various workplace industrial relations surveys, the most significant body of research carried out in Britain during the 1980s, reflect this traditional focus on procedural and substantive workplace rules.

As a result of the emphasis on the procedural nature of industrial relations and, to a lesser extent, substantive outputs, little attention has been directed at the actual process of industrial relations, that is, the nature of the relationship between management and workers as a result of the rule-making activities. As Roche (1986) observes, Dunlop's system is geared literally to the study of rules alone and ignores or overlooks other social processes in an organisation, such as the balance of power between unions and managements, the issue of control in the workplace, and levels of trust between the parties. A cogent and long-standing criticism of this approach, in particular the emphasis on procedural rules, is that it is more concerned with a descriptive approach in explaining how unions and management work within given rules and institutions than with seeking to explain why employment relations develop as they do (see Margerison, 1969).

However, economic developments since the 1970s have served to focus the study of industrial relations more closely on employment relations. Three sets of economic influence have exerted pressure on industrial relations in the developed industrial countries since the 1970s. First, macroeconomic forces that determine domestic wage and price changes are increasingly affected by expanding global competition in product markets; secondly, with regard to the structure of financial markets, the market for corporate control and access to capital is increasingly emphasising short-term returns to capital over long-term development, particularly in the United States and the UK; finally, technological change, primarily production function influences, has changed the optimum scale and nature of production (Mitchell and Zaidi, 1991). In particular, the inter-relationship between technological developments and increased competition is viewed by some academic commentators as rendering traditional mass production systems and their supporting institutions redundant (Piore and Sabel, 1984; Marshall, 1992). While the standardised mass-production system was production driven, the competitive environment of the 1990s is largely consumer driven. The altered economic conditions of the 1980s and 1990s, Marshall claims, do not just change the "magnitude" of the requirements for economic success, but also alter the necessary structures and policies. These new structures and policies centre on developing three key factors at firm level: product quality, productivity and labour flexibility.

According to Piore and Sabel (1984), these developments herald a new industrial revolution and a major restructuring of capitalism. The economic viability of firms depends on their ability to restructure in order to withstand increased global competition and the fragmentation of mass markets. In the 1970s and

1980s, both firms and national economies that were capable of offering more diverse and customised products fared better than more traditional producers of standardised mass products (Streeck, 1992). Firms that are flexible enough to engage in small-batch or customised production can command higher profit margins and are less vulnerable in their market position. Alternatively, traditional producers of standardised mass products faced greater competition from low-cost economies in developing countries, particularly in the area of labour costs. Labour-intensive industries, such as textiles, are especially vulnerable to this type of competition. In general, Piore and Sabel (1984) argue, firms that compete in standardised mass markets must be able to reduce wages and operation costs in order to survive. Whereas firms involved in producing for discrete or specialised market segments are able to give employees significant benefits in the form of enhanced employment security and high wage levels (Tailby and Whitson, 1989). Consequently, firms require new systems of work organisation, employment contracts and working time arrangements to provide the flexibility necessary to adjust to the recessionary conditions of the 1980s (Rubery and Wilkinson, 1994) and to the fragmentation of mass markets. This holds regardless of whether a firm is competing on the basis of low costs or product innovation and quality. In either case, labour flexibility is essential, albeit in different forms. The impact of these economic and organisational changes on employment relations has been vigorously debated, regarding the extent to which a new type of industrial relations has emerged where, in the face of external market pressures, management and unions collaborate and employees exhibit a new realism, which reflects their acceptance of the link between market forces and their employment conditions.

NEW INDUSTRIAL RELATIONS

Hyman (1989) argues that it is the increasingly competitive and vulnerable nature of product markets, rather than the threat of unemployment in the exposed sector of the economy, which is creating a "new realism" among workers concerning the fragility of their jobs and living standards. Roche and Larraghy's (1990) study of the determinants of annual trade union growth (1930–

84) indicated that unemployment had little effect on employees' disposition to unionise. They suggest that employees and employers may have become "inured" to prevailing rates of high average unemployment, which, in effect, may reduce the deterrence effect of unemployment. In any case, the key factors related to union growth were the rate of change in earnings and the rate of change in the actual number of people at work. Both of these factors, earnings and the number employed, are clearly related to product market considerations in the exposed sector of the economy. New realism according to Hyman (1989: 196) "represents an acceptance or even the active pursuit of forms of production organisation which sustain the employees' market position". However, the consequences of adoption by employees of this "new realism" affects not just the substantive aspects of the employment relationship, but also the procedural aspects including union organisation. In practice, it is impossible to separate industrial relations institutions from the organisation of production, particularly in times of fundamental change in the organisation of work (Terry, 1989). According to Terry (1989) there are two opposing views in relation to substantive changes in the way that work is organised. The first maintains that workers left in traditional full-time employment in manufacturing-based unions are broadly exerting the same level of influence in the introduction of new technology, work organisation and flexibility as previously. The alternative view is that a new realism, as described above, has arrived, where workers must accept and adapt to the new realities of an increasingly complex and competitive environment.

New Realism on the Shopfloor

A number of difficulties arise in analysing whether in fact such a shift is occurring in the conduct of industrial relations. Firstly, there are difficulties in measuring the complex factors involved which include: changes in managerial strategies; employee values and attitudes; employment practices and the interaction of management and labour. Few research agendas can encompass all of these areas, with the result that reliance is placed mainly on the inevitably limited number of case studies (see Storey, 1989; 1992). While the various Workplace Industrial Relations Surveys

(WIRS) are comprehensive and make an invaluable contribution to changes in industrial relations in Britain, they do not provide data on employee attitudes or patterns of labour–management relations. Secondly, there is the need to provide a theoretical framework which can explain the shift in industrial relations which goes beyond the simple shopping-basket list of causes such as demographic changes, labour-market changes, product-market changes, levels of education, the search for more satisfying work, economic recession, consumer sophistication and managerial values/ideology. Such a framework must specify the essential concepts and the relationships between the concepts in order to provide an explanation of the shift in industrial relations. Terry's (1989) analysis of change in shop-floor industrial relations is an attempt to provide such a framework and represents a major advance on the previous, and usually all-embracing, recipe approaches to specifying cause and effect relationships. He argues that the principle component driving the logic of change in industrial relations is the role of the product market, which structures, managerial strategies, the dynamics of shop-floor industrial relations and the response of shop-floor unionism (see Figure 1.1).

Figure 1.1: Markets and the Logic of Change in Industrial Relations

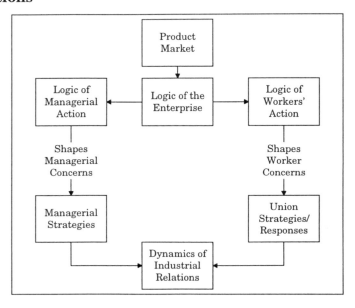

The logic of the enterprise is defined by the demands of the product market, which are a function chiefly of the level of competition, the technology of the enterprise and the necessity for product and quality innovation. In turn, the logic of the enterprise is the source which structures both the logic of managerial action and the logic of workers' action. Product markets in the 1960s and 1970s (compared to the 1980s) were less competitive and exerted little pressure on companies, and the emphasis was on producing as much as possible. The logic of the old industrial relations developed within a particular economic context of growth and stability accompanied by relatively slow technological change and production innovation. In this situation, the concerns of workers and shop-floor unionism focused on the distribution of the surplus from production in terms of improving basic earning, bonuses, overtime and fringe benefits such as pensions and sick-pay schemes. At the same time, shop stewards and workers vigorously defended the gains won and the status quo (such as customs and practice) from any encroachment by management. Given workers' priorities, these actions had a clear logic and also reflected managerial priorities of ensuring production scheduling at all costs and, as a consequence, giving priority to achieving stability in industrial relations. There was no obvious rationale for workers or their unions to concern themselves with the logic of the enterprise — that is, with the methods of production or the external product market — except to the extent that they impinged on issues of distribution.

Changes in product markets, such as increasing competitiveness, higher quality standards and consumer sophistication are now exerting pressures on companies, which have altered the logic that connected actors, actions and goals to a new logic that calls for a different course of action. The consequence of this logic is the emergence of a new set of employee attitudes towards the market (a new realism) and more co-operative patterns of labour–management relations (the new industrial relations). However, while the pressures of the market provide positive reasons to management to reduce labour costs, expand market share, increase profits and grasp new opportunities to introduce change, they provide, at least initially, negative reasons for worker

acceptance of the reorganisation of production in order to retain their earnings and remain in a job. Furthermore, market
pressures make clear the link between worker efforts, company
fortunes, employee earnings and employment security which
demands a logic of action that is fundamentally different from
past behaviour. New realism is simply the realisation among
workers and their unions that jobs and working conditions are, in
the first instance, dependent on market forces. Earnings and
security of employment are seen as contingent on company performance in the market, which in turn often demands change in
the way that work is organised and the level of effort required
from workers.

More complex technology, requiring closer monitoring and
attention, sophisticated quality systems and constant product
changes, requires more worker involvement and commitment
than previously. From the individual employee's perspective such
changes may be beneficial and liberating, improving working conditions, giving more intrinsically interesting work, allowing more
discretion in doing the work and more training and development,
which can enhance the employee's market position. Alternatively,
such changes in work organisation may be detrimental for the
individual, intensifying work effort and creating more effective
and closer monitoring systems.

Threats to Union Commitment

In either situation, Terry (1989) argues, this new logic of action
poses major problems for existing forms of workplace trade-union
organisation, creating both an institutional and ideological crisis
for unions. New structures set up by managements for communicating directly with employees are perceived as a potential threat
to existing union structures. Employee participation programmes
such as quality circles and autonomous work teams threaten to
marginalise the role of the shop steward. There is conflicting
evidence that such human resource management initiatives are
detrimental to trade unionism. Three possible relationships can
be discerned in the literature. First, such practices exclude unions
either directly or indirectly through the use of suppression and
substitution tactics. Secondly, they marginalise union organisa-

tion and activities. Thirdly, they actually encourage co-operation between management and unions and are therefore compatible with unionisation. The underlying logic of the human resource management approach to employment relations with its emphasis on building employee commitment and identity with the organisation is held to be incompatible with the collectivist ethos of unionism (Guest, 1987). As a result, the unions, an alternative source of employee identification, are either excluded or marginalised. In relatively highly unionised countries such as Britain and Ireland, union exclusion strategies are more likely to be high-risk strategies for employers where there is always the possibility of a resurgence in union strength in the long term. According to Smith and Morton (1990: 30), in Britain "the more common policy of employers is the implementation of partial exclusion policies the object of which is to marginalise trade unions even while recognising their continued right to operate". Marginalisation is achieved through the strategic management of certain critical employee processes. The emphasis on more direct communication with individual employees can, for example, be viewed as a usurpation of the "voice" function of trade unions. Workers' collective solidarity is more difficult to preserve where performance related pay is extensive and wage rates vary across similar occupations and related grades.

The ideological crisis occurs as a result of employee acceptance and commitment to the logic of the enterprise — that is, to an agenda of change set by management. The old industrial relations was based on a bargained compromise borne out of a mutual restraint based on low trust and limited expectations (Dunn, 1990). Metaphors such as the "Frontier of Control", "them and us", "digging in" and "wage offensive" are apt descriptions of the old industrial relations. In the new industrial relations the agenda is set by management and is focused on developing employee flexibility, co-operation and, above all, commitment to the firm. Dissent or mere lack of enthusiasm is perceived as jeopardising the whole enterprise, and there is no place for the old industrial relations, for demarcation disputes, for withdrawals of labour or for live and let live (Dunn, 1990). Thus the emphasis is on flexibility, change and commitment, accompanied by a vision that is upbeat and optimistic. In contrast, the old industrial relations is both irrelevant and destructive in the new competitive environment.

Commitment to this agenda tends to blur the conflict of interests traditionally associated with the employment relationship and, as a consequence, reduces the relevance of union membership and collective bargaining. The conflict of interests in the new logic is transposed to a conflict that originates in the product market. Thus, employees are not in conflict with their employer but with the company's competitors, with, as Basset (1986) argues, the replacement of the class struggle with the struggle for markets. Accordingly, the focus of trade unions becomes localised and essentially enterprise based. Thus, it is argued, "new unionism" or enterprise-based unionism poses problems for the cohesiveness and solidarity of national-based unions.

Industrial Relations in Irish Firms: A New Order?

The central focus of this book is the measurement and evaluation of change in workplace industrial relations structures and the relationship between management and labour. A central and integrating theme throughout is the extent to which a new type of industrial relations has emerged in Irish manufacturing companies, and whether this has caused an institutional or ideological crisis for trade unions. A comprehensive analysis of industrial relations must include both the structural characteristics of workplace relations and the dynamics of the relationship between labour and management. Structure refers to the institutions of collective bargaining, that is, the established worker representative and bargaining structures from which emerge the rules regulating the employment relationship and governing the organisation of work. It was the operation of these institutions, structures and procedures that was a cause of particular concern to the Commission on Industrial Relations set up in 1978. These concerns were also reflected in the report of the Donovan commission on industrial relations in Britain (1968) and were based on the assumption that the creation of a formal system of industrial relations at the workplace was the most effective way to achieve good industrial relations (Purcell, 1981).

The key features identified by the Irish Commission as causing a poor industrial relations environment, such as multi-unionism and the lack of, or non-adherence to, formal industrial relations procedures, have been addressed since with some success. However, it is open to question whether this has transformed industrial relations at the workplace from the traditional predominant pattern of confrontational and adversarial relations. Critics of the formal system approach argue that the existence of recognised and comprehensive procedures, codes of practice and established bargaining fora does not necessarily lead to orderly industrial relations or a high level of co-operation between management and workers. The manner in which these mechanisms are used, both at the formal and informal level, is a more fundamental determinant of industrial relations in an organisation.

DATA SET

The data set analysed in the following chapters comprises 17 manufacturing companies, spread across four industrial sectors: textiles, chemicals, engineering, food and drinks. To retain confidentiality, the names of the companies have been changed, but their sector can easily be identified from their pseudonyms. A particular company can thus be tracked throughout the book. Although we provide many relevant comparisons across many issues, the reader can quite easily refer across the chapters in order to gain a more comprehensive grasp of a company's industrial relations in total. The companies are evenly distributed geographically, and almost equally divided between urban and rural locations. Thirteen companies are in the medium/large category and four are defined as small — that is, companies with less than 100 employees (see Table 1, Appendix).

The selection of these particular companies resulted from information provided by the Labour Relations Commission. Approximately half of the companies were selected because of a history of frequent third-party intervention and the perceived adversarial nature of their industrial relations generally. The remaining companies have a low level of third-party intervention and are perceived as having relatively "co-operative" industrial relations. A comparison of these two groups would, it was hoped, provide some explanation for the different climate of industrial relations across these companies and also provide a clue to the factors which are conducive to improvements in a company's climate of industrial relations. However, it should be stressed that the initial selection criteria for the companies had no biasing influence on the subsequent research. Companies were not categorised and defined in terms of the initial selection criteria. Indeed, in at least one case, the initial categorisation of a company proved to be wholly inaccurate.

An evaluation of company-level industrial relations provides particular problems, as traditionally the main actors — labour and management — are seen to have both mutual and conflicting interests. Such terms as good and bad industrial relations or orderly and disorderly relations are prone to be value laden with a propensity to reflect a particular interest or perspective, be it management or labour. Good industrial relations tends to be simplistically associated with the absence of overt conflict. This is a particularly serious error when overt conflict is defined as encompassing not only strikes, but also the incidence of third-party intervention and even grievance rates. Conflict is too often seen as inimical to good union–management relations or even an indication of pathological relations in the workplace. However, the expression of conflict can be constructive in many circumstances, allowing the exchange of diverse opinions and the constructive management of conflicting interests. It is essential, therefore, to use a wide range of indicators when evaluating a firm's industrial relations.

Data were collected through interviews with key personnel in each company. The minimum number interviewed in each company included: the personnel or human resources manager, a line manager, two shop stewards (usually the senior stewards) and the main union official responsible for the plant. Additional interviews were often conducted with the finance manager and the senior production manager. Economic data on each company were collected using a structured questionnaire which was completed by a senior manager. A third source of data collection was through an employee survey in the medium/large companies. Access to conduct an employee survey was permitted in nine of the 13 medium/large companies. The size of survey conducted and the manner in which it was carried out varied across the nine companies. For logistical and practical reasons, it was not possible to conduct a proper random survey in all of the companies. Thus, the small sample size in some of the companies and the way in which the questionnaires were distributed is a weakness which, in the circumstances, was not possible to overcome (Table 1, Appendix).

Apart from these qualifications, the employee survey represents a unique and substantial survey of 402 employees in total, which can provide further insights into the industrial relations climate in a company, in addition to the other sources described above. This use of multiple research methods, interviews, economic data and a quantitative survey should render a comprehensive understanding of the phenomena under analysis. In general, the quantitative results are used to underscore the qualitative data. Triangulation as a research approach — that is, the use of multiple research methods — allows for more confident interpretations of complex phenomena, and leads to more comprehensive and holistic explanations than the use of a single research method (Tick, 1979).

Along with the use of multiple research methods, different levels of analysis are used to provide a comprehensive account of the economic and industrial relations changes in the manufacturing sector. In the final section of Chapter 1 there is a brief review of the industrial relations and economic performance for the manufacturing sector as a whole. The trends in strikes activity, labour productivity and employment changes that have occurred since the 1950s are outlined. Secondly, establishment-level changes in the collective-bargaining arrangements in the selected companies are addressed. Chapter 2 focuses on changes in union structures at the workplace; the resolution of disputes; and mechanisms of arbitration in the context of changes in the macro industrial relations environment. Chapter 3 examines changes in the substantive aspects of the employment relationship. These include flexibility, benefits, occupational structure, work effort and employee attitudes towards management. The chapter assesses whether these reflect a new realism among employees. Establishment-level changes in the relationship between labour and management over time are also evaluated.

Chapter 4 charts the changes over time in each company's industrial relations pattern, and concludes with an analysis of the causal factors affecting the patterns. Chapter 5 focuses on the problems of union–management co-operation and compares companies that have moved towards more co-operative relations with companies that can be defined as having adversarial industrial relations. Finally, two related topics — the personnel function and industrial relations in small companies — are considered in the context of the foregoing analysis. Given the centrality of the personnel function to the labour–management relationship, Chapter 6 attempts to establish the extent to which the personnel function has the capacity to act as a strategic lever to bring about change in industrial relations. Chapter 7 focuses on industrial relations in small firms. The rationale for considering small firms separately is that small firms are not just scaled-down versions of large firms, but have characteristics which are different from medium/large firms.

INDUSTRIAL RELATIONS AND ECONOMIC PERFORMANCE IN THE MANUFACTURING SECTOR, 1960–92

Industrial Relations in Ireland during the 1960s and 1970s were generally perceived at that time to be in a state of disorder (Commission on Industrial Relations, 1981). Throughout this period industrial disputes increased in number and length (Kelly and Brannick, 1987). In particular, there was a notable rise in the incidence of unofficial disputes, which was of particular concern to the commission. However, the number of strikes and man-days lost (MDL) has declined considerably throughout the 1980s in the manufacturing sector (see Figure 1.2)

During the 1980s, there was a dramatic decline in all indices, which has continued into the 1990s. Two particularly disruptive periods occurred from 1964 to 1968 and 1974 to 1979. In general, the entire period from 1971 to roughly 1985 was comparatively high in the number of man-days lost. Although the frequency of

Figure 1.2: Man-Days Lost in the Manufacturing Sector, 1960–92

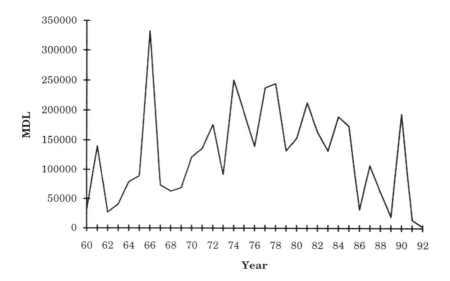

Source: Strikes Data Bank, Dept. of Industrial Relations, UCD.

usage of the conciliation service and the labour court is not available for the manufacturing sector alone, the overall pattern of usage should not differ significantly from the trends for all industrial sectors (see Figure 1.3).

Since 1971 the relationship between the number of disputes referred to conciliation and the number of labour recommendations issued by the labour court has remained constant. However, from 1990 the use of the conciliation service has increased at a faster rate. Usage of the conciliation service and the labour court proper increased gradually from 1971 to 1983, then declined in the period 1983–89, before once again rising. While several factors such as the economic climate and the development of employment and trade-union legislation affect the use of the conciliation and labour-court services, there also appears to be a close relationship between periods when national wage agreements are in operation (1970–80 and again from 1987 onwards) and increasing usage of the labour court and the conciliation service.

Figure 1.3: Labour Court Recommendations and Referrals to Conciliation, 1971–92

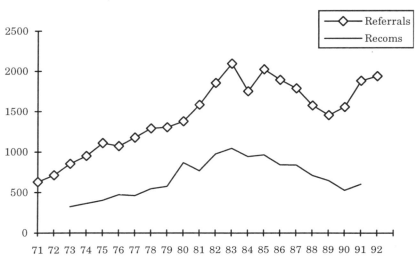

Year

Economic Performance in Manufacturing, 1953–89

Between 1953 and 1989, the volume of goods produced by the manufacturing sector increased by a factor of 7.03,[1] a large increase, even allowing for the relatively low volume of output in the immediate post-war era. In money values, this represented almost a six-fold increase in gross output at constant prices (1953 is the base year).[2] More impressively, net output, or value added after fixed costs are deducted, increased by almost a factor of 10 at constant prices. However, overall employment in manufacturing only increased by 30 per cent. As we would expect, the pattern of change over this period (1953–1989) varies considerably (see Table 1.1).

---

[1] This is the real increase in the amount of goods produced and is calculated by allowing for price increases and inflation.

[2] Gross output and net output are calculated in current money terms. They have been adjusted to constant prices using the Wholesale Price Index which increased by a factor of 10.31 in the period 1953–89. The Wholesale Price Index refers to the price of goods at the factory gate. For a more comprehensive discussion of these terms see Kirward and Gilvray (1983).

Table 1.1: Changes in Net Output,* Employment and Assets Added in the Manufacturing Sector, 1953–89

	Net Output		Employment		Net Output per Worker		Assets Added
	% increase in decade** (000)	% yearly increase†	% increase in decade	% yearly increase	% increase in decade	% yearly increase	£(000)
1953–60	27% (23,216)	3.4%	5.4%	0.7%	20.6% (123)	2.6%	63,070
1960–70	121% (131,853)	12.1%	31%	3.1%	69.0% (497)	6.9%	236,425
1970–80	89% (213,546)	8.9%	13.7%	1.4%	66.1% (804)	6.6%	532,955
1980–89	86% (390,571)	8.6%	-15.5%	-1.7%	120.0% (2,429)	12.0%	584,147

* **Gross output** represents the selling value of goods actually produced in the year, as reported by the businesses themselves, irrespective of whether sold or put into stock. **Fixed costs** (or industrial input) are defined as the cost of materials, industrial services and fuel and power used in the year. **Net output** is defined as gross output less fixed costs.

** The percentage increase is calculated as follows: year 10 – year 1 / year 1. The real money increase in output per worker at constant 1953 prices is in brackets.

† These are crude yearly averages, as the compound effect of each cumulative yearly increase is ignored, and they are thus slight overestimates of the actual increases particularly in the latter years of each decade.

Source: Statistical Abstracts 1950–79; Census of Industrial Production, 1979–89.

After the stagnation of the 1950s, net output rose rapidly in the three succeeding decades. Although the yearly rate of increase was highest in the 1960s, the actual increase in net output added in constant prices in the 1980s was three times that added in the 1960s. Despite the less buoyant economic climate in the 1980s, the average yearly rate of increase in net output was maintained at similar levels to the previous decade. During the same decade, employment in manufacturing fell by 15.5 per cent or an average yearly decline of 1.7 per cent. It was only during the 1960s that employment increased at a relatively high yearly average of 3.1 per cent. The period 1970–89, when net output rose fastest in real terms, had an overall net decrease in employment of 3.9 per cent.

The higher net output of this period is mainly a result of increased investment in capital assets, which increased the productivity of labour. However, the phenomenon of transfer pricing associated with foreign multinationals may have exaggerated net output. In 1974, all foreign industry accounted for 25 per cent of gross output; by 1985 this had grown to 50.2 per cent (Foley, 1991). The aggregate assets added each year more than doubled (2.7 times) in the 1960s and increased again by a factor of 1.25 in the 1970s (Table 1.1), and remained constant in the succeeding decade. Although investment in assets remained constant over these latter two decades, the increase in net output per worker almost doubled to 12 per cent per year in the 1980s. A number of factors can be advanced to account for this trend, though it is difficult to evaluate the exact impact of each separately.

Firstly, the cumulative addition of assets added from 1970 onwards clearly increased the net output per worker significantly. As a result, the proportion of net output accounted for by labour costs decreased rapidly, particularly after 1970. Labour costs absorbed 53.7 per cent of net output in 1955, but only 26.5 per cent in 1989 (see Table 1.2). The most dramatic change occurred

Table 1.2: Labour Costs as a Percentage of Fixed Costs* and Net Output, Selected Years, 1953–89

Year	% of Fixed Costs	% of Net Output
1950	20.6	51.6
1955	20.4	53.7
1960	21.0	52.4
1965	23.9	50.1
1970	27.7	48.8
1975	23.8	46.1
1980	24.4	43.7
1985	20.8	33.0
1989	20.9	26.5

*   Fixed costs are calculated as (gross output – net output) and include (i) industrial materials and services, (ii) materials for processing, (iii) ancillary goods and services, and (iv) all fuel and power.
Source: Statistical Abstracts 1950–79; Census of Industrial Production 1979–89.

between 1980 and 1989 when labour costs decreased from 43.7 per cent to 26.5 per cent of net output, a reduction of 40 per cent. However, the cost of labour as a percentage of fixed costs has remained remarkably constant at approximately 21 per cent.

Labour costs (at constant 1953 prices) have increased by a factor of four between 1953 and 1989. As Table 1.3 indicates, the 1980s had the lowest percentage increase in the real costs of labour compared to the previous three decades. Thus, while output per worker increased substantially, labour costs were tightly controlled, increasing by only 12.6 per cent in this period. However, the actual labour costs per employee increased by 33 per cent. This discrepancy between overall labour costs and the cost per employee is explained by a significant decrease of 15 per cent in manufacturing employment, accompanied by capital investment in new plant and machinery. Since capital investment in terms of assets added was similar in both the 1970s and the 1980s, a further factor in the increase in net output and a decrease in labour costs may have been the more productively efficient use of labour and capital in the 1980s. Productive efficiency may have improved both through changes in the way that work is organised and through increased effort levels from employees. This is a plausible argument given the economic recession of the early 1980s and the increasing competition in national and international markets, which created a difficult economic environment for manufacturing companies (see Table 1.3).

Table 1.3: Changes in Total Labour Costs and Labour Costs per Worker, 1953–89

	Labour-Cost Increases (%)*	*Cost per Worker Increases (%)*	*Employment Changes (%)*
1953–1960	27	21	5.4
1960–1970	106	58	31
1970–1980	69	49	14
1980–1989	12.6	33	−15.5

*   Percentages are calculated using constant 1953 prices for all years.
Source: Statistical Abstracts 1950–79; Census of Industrial Production 1979–89.

A second factor contributing to the increase in net output per worker in the 1980s was the increased establishment and importance of foreign-owned companies in the Irish manufacturing sector. Between 1978 and 1988, the number of foreign-owned firms in Irish industry increased by 22 per cent and their share of employment increased from 35.3 per cent to 42 per cent (Ruane and Gibney, 1991). Output per worker in foreign-owned firms tends to be superior to indigenous firms. Output per employee in North American industry in Ireland, for example, was 178 per cent of the Irish figure in 1973–74 increasing to 343 per cent in 1985. Foreign firms' share of net output increased from 58.1 per cent to 65 per cent in the short period 1983–87 (Foley, 1991).

Thirdly, the reduction in the number of strikes and man days lost may also have contributed to the improvement in worker productivity. The effects of strike activity on national productivity and lost output has received considerable attention (see Hirsch and Addison, 1986; Knight, 1989; Freeman and Medoff, 1984, for a review of the literature). Most of the studies report that industry losses from strikes are in fact quite small when aggregated across all industries. However, for those particular firms involved in a strike, the costs can be extremely high and serve as a motivating factor in their avoidance (Hirsch and Addison, 1986). In the Irish manufacturing sector there appears to be no relationship between the number of man days lost and the number of strikes and net output per worker (see Table 1.4).

Net output per worker is negatively related to the number employed, as expected, and is also negatively related to the proportion of net output allocated to labour costs. This latter relationship is a result of the decreasing secular trend in labour costs as a proportion of net output evident over the period 1953–89. It is interesting to note that whereas 50 per cent or more of the value added in manufacturing companies at the aggregate level was absorbed by labour costs in the 1950s, by 1989 this had fallen to 26.5 per cent of the value added. Although there is an absence of a statistical relationship between indices of industrial disruption and net output per worker, it would be erroneous to assume that the climate of industrial relations has no impact on a

Table 1.4: Linkages between Industrial Relations and Economic Indicators, 1953–89 (Pearson Correlation Coefficients 2-tailed Significance)

	MDL	NTWK	STRIKES	EMPLOY
NTWK	NS			
STRIKES	0.66***	NS		
EMPLOY	NS	-0.32*	NS	
WAGNET	NS	-0.46**	NS	NS

N = 36
*   P < 0.05
**   P < 0.01
***   P < 0.001
NTWK   =   Net Output per Worker
EMPLOY =   Numbers Employed in Manufacturing
WAGNET =   Wages or Labour Costs as a Proportion of Net Output.
NS   =   No significant correlation.

company's economic performance. The share of net output or value added between capital and labour is a fundamental issue in the industrial relations process. Collective bargaining is ultimately about regulating, maintaining and bargaining over effort levels and rewards.

Changes in the Employment Structure, 1979–89

Apart from the decline in employment of 15 per cent in manufacturing already noted, several changes are discernible in the employment structure between 1980 and 1989. Manual operatives declined as a proportion of all employees from 76 per cent to 72 per cent in 1989 (see Table 1.5).

This was particularly pronounced for male manual operatives who declined as a proportion of all manual from 71 per cent in 1979 to 68 per cent in 1989. In real terms, this means a smaller share of a declining employment base. Conversely, the female proportion of manual operatives has grown by 3 per cent. Average manual wages also declined from 71 per cent to 67 per cent of the average white-collar wage/salary. Despite the large prescriptive literature advocating flatter, less hierarchical organisational

Table 1.5: Changes in the Employment Structure, 1979–89 (Selected Years)

	Manual Operatives as a % of all Employees*	Manual Wages as a % of White-Collar Work	Span of Supervision[†] (manual)	Managerial and Admin/ Tech as a % of Staff
1979	76	71	17.7	53
1983	75	69	18.3	52
1986	73	68	17.5	53
1989	72	67	17.3	54

* Excluding supervisors. Employees are divided into four main categories in the Census reports: Industrial Workers; Supervisors; Clerical Staff; and Administrative and Technical Staff (Administrative refers to managerial and senior administrative positions).
† Number of manual workers per supervisor.
Source: Census of Industrial Production, 1979–89.

structures, there is little evidence of any reduction in the number of manual employees per supervisor during the 1980s. Similarly, the proportion of managerial and technical positions among white-collar employees has changed little. However, females accounted for only 10 per cent of these managerial and technical positions in 1979, which increased during the decade to 14 per cent in 1989 (Table 1.6).

Table 1.6: Changes in the Gender Structure of Employment, 1979–89

	Females as a % of Manuals	Females as a % of Clericals	Females as a % of Admin/Tech	Females as a % of Supervisors
1979	29	63	10	14
1983	30	60	11	14
1986	31	59	12	15
1989	32	58	14	16

Source: Census of Industrial Production, 1979–89.

A shift also occurred in the number of female supervisors and, more conspicuously, in the percentage of females working in routine clerical occupations. Even allowing for these shifts, females are still underrepresented in managerial, technical and supervisory positions, given their overall share of employment in the manufacturing sector.

Overall the 1980s decade was one of significant change in Irish manufacturing. There was an enormous leap in productivity per worker, and at the same time considerable reductions in the numbers employed in manufacturing. The average size of foreign firms declined from 106.4 employees in 1978 to 90.9 in 1988, and in Irish firms from 32.2 to 17.5 (Ruane and McGibney, 1991). A majority of firms shed employees during this decade (a common experience in the companies in this study). Increasing international competition, company downsizing and the introduction of new forms of technology generated a need for greater flexibility in work organisation, which often demanded new skills or the amalgamation of old skills in new combinations. Despite these changes and challenges, the incidence of strikes and the number of man days lost in manufacturing companies declined dramatically, particularly in the latter part of the decade and into the 1990s. A critical industrial relations question is whether the reduction in strike activity is an enduring phenomenon or a consequence of a severe economic recession and high unemployment. Furthermore, it is not clear whether this industrial peace has shifted industrial relations away from the traditional adversarial approach towards more co-operative labour–management relations. These questions are central to this study and inform much of the subsequent analysis in this book.

Chapter 2

INDUSTRIAL RELATIONS PROCEDURES AND UNION STRUCTURE

Debate on industrial relations issues and trends in Ireland has generally been conducted in the context of, and compared to, industrial relations trends in Britain. There are obvious reasons for this connection, such as proximity, similarity of industrial relations structure, historical considerations and close economic ties. Despite membership of the European Union, this relationship remains strong. Thus, we would argue, it is appropriate to compare changes in union structures and workplace procedures in Ireland with industrial relations changes and trends occurring in Britain. Furthermore, such a comparison also allows the question of continuity and change to be more sharply posed. At the macroeconomic and societal level, few would argue against the decline in trade union status and power in Britain. Rose (1993) identifies five central trends at the macro level in British industrial relations since 1980.

1. **Exclusion**: Unions have ceased to be involved with employers and the government in tri-partite bargaining over the economy. A consequence of this is that the unions have lost their advisory roles in official policy bodies.

2. **Pacification**: The number and severity of strikes declined in the 1980s, and by the early 1990s Britain was a relatively strike-free country.

3. **Juridification**: A succession of legal acts removed many of the traditional legal immunities arising from the 1906 Act. Unions' activities by the 1990s were tightly controlled.

4. **Contraction**: Union membership declined from over 13 million in 1979 to 10 million in 1990, a fall of 23 per cent.

5. **Demoralisation**: The credibility of unions as bargainers and independent sources of power was further eroded by managerial strategies which marginalised the unions.

Judged against these macro-level trends, industrial relations in Ireland during the 1980s has remained relatively unchanged. After three national tripartite agreements covering the period 1987 to the present, the trade unions participate in a wide range of government policy groups. Their legitimacy and high national profile have not changed since 1980, and, if anything, have been enhanced. However, like Britain, industrial conflict in Ireland has declined substantially, with the Irish manufacturing sector being virtually strike-free. In terms of legal restrictions on trade unions, there is no comparison in Ireland with the raft of trade-union legislation in Britain. Although the Industrial Relations Act, 1990 has been criticised for its potential ability to control and constrain legitimate union activity (Wallace, 1991), it nevertheless retains the basic immunities of the Trades Dispute Act, 1906, albeit in a more restricted fashion. Union membership in Ireland during the 1980s has not declined as rapidly as membership in the UK (see Figure 2.1). The contrast between the two countries is particularly evident after 1987.

Apart from a decline in strike rates since 1985, the collective bargaining system in Ireland does not appear to have changed substantially since 1980. Since managerial strategies operate at the establishment level, they are considered below in the context of workplace industrial relations

The consensus concerning the broad macro trends in British industrial relations is, in contrast, conspicuously absent regarding changes at the workplace level. At the workplace level there is considerable disagreement regarding the position of the union. A number of writers have argued that, despite the macro trends, industrial relations at the workplace have not changed substantially (Marsh, 1992; Batstone, 1988; Millward et al., 1992). Formal shop-steward structures and the collective bargaining

Figure 2.1: Percentage Change in Union Membership in the United Kingdom and Ireland, 1980-91

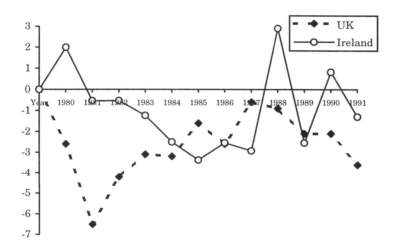

Source: Blyton and Turnbull, 1994: 106;and Roche, 1992.

system remain intact: for example, the ratio of shop stewards to union members was 1 to 22 in 1984 and 1 to 20 in 1990. Batstone (1988) identified three styles of management strategy which were claimed to be prevalent in the UK in the 1980s: a strategy of confrontation with unions, a strategy encouraging employee commitment to the organisation and a strategy emphasising flexible labour contracts. The end result of these strategies is the exclusion or marginalisation of trade unions in the workplace (Smith and Morton, 1993; 1994). However, the evidence according to Batstone (1988) is inconclusive. Apart from a small number of major confrontations with trade unions, notably in the printing and coal-mining industry, few employers actually took an oppositional approach to unions. In unionised establishments in Ireland, there are no incidences of such confrontation between unions and employees aimed at marginalising or excluding trade unions.

A second strategy and an alternative to confrontation comprises a set of employee-involvement techniques usually subsumed under the rubric of human resource management. Human resource management practices, it is claimed, are often incompatible with the independent collective organisation of workers (Guest, 1987; Hyman, 1989; Fiorito et al., 1987; Smith and Morton, 1993). Human Resource Management, with its emphasis on building employee commitment and identity with the organisation, is held to be incompatible with the collectivist ethos of unionism. However, in a survey of over 200 medium and large companies in Ireland, HRM practices were found to have no impact on union density levels (Turner, 1994) and, apart from type of payment systems, no impact on union recognition (Roche and Turner, 1994). Furthermore, the extent and use of numerical flexibility (the proportion of employees on part-time, temporary or casual/fixed-term contracts of employment) had no significant relationship with the level of unionisation in a company (Turner, 1994).

Proponents of continuity, however, may be underestimating the actual decline in union power at the workplace. Those who see change occurring in the position of trade unions at the workplace in Britain can base their case on the strong evidence of decline emerging from the 1990 Workplace Industrial Relations Survey (Millward et al., 1992). In particular, the exponents of the change thesis in workplace industrial relations emphasise the control that managements now have in the workplace (Kessler and Bayliss, 1992; Smith and Morton, 1994; Storey, 1992). An important instance of this is that managements now communicate directly with workers, and the shop-floor union structure is being bypassed or ignored.

During the period 1981–84 there is strong evidence from the British workplace industrial relations survey of restrictive practices being dismantled in unionised establishments (Wadhwani, 1990). Case studies also reveal that managements during the 1980s made significant changes in work organisation (Storey, 1992) and that shop stewards were less assertive and autonomous than previously (Terry and Edwards, 1988). Whether the changes at the workplace represent enduring long-term adjustments in labour–management relations or are temporally related to the fluctuations in the business cycle is at the heart of the continuity/ change debate. In any case, a critical contribution to this debate involves the measurement and assessment of change in union structures, workplace procedures and labour–management inter-action. In order to assess the extent of change in these areas in the companies surveyed, union structures and procedural mecha-nisms were divided into organisational indices of shop-floor union structure and substantive indices of union influence (see Terry, 1986). Organisational indices refer to aspects such as shop-steward structure, union density and support by management for steward organisations. Substantive indices refer to the extent of conflict, official and unofficial strikes, third-party intervention, and union bargaining strength.

UNION PRESENCE AT THE WORKPLACE

Shop stewards are an essential part of union government, par-ticularly at the workplace level, providing a link between union members and the national union. Given their central importance to workplace industrial relations, the extent of research on shop stewards in Ireland is remarkably sparse. Murphy's (1981) account of a steward section committee provides an invaluable insight into the workings of a steward committee, but little is known about the general existence of steward committees or the activities and role of such committees. A survey of shop stewards in 24 establishments in 1987 reveals the complexities and pressures of the shop steward role (Flood and Turner, 1993). The stewards interviewed fell broadly into three categories: 13 per cent of the stewards were propelled into office because no one else was willing to take on the job; 11 per cent were nominated by members external to the work group; and the remaining 76 per cent were elected in contested elections. This is also reflected in the findings of Wallace (1982) that 65 per cent of stewards were elected unopposed or appointed without a contest, as distinct from 35 per cent who were elected. Furthermore, in that study, 67 per cent of respondents indicated a difficulty in getting members to take on the role of shop steward. However, the strength of oppo-sition in these contested elections is open to question since there was a marked initial reluctance to take on the steward role (see Table 2.1).

Table 2.1: Motivation, Commitment and Satisfaction of Stewards

Initial Motivation to Take on the Job as Steward		Willingness to Abdicate Steward Role		Feelings about Work as a Steward (Role Satisfaction)	
Wanted it very much	18%	Very glad to pass job on	62%	Enjoy most of the time	59%
Had mixed feelings	50%	Cannot decide	3%	Fifty-fifty	27%
Did not want it	32%	Prefer not to give it up	35%	Enjoy it hardly ever	14%

N = 38
Source: Flood and Turner, 1993: 98.

Indeed, over 60 per cent of the sample indicated a willingness to give up the role, provided that a suitable replacement was available to take their place. Despite this reluctant activism, 60 per cent of those interviewed expressed role satisfaction, which underscores the fact that the factors that propel reluctant stewards in and out of role occupancy and the satisfaction that stewards derive from the role itself are very different. Furthermore, shop stewards' experience and length of time in the role do not indicate a serious turnover problem. While 24 per cent of stewards had less than two years' experience as shop stewards, 76 per cent had more than three and 52 per cent more than six years' experience. The majority of stewards in this study have more experience when compared with the stewards in the Batstone et al. (1977) study, where 25 per cent had been in the role for one or less years, 40 per cent for two to four years and 35 per cent for over five years. Research into steward stability indicates that a low rate of turnover is related to a high level of support both from full-time officers of the union and from union members in the workplace (Winch, 1981). The low initial motivation of many stewards, their willingness to pass on the job and the relatively high satisfaction level with the role indicates the complexity of a position which is rewarding, but at times difficult and stressful. Sectionalism and disunity among members were frequently cited as problems faced by stewards in executing their role (see Table 2.2), and stewards viewed their members' union expectations as primarily instrumental, with 41 per cent of respondents rating their members' expectations of the union as unrealistic. The attitude of management is an equally important factor. Stewards who received assistance from management in executing their role reported higher levels of satisfaction than their counterparts facing obdurate managerial opposition. Time spent on union duties is also associated with role satisfaction, which would seem to indicate that freedom to spend sufficient time on union affairs adds significantly to the ease of executing the role.

Table 2.2: Problems Faced by Stewards in Executing Role

References to:	*Per Cent*
Sectionalism/disunity	24
Attitude and opposition of management	24
Unrealistic expectations of members	17
Union-job role demands	11
Consistent opposition from members	24

N = 29
Source: Flood and Turner, 1993: 99.

As a result of the difficulties of the role, a number of stewards experienced ambiguity and psychological strain in it. Although 70 per cent of respondents are sure of what is expected of them as shop stewards, 30 per cent were often unsure and 44 per cent experienced some psychological strain as measured by the extent to which they worried about union duties outside ordinary working time. Two significant findings emerge from this research. Firstly, the job of a shop steward is a complex and difficult role, if a rewarding one, and requires particularly competent and committed union members to undertake it. Secondly, the attitude and response of management to the shop steward is an important factor in relation to the pressure experienced by stewards and their effectiveness as stewards. In the following section, the shop-steward structure, management attitudes and the extent of interaction between the shop steward and union members are addressed in the 13 medium/large establishments which participated in the present study.

Steward Structures

A notable feature of the steward structure in the companies surveyed is the informality of their organisation. While all the stewards surveyed reported the existence of a steward committee at their workplace, the degree of formality with which the committees operated in terms of regular meetings, agendas and recorded minutes was extremely low. This reflects a preference on the part of most stewards for an informal approach in which meetings are held only as the need arises. In practice, stewards meet on a regular day-to-day basis in the course of their work and at break times. Only one steward committee reported regular formal fortnightly meetings of stewards (see Table 2.3) while, with three exceptions (Clothing Ltd., Textile, Packfoods), stewards reported a considerable amount of informal meetings all of the time and as issues arose.

Table 2.3: Shop-Steward Structure and Facilities

Formal Meetings between Parties		*Informal Meetings between Parties*		*Manner of Steward Election*		*Elections Contested*	
Every 2 weeks	1	All of the time/ As issues arise	10	Secret ballot	10	Contested	7
Every 1–2 months	4	Every 1–2 months	2	Show of hands	3	Not contested	6
Every 3–4 months	2	Seldom	2				
As issues arise	1						
Never	5						
N	13		13		13		13

Source: Company interviews.

Election of shop stewards took place either on a yearly or two-yearly basis. The formal method of election of general workers was by secret ballot in all companies (SIPTU members in Burchocks being the exception — using a show of hands). In the case of craftworkers, where numbers are small, the nomination and election of stewards tended to be a more informal and consensual process. Altogether there appeared to be contested elections in seven companies. The extent to which shop-steward elections were actually contested, however, varied considerably even in these companies. Few of the elections were seriously contested even among the general workers. However, in two companies, Mineral Ltd. and Electro Engineering, the recent elections of shop stewards were vigorously contested, and virtually a new steward committee elected in each company.

Apparently it is only where a particularly urgent issue(s) arises to be solved (and there is disagreement among the membership on the matter) that elections assume greater importance. In the absence of a contentious issue, there appears to be a low initial motivation to take on the role of shop steward, confirming the findings of Flood and Turner (1993). All the stewards interviewed reported no difficulties in getting time off for union courses and meetings (although Clothing Ltd. shop stewards felt that it was given grudgingly) or in disseminating union information to members. The most preferred method of communicating routine union information was by notice board, followed by word of mouth — again indicating the importance of informality in the steward structures. All of the stewards interviewed had attended a union training course, which appeared to be the general case for the majority of stewards in the companies surveyed. Interestingly, given the importance of the steward role, only two companies provided in-company courses for their shop stewards. Such in-company courses would, obviously, pose difficult problems for shop stewards and their union, which could be diffused if senior stewards were involved in the development and instruction on these courses. Newly elected stewards at one company appeared to have initial difficulties in adapting to the role.

Relations with Management

In 11 companies, stewards felt that their relations with management were very good, good or satisfactory (see Table 2.4). However, in one company with two general unions there was a difference of opinion between the two stewards representing the unions as to whether relations were satisfactory or unsatisfactory. Apart from this, stewards in only two of the companies, Lola

Drinks and Senchem, stated that relations with management
were not very good (the reasons for these views are explored
later). Similarly, the personnel managers in two companies,
Senchem and Textile, reported that relations with their shop
stewards were poor or unsatisfactory.

Table 2.4: Union Relations with Management

Relations with Management		Off-the-Record Discussions	
Very good	3	Very common	2
Good	6*	Fairly common	4
Satisfactory	2	Not very common	3
Unsatisfactory	1*	Very rare	4
Not good at all	2		
N	13	N	13

*   Packfoods answered twice for 2 unions.
Source: Company interviews.

Whatever the causes of poor relations, they did not arise from any
interference by management in stewards carrying out union
business. Formal scheduled meetings between shop stewards and
management tended to occur only when an issue arose which
demanded a meeting between both parties. There were no
instances of regular formal meetings which took place regardless
of whether there was a specific issue to be discussed or resolved.
In practice, companies do have extensive formal meetings with
stewards, particularly over flexibility issues and the introduction
of specific programmes which can effect the way that work is
organised. In one company, for example, a flexibility agreement
took four years to complete, while in another company the introduction of a total quality management programme led to regular
and ongoing meetings between management and shop stewards
over a period of two years. Nevertheless, in the absence of specific
issues to be discussed, there was no provision for regular formal
meetings between management and stewards in any of the
companies surveyed.

Contact between shop stewards and management, especially
the personnel manager, tends to be of an informal nature. In 10 of

the companies the shop stewards had regular meetings at least monthly with the personnel manager to sort out industrial relations issues. Indeed, regular off-the-record discussions were described by stewards in six companies as either very common or fairly common. What emerges is the importance of, and in many cases a preference for, the informal process in the relations between stewards and management, for resolving industrial relations problems (see Table 2.4).

Stewards in nine companies considered the information they received on company performance to be at least satisfactory, while stewards in four companies regarded it as poor. The shop steward in Clothing Ltd. for example felt that the information was given only as a bargaining ploy, and was usually too late and of suspicious validity. Practices varied substantially across the companies, with one company, Electro Engineering, providing more comprehensive information to the shop stewards, especially the convenor, than to employees. The most common issues with which stewards had to deal in the previous three years were issues of flexibility (such as the introduction of quality-management systems), followed closely by changes in custom and practices (particularly the issue of seniority) and pay issues (see Table 2.5).

Table 2.5: Disclosure of Information, Issues and Bargaining Arrangements

Disclosure of Information		Commonest Issues		Bargaining Arrangements	
Very good	3	Work flexibility	6	All unions jointly	1
Good	1	Custom & practice*	5	Some jointly	1
Satisfactory	5	Pay issues	5	All separately	11
Poor	2	Manning levels	4		
Very poor	2	Discipline/ overtime issues	3		
N	13			N	13

* Includes seniority issues.
Source: Company interviews.

Undoubtedly, the increasing emphasis on flexibility and changes in the way that work has traditionally been organised has increased pressure on shop stewards. An extreme example of this pressure was the negotiation of a flexibility agreement which severely curtailed over-time in one company. Although the agreement was recommended by the shop-steward committee and narrowly accepted by the work force, the criticism and accusations levelled at the committee led to their voluntary resignation and the election of an entirely new committee of shop stewards. Despite this increasing pressure there is little evidence of any serious threat to the established union structures at the workplace. The presence of dual or alternative structures to the collective bargaining process, such as joint participation between management and labour, which might pose a threat to the established union structure existed in only two companies. Even in these companies the participation structures were only in the initial development stage and essentially depended on union support for their survival.

An interesting feature of workplace union structures is the negotiation of separate agreements between management and general and craft workers. Only in one company did stewards representing general and craft workers negotiate some, but not all, issues jointly. Traditionally, the divide between craft and general workers in terms of remuneration, fringe benefits and working conditions has been carefully monitored by craft workers to ensure that the differential remains between the two (in a number of companies there was an explicit percentage difference maintained, usually in the region of 15–20 per cent of wages). On the evidence of the companies surveyed here, there appears to be no change in this area.

SHOP STEWARD AND UNION MEMBERSHIP INTERACTION

Finally, the employee survey carried out in nine of the companies sheds some light on the relationship between shop stewards and union members. Excluding white-collar employees, there were 284 manual employees, of whom 271 indicated that they were union members, 11 failed to answer and 1 reported not being a union member. Almost all of the respondents (99 per cent) reported knowing who their shop steward was, and 91 per cent knew the name of their external trade union official. Respondents were also asked how often they consulted with their shop steward. A significant proportion (39 per cent) consulted their steward on average at least once a month, 18 per cent consulted about once every six months, 6 per cent once a year, and 37 per cent rarely consulted their shop steward. There was no significant statistical difference in the level of consultation between members and stewards across the nine companies. It could plausibly be argued that employees who consult their stewards more often are either more dissatisfied with the grievance procedures for settling disputes or are generally less satisfied with their work. However, there is no statistically significant difference in the level of consultation between those who are satisfied with existing grievance procedures and those who are dissatisfied (see Table 2.6).

Table 2.6: Level of Consultation and Satisfaction with Grievance Procedures

Consultation Average with Steward	Satisfied with Procedures (%)	Dissatisfied with Procedures (%)
Once a month	39	42
Once a year	28	16
Less than yearly	34	43
	100 (173)*	100 (77)

N = 250
Chisq: 4.6
Sig.: 0.1
* Number of employee responses in brackets.
Note: Here and in the following tables a chi-square score is reported where appropriate. The chi-square test is a statistical method of testing for the presence or absence of a relationship between two variables. A significance (Sig) level at or below 0.05 indicates a 95 per cent probability that there is a relationship between two variables. Conversely, significant levels above 0.05 lower the probability that there is a relationship between two variables.
Source: Employee Survey.

While a slightly higher percentage of those dissatisfied with grievance procedures are likely to consult their stewards regularly, it is also the case that in this dissatisfied group there is a higher percentage who rarely consult with their shop steward.

Again there is no significant statistical difference between levels of consultation and satisfaction with work (see Table 2.7).

Table 2.7: Levels of Consultation with Stewards and Satisfaction with Work

Consultation Average with Steward	Satisfaction with Work		
	Most of the time (%)	Sometimes (%)	Rarely / Never (%)
Once a month	38	34	60
Once a year	26	21	15
Less than yearly	36	45	25
	100 (195)	100 (47)	100 (20)

N = 262
Chisq: 5.3
Sig.: 0.25
Source: Employee Survey.

A notable feature of the responses is the large percentage (74 per cent) of employees who liked the work that they did all or most of the time. Even though there was a trend amongst those who were least satisfied also to consult their stewards regularly, the actual numbers involved were too small (20) to draw any conclusion. Given the large number in the satisfied category, it is a more reliable measure of the trend that those who consulted regularly with their steward were as likely to be satisfied with their work as those who rarely consulted. Lastly, there was a tendency, though not statistically significant, for employees with longer service in the company to consult more regularly with a shop steward (see Table 2.8).

While 40 per cent of employees with two or less years service consulted regularly, 45 per cent of those with more than 15 years regularly consulted with their steward. Conversely, only 28 per cent of long-service employees rarely consulted with the steward, compared to 55 per cent for new employees. However, the number of employees with short service records was relatively small and may be biasing the trend. The age of respondents was more evenly distributed and confirms the finding that older workers are more likely to consult with their stewards on a regular basis.

Table 2.8: Levels of Consultation and Length of Employment Service

Consultation Average with Steward	Service Years (in %)				
	0–2	3–5	6–10	11–15	+15
Monthly	40	34	29	29	45
Yearly	5	22	29	24	27
Less than yearly	55	44	42	47	28
	100 (20)	100 (41)	100 (31)	100 (34)	100 (135)

N = 261
Chisq: 13.25
Sig.: 0.1
Source: Employee Survey.

Table 2.9: Levels of Consultation and Age

Consultation Average	Age: 15–25 (%)	Age: 26–35 (%)	Age: 36–45 (%)	Age: 46–55 (%)	56+ (%)
Monthly	27	35	41	46	55
Yearly	18	23	21	34	27
Less than yearly	55	42	38	20	18
	100 (33)	100 (77)	100 (89)	100 (50)	100 (11)

N = 260
Chisq: 13.8
Sig.: 0.085
Source: Employee Survey.

It is not surprising that older workers are more active union members since they are more likely to have an in-depth knowledge of collective agreements and organisational rules generally. As such they are effective monitors of these agreements and are more likely to spot breaches of an agreement or the long-term implications of workplace changes. Conversely, younger workers may be less committed to the union and have more opportunities to exit from the company and seek alternative employment. If this is the case, older workers could be expected to rank the importance of the company higher in their life interests compared to younger workers. Indeed, this appears to be the case.

Older workers are more than twice as likely to rank their firm as the second most important priority in their lives, compared to workers in the 15–35 age group (see Table 2.10).

This statistically significant relationship is true for all employees regardless of occupational status (blue or white collar).

Table 2.10: Age and Ranking of Firm*

Firm Ranked	Age		
	15–35 (%)	36–45 (%)	45+(%)
Second	14	25	35
Third	16	24	20
Fourth	41	22	18
Fifth	29	29	27
	100 (105)	100 (79)	100 (51)

N = 235
Chisq: 17.4
Sig.: 0.0078
*   Respondents were asked to rank five social categories in order of impor-
    tance, with the most important scored one and least important scored
    five. The five areas were: social life; family; religious/church beliefs;
    friends and their firm.
Source: Employee Survey.

Table 2.11: The Impact of Age and Salary Level on Firm Ranking (Stepwise Regression)
Dependent Variable: Firm Ranking (1 to 5)

Independent Variables	Beta Coefficient
Salary	-0.275***
Age	-0.12*
Occupation	-0.02 N.S.
R^2	0.10
F ratio	16.7***

N = 294
***   Sig. < .001
**   Sig. < .01
*   Sig. < .05
Source: Employee Survey.

However, the relationship is modified when employee salary levels are taken into account. It is possible to evaluate the impact of age, controlling for salary level, on employees' ranking of their firm.

Table 2.11 indicates that both high salary and increasing age are negatively related to ranking the firm lower in priority (i.e. ranking the firm fourth or fifth). However, a unit rise in salary is more than twice as important as a unit increase in age in determining a respondent's ranking of the importance of his firm. While age is still a significant factor, it is the salary level which is the stronger influence on how employees perceive the importance of the firm.

PROCEDURES, STRIKES AND THIRD-PARTY INTERVENTION

A procedure agreement can be defined as a jointly agreed set of written rules designed to influence the behaviour of management, employees and trade unions in a defined work situation (Hawkins, 1979; Wallace, 1989). It generally relates to matters arising from wage claims, grievance issues and disciplinary actions. The Commission of Inquiry on Industrial Relations (1981) regarded the absence of formal written procedures in many firms as a major source of industrial relations problems, and urged that the development of agreed and comprehensive codes of practice be regarded as a major priority. However, the few surveys which have addressed this issue show that the great majority of medium and large-size firms have formal procedures in place. Gorman et al. (1975) found that more than 75 per cent of large firms (500+) and 66 per cent of medium firms (100–499) had formal procedures for claims, grievances and disciplinary action, while a survey of 141 firms in the manufacturing sector in 1984 indicated that 95 per cent of unionised companies had procedure agreements in place (IDA, 1984). Wallace and O'Shea (1987) found that 67 per cent of the companies in a study of unofficial strikes possessed a written procedure agreement.

These results cast some doubt on the Commission's analysis, since procedure agreements appeared to be a widely established feature in most firms. However, the Commission's (1981) prescription for legally binding procedure agreements reflected a concern with the observance of such agreements. Wallace and O'Shea (1987), for example, found that the vast majority of respondents reported that the terms of the procedure agreement had been broken as part of the unofficial strike. In the case of Tirown Sweets — one of the case-study companies in this study — the experience of unofficial strikes in the 1970s and early 1980s led to the signing of a legally binding procedure agreement by each employee. The agreement, registered under the Industrial Relations Act, 1946, resulted from the threatened closure of the factory following a nine-week strike. Appropriate procedures do not, of course, guarantee good industrial relations, but they do allow for a framework that regulates industrial relations between management and labour.

Although the procedural agreement was breached in most cases in Wallace and O'Shea's study, 57 per cent of respondents claimed that the agreement was used at some stage. While procedures do not determine policy decisions — that is, the actual substance of the employment relationship relating to the terms and conditions of employment and the organisation of work — they are, according to Kessler (1993), an essential instrument for carrying into effect a sound industrial relations policy. The Commission's (1981) emphasis on formal, binding, procedures reflected a concern with the large number of strikes occurring in the 1970s. A more worrying factor was the high number of unofficial strikes — that is, strikes not mandated by the relevant union authority. This trend is evident in the strike records of the case-study companies (see Table 2.12).

Taking all strikes together, 75 per cent of these were unofficial, with the period 1981–85 accounting for more strikes than any other period During this time, formal, written procedural agreements setting out the steps to be followed when a grievance arose existed in all companies. The absence of formalised procedures, therefore, can not be linked to the incidence of unofficial strikes. There is a pronounced downward trend in both official and unofficial strikes. Indeed, all of the companies have been strike-free since 1990.

Table 2.12: Official and Unofficial Strikes, 1971–93

Year	Official	Unofficial	Number of Firms Included
1971–75	1	12	8
1976–80	5	11	10
1981–85	8	19	11
1986–90	1	4	13
1993	0	0	13
Total	15	46	13

Source: Strikes Data bank, Department of Industrial Relations, University College Dublin.

Historically, the strike rate varied substantially across the companies, with two companies alone accounting for 73 per cent of the official strikes and 61 per cent of unofficial strikes. Omitting these companies from the strike statistics would give an average number of two strikes (official and unofficial) per company for the entire period 1971–93. Both of the strike-prone companies fall into the category of import-substitution companies as defined by Kelly and Brannick (1988). These were companies, mainly British, which set up in Ireland in the 1930s in order to avoid the high tariff barriers and to manufacture goods especially in the food, drink and tobacco sectors, for consumption in the Irish market. Thus, the set-up decision was guided by the government's protectionist economic policies, and also the comparatively lower labour costs in Ireland.

Using a comprehensive databank of strike statistics covering the period 1960–84, Kelly and Brannick (1988) found that while British companies had fewer and shorter strikes than Irish companies and other foreign companies prior to 1970, this changed dramatically in the 1970s, with British companies experiencing larger strikes, greater numbers of workers involved and man-days lost than Irish or foreign companies. Kelly and Brannick's (1988) explanation of this sudden change in the strike-proneness of British import-substitution companies stresses the centrality of changing market conditions. The lifting of trade barriers effected by the Anglo-Irish Free Trade Agreement in 1965, followed by entry into the European Economic Community in 1973, substantially changed the economic position of the import-substitute companies. These developments undermined their competitive advantages and allowed greater competition from foreign companies. A consequence of the increased competition and pressure for change in these companies is a significant factor accounting for the high rate of strike activity. The traditional relationship between management and labour came under considerable strain as managements attempted to adapt to the changed market conditions. Moves to reduce labour costs through redundancies, the elimination of restrictive works practices and the intensification of work effort inevitably resulted in conflict as employees attempted to maintain their existing working conditions and employment security. The erosion of market position is indicated by the fall in employment experienced by British companies in the food sector — employment declined from 5,300 in 1973 to 3,800 in 1983 (Kelly and Brannick, 1988).

Many of these companies ceased operation and of those that have survived as manufacturers it is with much-reduced work forces and usually under new ownership. Both of the strike-prone case-study companies in our survey changed ownership in the 1980s. It is interesting to note the contrasting experiences of these companies in terms of their business/managerial strategies and employment performance. There are dramatic differences in employment patterns between the companies, with a continuous decline in employee numbers in Tirown Sweets, compared to a rise in employee numbers in Burchocks (see Table 2.13). Both of these companies compete in the same product market, thus excluding market changes as an explanation of the contrasting employment trends. In the national context, the manner in which these companies coped with the shift away from protected markets to more open free trade, and the related business strategy pursued, was the key to their ability to adapt successfully to the changes.

Tirown Sweets has essentially pursued a strategy of disinvestment. The first instance of any sizeable investment since the factory was established in the 1930s occurred in 1986/7. However, the new plant and factory, set up in 1986 to replace the older

Table 2.13: Changes in Employment, 1976–94 (Selected Years)

Year	Tirown Sweets	Burchocks
1976	785	1,750
1980	628	n/a
1986	516	1,275
1988	186	n/a
1990	190	1,459
1994	198	1,575

n/a = figures not available.
Source: Company data files.

factory, had a much lower production capacity. In 1986, 45 per cent of total sales (approximately 27,000 tonnes per year) were manufactured in the old factory, whereas by 1993 only 7 per cent of total sales (approximately 11,000 tonnes) were manufactured in the new factory. Imported products from the UK account for the remainder of total sales. This marks a shift from a manufacturing to a mainly warehousing process. According to senior managers interviewed, the lack of investment resulted from three factors: the Irish market was considered too small to justify a large investment; there were greater economies of scale available in the UK plants; and a major rationalisation of these plants occurred in the 1980s.

Burchocks has pursued a distinctly different strategy investing continuously in new plant and machinery since 1980. Production capacity of the factory increased from 30,000 tonnes in 1980 to 45,000 tonnes by 1993. There is a research and development ethos in Burchocks encouraging and facilitating new-product development, which is absent in Tirown Sweets. Furthermore, Burchocks has a board of directors, while in Tirown Sweets the managing director and senior management were directly answerable to the UK board of directors. Consequently, the capacity of Burchocks to develop its own business strategy independently of the parent company was enhanced. The strategy chosen to cope with the shift to free trade was to expand and develop into an exporting company, to the extent that exports now account for over 80 per cent of units produced. The contrasting example of these companies highlights the different approaches adopted to cope with increasing competition and the dismantling of tariff barriers. Although both companies experienced similar industrial relations climates, characterised in the 1970s by high official and unofficial strike rates, their subsequent histories are dramatically different.

REFERRALS AND THIRD-PARTY INTERVENTION

Comparing 1986 to 1993, the number of referrals for all companies has remained approximately at the same level. Over this period referrals to conciliation service within the Labour Court (and since 1990 to the Labour Relations Commission) averaged 44 per year, rising to a high of 65 in 1991 and declining to 50 in 1993 (see Table 2.14). There is no evidence of a change in the companies in their use of third-party machinery. A clear and declining use of the Labour Court proper is apparent during the period 1980–90.

Shop stewards in six of the companies believed that the services provided by the Labour Relations Commission were not effective, while only one personnel manager expressed this view. The reason advanced for believing it to be ineffective was not the delivery of the service itself, but dissatisfaction with the outcomes. Stewards in this category felt that they "lost too many cases" or that the process was "drawn out" and gave "an inconclusive or unfavourable result" or more generally that it was "ineffective for employees". This confirms the findings on shop-steward attitudes towards the conciliation service in Wallace and O'Shea (1987). *All* of the stewards and the personnel managers interviewed, including the most frequent users of the service, expressed a desire to avoid using third-party intervention in favour of solving problems at the workplace itself. In practice, the vast majority of grievances, both individual and collective are solved within the company and without recourse to third parties.

A distinction between issues referred to a third party must also be made in terms of the importance or critical nature of the issue. An example of this can be gleaned from a breakdown of third-party issues carried out by the personnel department in

Burchocks who are the most frequent user of the Labour Relations Commission. At least 50 per cent of the cases referred to conciliation dealt with individual grievances, many of which the chief stewards recognised as being trivial. The presence of two unions for the general workers and the ensuing competition for members tended to reinforce the policy of taking a large number of individual issues to the Labour Relations Commission. In many cases, the stewards preferred to support members' grievances, rather than deter them from going to conciliation, even if the outcome was obviously going to favour the company.

Table 2.14: Company Referrals (1986–93) and Recommendations (1980–93)

	Company Referrals to Conciliation	Labour Court Recommendations
1980	n/a	17
1981	n/a	16
1982	n/a	14
1983	n/a	10
1984	n/a	24
1985	n/a	28
1986	47	18
1987	35	19
1988	31	19
1989	34	9
1990	40	12
1991	65	—
1992	52	—
1993	50	—

N = 13 companies.
Source: Labour Relations Commission Referral Documents and Labour Court Annual Reports.

A number of the personnel managers interviewed perceived the Labour Relations Commission as an important safety valve allowing the parties to get the issue into a public forum which provided some "objectivity" in dealing with the issue. Thus a large proportion of cases referred to the Labour Relations Commission can be classed as *trivial or minor issues,* which from the personnel managers' perspective act as a safety valve, reducing frustration on the shop floor and also allowing the union to be publicly seen to represent its members.

A second category of issues referred to the Labour Relations Commission can be described as *tactical issues,* for either the unions or management. Three of the personnel managers explicitly mentioned this as a prevalent strategy for both management and unions. In these cases, the Labour Relations Commission is used as an extension of the bargaining process between management and unions at company level. A consequence of this strategy is that both parties are unlikely to shift their respective positions in negotiations at the company level, since referral to a third party will inevitably require both parties to make concessions to solve the dispute. A further advantage for both parties is their freedom to reject any solution proposed by the third party. Many minor or trivial issues referred to the Labour Relations Commission may also have a tactical purpose, either paving the way for concessions or gains in other areas, or as part of a more complex set of negotiations.

The third category of disputes referred to the Labour Relations Commission can be defined as *substantial issues* of disagreement between management and labour, which are seen by both parties as fundamental to their interests. These cases are often intractable and difficult to resolve, and conciliation meetings between the parties can extend over a long period of time. From the present statistics provided by the Labour Relations Commission, it is impossible to distinguish between these three referral categories. In the absence of such an analysis of the cases referred, any interpretation of the significance of frequent users of the conciliation service must be treated with caution. Both stewards and personnel managers expressed a reluctance to use the Labour Court itself. This was more pronounced among the stewards who believed that in the present economic climate the recommendations of the Labour Court tended to favour the employer rather than the employees. What emerges from the use of third-party intervention by the companies is a shift towards more settlements at the conciliation stage, and less resort to the Labour Court. This, of course, reflects the explicit strategy of the Labour Relations Commission to settle as many cases as possible at the conciliation stages.

At the company level, formal discipline and grievance procedural agreements were established in each company. In general, formal disciplinary procedures were rarely used. When they were used, all the personnel managers interviewed believed that they were effective. In contrast, two of the line managers interviewed felt that the disciplinary procedures were not effective, while shop stewards in four companies also described the procedures as ineffective. However, it must be stressed that formal disciplinary procedures were rarely invoked in any of the companies and were not a priority or contentious issue among any respondents. Grievance procedures, on the other hand, can be expected to operate more frequently and receive a more critical evaluation. Again, all personnel managers found the grievance procedures to be effective. Similarly, line managers also believed that the procedures were effective. However, stewards in four companies claimed that they were ineffective. Thus, shop stewards in four companies were dissatisfied with the way the procedures were working.

Research in this area has generally shown that managers are more likely to be satisfied with procedures than shop stewards (Daniel and Millward, 1983; Wallace, 1982). Steward dissatisfaction can perhaps be traced to the way in which the procedures operate, particularly in relation to the issues of maintaining the status quo — that is, that changes in employment conditions, such as the reorganisation of work, will not, if challenged, be put into effect until agreement has been reached between the parties or until the procedural process has been exhausted. Only two companies, Senchem and Mineral Ltd., had such a status quo clause included in their procedural agreements. Wallace (1989) argues that procedures without a status quo clauses are severely defective, but goes on to say that the effectiveness of procedures depends more on the climate of trust. The evidence here tends to confirm the latter point — that the effectiveness of procedural agreements depends more on the climate of trust between management, stewards and employees — but not the former

position — that procedures without status quo clauses are
defective. Results from the employee survey indicate that
Senchem and Mineral Ltd. had the lowest satisfaction levels with
grievance procedures and the most negative attitudes towards
management (see Table 2.16). By a climate of trust is meant that
stewards and workers can trust that management will not try to
bring about substantial changes in employment and work conditions without consulting and negotiating on the changes, and
will attempt to solve problems quickly and effectively in terms of
existing agreements. In the following section, employee satisfaction with procedural agreements is examined in the context of
the level of trust between management and employees. Overall
there was a substantial minority, particularly of manual workers,
who were dissatisfied with discipline and grievance procedures
(see Table 2.15).

Table 2.15: Employee Satisfaction with Procedures

	Discipline Procedures (%)		Grievance Procedures (%)	
	Manual	White Collar	Manual	White Collar
Satisfied	74	87	69	84
Dissatisfied	26	13	31	16
Total	100 (274)	100 (113)	100 (269)	100 (111)

Source: Employee Survey.

Since, as we have noted, disciplinary procedures were not regarded as a contentious issue, the following analysis focuses only
on grievance procedures. The analysis also concentrates only on
manual employees because of the larger proportion of this group
who are dissatisfied with grievance procedures. Table 2.16 indicates the mean score for the nine companies in which the employee survey was administered (a 1 indicates complete satisfaction of employees with the grievance procedures). There is a
statistically significant difference between Senchem and Mineral
Ltd. and other companies such as Dairyfood, Burchocks, Micro
Engineering, Electro Engineering and Chemton. Chemton has a
mean that is three times that of Senchem. Despite this difference,
both companies are low or rare users of the Labour Relations

Commission. In fact, there are two companies, Dairyfood and Burchocks, which are frequent users, and these have higher satisfaction levels with grievance procedures than low-user companies. Therefore, it would be inaccurate to claim that frequent use of third-party intervention indicates dissatisfaction with procedures or, by extension, that industrial relations are bad or disruptive in these companies. Indeed, the example of Burchocks indicates that the opposite can be true.

Table 2.16: Employee Satisfaction with Grievance Procedures

Company	Mean: 0 = low satisfaction 1= high satisfaction	Third-party Intervention Level
Senchem	0.3226	Low
Mineral Ltd.	0.3636	Frequent
Packfoods	0.627	Moderate
Clothing Ltd.	0.75	Low
Dairyfood	0.7667	Frequent
Burchocks	0.8333	Frequent
Micro Engineering	0.86	Low
Electro Engineering	0.875	Low–Moderate
Chemton	0.8947	Low

N = 284 (manual employees only).
Source: Employee Survey.

It appears that perceptions of the effectiveness of procedures do not relate to the formal mechanisms per se, but are related to the climate of trust between management and employees. Two questions are used to evaluate this relationship. Respondents were asked whether they felt that management behaved fairly towards employees, and whether full teamwork was possible in their company. In both cases there was a significant statistical difference in results between those satisfied and those not satisfied with grievance procedures: 87 per cent of those who believed that management behaved fairly towards employees were also satisfied with grievance procedures. Conversely, of the respondents who disagreed with the statement that management behaved fairly towards employees, only 41 per cent were satisfied with procedures, while 59 per cent were dissatisfied.

Employees who perceived management to be fair, and who perceived also that full teamwork was possible, were almost twice as likely in both instances to be satisfied with grievance procedures. It appears that the nature of the relationship between management and employees is closely related to employee perceptions of procedures. Where there was a reasonable level of trust between management and employees, the settlement of most grievances was likely to be achieved without recourse to the formal grievance procedure. The effectiveness of having an explicit "status quo" clause received little support, since Mineral Ltd. which had the

Table 2.17: Satisfaction with Procedures and Perceptions of Management Fairness

Procedures	Management Behave Fairly towards Employees (%)		
	No	No Opinion	Yes
Satisfied	41	76.5	87
Dissatisfied	59	23.5	13
Total	100 (91)	100 (34)	100 (138)

Chisq: 56.8
Sig.: 0.000
N = 269
Source: Employee Survey.

Table 2.18: Satisfaction with Procedures and Perceptions of Teamwork

Procedures	Teamwork Possible (%)		
	No	No Opinion	Yes
Satisfied	47	64.5	84
Dissatisfied	53	35.5	16
Total	100 (89)	100 (31)	100 (146)

Chisq: 34.7
Sig.: 0.000
Source: Employee Survey.

second lowest mean grievance satisfaction rate was the only company with an explicit "status quo" clause in the formal grievance procedure. It may be that status quo clauses would work effectively in companies with high trust levels, but there is paradoxically no pressing need for them in such cases where, as already indicated, informal arrangements serve to lubricate the operation of the procedures. Employees in this company also held the most negative attitudes regarding the fairness of management and the possibility of full teamwork between management and employees. Indeed, Senchem and Mineral Ltd. were consistently more negative on all measures.

Given the lower response rate of Mineral Ltd. (N = 24), there is a possibility of sample error. One way of checking this is to increase the response rate by adding the white-collar responses, giving a response rate greater than 30 to N = 41. A one-way analysis of variance of the relationship between satisfaction levels with grievance procedures across the companies which included white-collar workers revealed a similar pattern of results to before. What is apparent from this analysis is the importance of the relationship between management and employees in terms of the level of trust between both parties, which goes beyond the formal adherence to procedures, and which in turn affects the perceptions of employees regarding the effectiveness of those procedures.

CONCLUSION

The findings here indicate strong continuity in union organisation and management acceptance of union legitimacy in the workplaces surveyed. Steward structures, facilities and training appeared to have changed little. Indeed, in most cases, the shop stewards were receiving more extensive training from their unions than previously. In the companies in which the employees were surveyed, a relatively high percentage consulted their shop steward at least once every month, confirming the continuing importance and centrality of the union structure at the workplace level. The most notable change was the decline in all strike indices to zero levels by 1990 for all companies. This had been accompanied by a steady and relatively unchanging use of third-party dispute mechanisms since 1986. These changes imply greater usage and observance of procedural agreements and, where agreement is not reached, the referral of issues to the labour relations commission. Industrial relations considerations still appear to be perceived as a central aspect of human resource management generally. Personnel managers were asked to evaluate the importance of industrial relations considerations in four major areas: capital investment decisions, changes in production methods, wages and conditions of employment, and redundancy matters. This question is based on the question used in the Industrial Relations Research Unit survey conducted in Britain in 1977/78 and reported in Batstone (1988) in which almost 1,000 manufacturing establishments were surveyed. Respondents were offered four response categories: play a central role; a very important role; considered; or no role at all. Overall scores for the case-study companies and the Industrial Relations Research Unit Survey (Warwick) are presented in Table 2.19.

Table 2.19: Centrality of Industrial Relations in Organisational Unions*

Centrality of IR	*Case-Study Companies*	*IRRU Survey***
(a) Fixed capital investment decisions	182	85
(b) Major changes in production methods	200	129
(c) Wages and conditions of employment	200	178
(d) Decisions to make employees redundant	150	169

* Responses have been scored so that replies in which industrial relations "play the central role" are weighted by 3, multiplied by 100 and finally divided by the number of firms in the survey to give the average score. At the other extreme, the replies in which industrial relations are not considered at all are scored at zero. Thus, if all respondents stated that such considerations were central, the total score would be 300, whereas if all reported that they played no role at all, the score would be zero.
** *Source*: Batstone, 1988.

Since the maximum possible score for each area is 300 (i.e. where all companies report that industrial relations is central to the decision), it can be seen from Table 2.19 that industrial relations considerations are viewed as being central or very important when decisions about changes in production methods and wages and conditions of employment are being considered and, perhaps surprisingly, when fixed capital investment decisions are being considered. Average scores on three of the areas are substantially higher for the Irish companies than the scores from the Industrial Relations Research Unit survey and indicate continuity in the attention given by personnel managers to industrial relations.

Chapter 3

CHANGES IN WORK ORGANISATION AND EMPLOYEE ATTITUDES

Stability or change in formal union workplace structures and in the procedural aspects of industrial relations is not necessarily a good indicator of what is actually happening at the workplace (Terry 1989, Dunn 1990). Substantive areas of employment, such as grading structures, effort levels, skill demarcations and payment systems may have undergone considerable change, while structural and procedural aspects of industrial relations remain unaltered. Over time, procedural clauses can come to constitute quasi *de jure* rights, which can act to constrain management even in periods of relatively low union power (Dunn and Wright, 1994). On the other hand, substantive areas of the employment relationship are not constrained in the same manner, since management has the formal right to direct labour in the production process with regard to the demands of efficiency and market considerations. Consequently, while the structure of union organisation and procedural agreements remains unchanged, the actual content or substance of the employment relationship may have gone through a transformation. Equally significant are employees' perceptions of employment changes.

In this chapter, the key substantive changes in work organisation in the case-study companies are examined, and, in those companies in which an employee survey was conducted, the findings on employees' perceptions regarding changes in work-effort levels and work satisfaction are presented. Employee perceptions of changes in work-effort levels and attitudes towards management are considered in the context of the predicted shift to a "new realism" in industrial relations. And, where there is employee acceptance of the logic of the enterprise, it is considered whether the traditional conflict of interests between employer and employee is blurred.

CHANGES IN WORK ORGANISATION

Substantive aspects of the employment relationship refer to the nature of the job and tasks performed, compensation, effort levels and working conditions generally. Thus, while procedural rules regulate the behaviour of parties to the collective agreements, the substantive aspects concern the behaviour of employees and employers as parties to individual contracts of employment (Flanders 1975: 86). Farnham and Pimlott (1990: 162) suggest that while there is a tendency for procedural aspects to have a separate and long-term existence, the substantive aspects tend to be altered more regularly to take account of changes in the employment relationship. In assessing changes in the substantive aspects of the employment relationship in the present study, we focus on the following key areas: flexibility, job/grading structure, effort levels and employee benefits. These are areas of inquiry that are central to the debate on substantive aspects of the relationship, and serve as good indicators of what is happening at workplace level.

Flexibility in the Workplace

Functional flexibility can be defined as the expansion of skills within a workforce, or the ability of firms to reorganise the competencies associated with jobs so that the job holder is willing and able to deploy such competencies across a broader range of tasks. This process may result in employees moving into higher or lower skill areas, or a combination of both. It is often referred to as multi-skilling. Elger (1991) notes that the most striking feature of the findings on functional flexibility in the influential International Manpower Survey of large firms in the UK is actually the modesty, rather than the radicalism of the changes involved, and the centrality of reduced manning levels, rather than upskilling. For craft maintenance activities, 75 per cent of their manufacturing panel reported a "small enlargement of a maintenance craftsman's job", and 57 per cent had gained limited craft overlap, sometimes requiring training but without violation of any group's "core trade".

The evidence to date from Ireland on functional flexibility suggests that while this form of flexibility is on the increase, it is largely confined to manufacturing industry (Suttle, 1988). While some organisations have taken a number of initiatives in the area of multi-skilling, it has been argued (Gunnigle and Daly, 1992) that "add-skilling" or "extra-skilling" may be more appropriate descriptions of these developments than multi-skilling. This argument is based on the evidence that functional flexibility among skilled workers largely involves those categories receiving training in and agreeing to undertake other prescribed tasks in addition to their traditional trade — for example, fitters undertaking electrical/instrumentation work. There is, of course. evidence of organisations claiming to have total functional flexibility in their operations. However, as Gunnigle (1992) notes, such functional flexibility would appear to pertain only in unskilled assembly-type work where their is a minimal training requirement and it is thus relatively easy to deploy workers across a large range of tasks as required. In the present research, our interviews sought to establish whether management had the optimum degree of flexibility from employees and whether working practices had been improved/made less restrictive in recent years.

Of the 13 personnel managers interviewed in the medium/large companies, six agreed that they had the optimum degree of flexibility to a large extent, while seven felt that this was not the case. However, 10 of the 13 believed that there had been improvements in the whole flexibility area in recent years, particularly in the area of work organisation. The more frequently cited areas in which greater flexibility was occurring included less restrictions on the introduction of new technology, greater transferability between sections/departments/shifts, greater amounts of teamwork (usually as a result of reorganisation) and wider responsibility for quality. As one personnel manager put it:

> In recent years the views of management and unions have tended to converge somewhat more than in the past. This is occurring on the basis that change is necessary for survival. Shop stewards, more than ever before, are beginning to

understand the wider issues of company performance and competitiveness.

The area in which most organisations are finding it difficult to gain agreement appears to be multi-skilling. A majority of personnel managers interviewed maintained that the union limited management's freedom in this area, and in those organisations where negotiations on multi-skilling had taken place, almost invariably they had been long and protracted. However, a number of respondents also highlighted the fact that management were equally limited by cost constraints and were reluctant to undertake a costly exercise to upgrade employees. A majority also highlighted a lack of resources allocated to training and development as an additional factor limiting action in this area.

Occupational Structure

Turning to the issue of the present job classification/occupational structure, a majority had been developed since 1981. A majority had between four and six grades for manual employees and no company had more than nine manual grades. This reflects a marked decrease in the number of manual grades in establishments since 1980. Movement towards a levelling of occupational structures is indicative of the general trend in functional flexibility noted above. Despite the changes in job flexibility and flatter grade structures, there was a high level of dissatisfaction among the employees surveyed regarding available promotional opportunities. Slightly more than 50 per cent were not satisfied with their chances of promotion (see Table 3.1).

Table 3.1: Satisfaction with Promotional Opportunities*

	White Collar	*Blue Collar*	*All Workers*
Satisfied	38%	25%	29%
No opinion	18%	21%	20%
Not satisfied	44%	53%	51%

N = 384
* Percentages are rounded to the nearest number.
Source: Employee Survey (9 companies).

The level of satisfaction was significantly higher among white-collar employees than blue-collar (which includes skilled and unskilled). A sharper difference emerges when the actual number of employees who had received promotion since commencing employment are considered. Overall, 37 per cent of the employees surveyed had been promoted. However, only 29 per cent of blue-collar workers had been promoted, compared to 54 per cent of white-collar workers, even though blue-collar employees tended to have longer service with the company (for example, 52 per cent of blue-collar workers had over 15 years' service, compared to 35 per cent for white-collar). For the majority of blue-collar workers (71 per cent) the chances of promotion were slim. Indeed, of the blue-collar workers with more than 15 years' service, only 32 per cent had been promoted since their employment began. Interestingly, there was little difference in promotional experiences between skilled and unskilled employees — 32 per cent compared to 28 per cent respectively. What emerges from this review of the occupational structure is a change towards a flatter grade structure for manual employees, with little movement between occupational levels, particularly for blue-collar workers.

Employee Benefits

Benefits (both statutory and voluntary) are estimated to constitute an additional 25–30 per cent on top of basic weekly pay for manual grades. However, the percentage add-on is primarily related to the level of fringe benefits voluntarily agreed at company level, particularly items such as pensions, health/insurance cover, and sickness benefit, and can therefore vary considerably between organisations. Voluntary fringe benefits refers to an ever-expanding group of facilities provided by an employer, the terms of which are set by unilateral decision or in negotiation with employees and their representatives. The most widely applicable schemes are pension plans and those schemes relating to employee health. Pension schemes in this context refer to those pensions provided by the organisation and governed by the Pensions Act, 1990. Most large companies have such schemes. A 1988 survey of 579 companies conducted by the Federation of Irish Employers found that 79 per cent of companies had a pension scheme for all or some employees. The majority of these schemes are contributory, with the normal rate of employee contribution at 5 per cent of annual earnings.

While there is no legal obligation on companies to provide sick-pay or health-insurance cover for employees, many organisations do undertake such schemes. A 1990 survey carried out by the Federation of Irish Employers found that of the 515 companies surveyed, 351 (68 per cent) had sick-pay schemes for full-time manual workers, and 424 (82 per cent) had schemes for white-collar grades. Also, over 75 per cent of private-sector companies have VHI schemes in operation for employees. The Federation of Irish Employers estimates that over half of the white-collar schemes and one-third of the manual-grade schemes incorporate an employer contribution to the cost of such schemes. Similarly, while there are no statutory requirements for the provision of canteen facilities, the Safety in Industry Act, 1980 requires that "where more than five people are employed, there must be adequate provision for boiling water and taking meals". In practice, the majority of medium/large employers provide some form of canteen facilities. These may be subsidised by up to half the economic costs of meals, often with tea/coffee facilities also being provided at subsidised rates. The present research reveals that a range of benefits, varying across organisations, is offered to employees (Table 3.2)

Table 3.2: Benefits Offered to Employees

Pension	*Bonus*	*VHI Contrib.*	*Subsidised Canteen*	*Sick Pay*	*EAP* Programme*
10	5	10	6	8	1

N= 11 (A number of respondents failed to answer this question).
* Employee Assistance Programmes.
Source: Company Interviews.

In a majority of organisations, the benefits were similar across all groups of employees, with union pressure being cited as one of the most common factors in securing these benefits. When asked to rate how competitive these benefits were, all personnel managers interviewed rated the benefits as very competitive or above average. However, there was a large proportion of employees who were dissatisfied with a number of benefits. In particular, there was a high level of dissatisfaction among manual employees concerning sick-pay schemes (46 per cent) and pension schemes (36 per cent).

Table 3.3: Employee Satisfaction with Benefits

	White Collar (%)	Blue Collar (%)	Total (%)
Sick Pay			
Satisfied	75	47	55
No opinion	12	7	8
Not satisfied	13	46	37
N = 392			
Pension			
Satisfied	65	52	55
No opinion	13	12	12
Not satisfied	22	36	32
N = 386			
Lay-offs			
Satisfied	38	45	43
No opinion	45	28	33
Not satisfied	18	27	24
N = 377			
Holidays			
Satisfied	69	71	70
No opinion	6	5	5
Not satisfied	25	25	25
N = 394			
Shift Arrangement			
Satisfied	30	57	49
No opinion	60	23	34
Not satisfied	10	20	17
N = 376			

Source: Employee Survey.

More manual workers were also dissatisfied with shift arrangements and lay-off arrangements, but these were primarily related
to blue-collar work and the percentage dissatisfied was relatively
low — 20 per cent for shift work and 27 per cent on lay-off
arrangements. Most employees, regardless of occupational status,
appeared to be satisfied with the holidays available.

CHANGES IN WORK EFFORT

It can be seen from the review of changes in work organisation
that most companies have experienced change in this area. The
logic of the new realism in industrial relations implies that either
employees will accept that they must make greater efforts in their
work, or they will be positively motivated to exert more effort to
protect jobs and earnings. In either case, employees will exert
more effort than in the past. A second question is the degree to
which changes in work organisation and the market environment
have made work more interesting, with less tight supervision and
more employee discretion. This is a particularly important issue
in the human resource management literature with its emphasis
on providing satisfying jobs and encouraging employee discretion
and commitment rather than compliance in fulfilling company
tasks and goals.

A comprehensive measurement of effort levels requires both
objective and subjective measures. According to Guest (1990) the
best way to measure effort is the subjective approach of simply
asking people if they are working harder. Edward and Whitson
(1991) in their survey of workers in four organisations relied on a
single straight question, which asked respondents whether they
thought that their work was getting harder. A more sophisticated
measure is used in the present survey. Work effort is measured
across four dimensions in terms of whether work:

(a) Is more difficult than before

(b) Requires more physical effort

(c) Requires more mental effort

(d) Leaves the employee more tired at the end of the day.

Respondents were asked to evaluate whether their work had changed in recent years. For the purposes of analysis, one factor is created from the four variables ($\alpha = 0.645$). However, it is interesting to note individual scores on the variables (Table 3.4).

Table 3.4: Changes in Effort Levels

		Yes	No	N
1.	Work more difficult than before	56%	44%	328
2.	More physical effort needed	39%	61%	331
3.	More mental effort needed	77%	23%	331
4.	More tired than before	66%	34%	331

Source: Employee Survey

A majority of respondents felt that their work was more difficult than before, especially in terms of the extra mental effort required, and that the work left them more tired at the end of the day than previously. Turning to the composite dimension of effort, only 11 per cent reported that their work had not changed on any of the dimensions, whereas 51 per cent of employees believed that their work effort had increased on either 3 or 4 of the dimensions. No two companies were significantly different on these dimensions. It could be argued that perceptions of working harder are related to such factors as age, gender and occupation. However,

Table 3.5: Changes in Work Effort and Occupational Status

Dimensions of Effort	Manual	White Collar	Admin / Tech	Professional
0	15%	6%	6%	4%
1	19%	11%	11%	17%
2	20%	24%	28%	13%
3	19%	38%	33%	44%
4	27%	21%	22%	22%
	100%(172)	100%(63)	100%(46)	100%(23)

Source: Employee Survey.

age, gender and occupational status had no (statistically) significant effect on perceptions of work effort, though professional
employees were more likely to report greater effort.

Overall, white-collar workers were more likely to report that
they were making more effort than previously — 58 per cent on
three or more dimensions, compared to 49 per cent for manual
workers — but the difference was minor and statistically not
significant. We can conclude that perceptions of changes in work
effort are relatively evenly distributed across all employees
regardless of age, gender and occupation. If there is a new realism
in industrial relations we would expect these perceptions of
greater work effort to be linked to an awareness of the struggle
for product markets and, perhaps, a higher priority being
accorded to the company by employees. Table 3.6 indicates that
there was *no* significant relationship between those who perceived that they were working harder and agreement with the
statement that employees and management co-operated in order
to compete against other companies with a similar product to
their company.

**Table 3.6: Work Effort and Awareness of Market
Competition**

Number of Effort Dimensions	In Competition against other Companies		
	Yes	No	No Opinion
0	10%	12%	11%
1	20%	8%	15%
2	24%	18%	13%
3	24%	31%	30%
4	22%	31%	30%
	100%	100%	100%
N	62%(199)	21%(67)	17%(53)

Chisq: 11.7
SIG: 0.17
Source: Employee Survey.

Indeed, there is a slightly higher percentage who disagree with
this statement and who also believe that they are working harder

than in previous years. Nor is there any evidence that working harder is related to how respondents rate the importance of the company in their life interests (Table 3.7).

Table 3.7: Work Effort and Company Ranking

Firm Ranked in Life Interests	*Dimensions of Effort*				
	0	*1*	*2*	*3*	*4*
First	0%	4%	2%	1%	0%
Second	18%	30%	26%	22%	22%
Third	27%	22%	18%	21%	22%
Fourth	27%	26%	32%	29%	25%
Fifth	36%	18%	23%	27%	30%
	100%(33)	100%(50)	100%(62)	100%(79)	100%(72)

N = 296
*   Respondents were asked to rank five social categories in order of importance with the most important scored 1 and least important scored 5. The five areas were: social life; family; religious/church beliefs; friends and their firm.
Source: Employee Survey.

A comparison of employees who indicated no change in work-effort levels with those who perceived a change in all four dimensions reveals only a slight difference. Eighteen per cent compared to 22 per cent ranked their company as the second most important factor in their lives, while 37 per cent and 30 per cent respectively ranked it as the least important. These results do not appear to support the view that employees are working harder because they perceive the importance of the market struggle or because they are more committed to their company. Nevertheless, a majority of employees claimed that they were working harder than before, which provides some support for the argument concerning a new realism in Irish industrial relations. However, as we have seen, these perceptions were not significantly related to how important employees ranked their company or whether they believed that they should co-operate with management in order to compete against other companies.

CHANGES IN WORK SATISFACTION

Respondents were asked to assess whether their jobs had improved along four dimensions:

(a) Has become more interesting

(b) Is less tightly supervised than before

(c) Gives more freedom to decide how to do work

(d) Is more enjoyable to do.

The four dimensions have been grouped together as one factor (α = 0.68) measuring the extent of improvement in respondents' jobs. As Table 3.8 indicates a large proportion of employees believed that their job had improved on at least one dimension in recent years.

Table 3.8: Changes in Work Satisfaction

	Dimensions of Satisfaction	Yes	No	N
1	More interesting	59%	41%	100% (328)
2	Less tightly supervised	41%	59%	100% (327)
3	More freedom in work	49%	51%	100% (329)
4	More enjoyable to do	46%	54%	100% (328)

Source: Employee Survey.

Only 22 per cent reported no change in any of the dimensions, while 37 per cent of employees believed that their job had changed on three or four dimensions. These results do not differ significantly according to age or gender, though there is a significant relationship between salary level and increased satisfaction with work.

While only 2 per cent of employees earning above £18,000 reported no positive changes in their work, the corresponding proportion for employees earning £5,000–£10,000 was 33 per cent. Even so, there was a significant number of respondents at the lower salary levels who experienced improvements in their jobs,

Table 3.9: Changes in Satisfaction with Work and Salary Level

Dimensions of Satisfaction	Salary Levels				
	5–10,000	10,100–12,500	12,600–15,000	15,100–18,000	18000+
none	33%	21%	26%	21%	2%
1–2	46%	49%	43%	32%	33%
3–4	22%	30%	31%	46%	64%
	100%(46)	100%(83)	100%(65)	100%(28)	100%(42)

N = 246 (A large number of employees failed to indicate their salary level.
Chisq: 27.2
Sig.: 0.000
Source: Employee Survey.

particularly on at least one or two of the satisfaction dimensions. Significant differences also existed in responses across the companies (Table 3.10).

Table 3.10: Average Factor Scores across Companies
(four dimensions combined: 0 = no on all dimensions, to 4 = yes on all dimensions)

Company	Mean Satisfaction Score (range 0–4)	N
Clothing Ltd.	1.25	12
Dairyfoods	1.67	39
Mineral Ltd.	1.68	37
Mitchell's	1.82	65
Burchocks	1.97	31
Micro Engineering	1.99	73
Senchem	2.12	32
Chemton	2.6	15
Electro Engineering	2.94	18
All Respondents	1.94 (average)	322

Source: Employee Survey.

Overall, we can conclude that significant differences in responses occurred both between the companies, and according to a respondent's salary level (occupational position also is related but salary has the greater influence with a higher Pearson correlation with positive changes in work satisfaction than occupation: 0.26*** compared to 0.18**).

Since, as we have argued, an indicator of a new realism in industrial relations is that employees will either be resigned to working harder *or* be positively committed to working harder, if commitment is the predominant reason for greater work effort rather than mere fatalistic acceptance of market realities, then those who are working harder should also have a more positive perception of their jobs. Conversely, no relationship between effort and job improvement indicates a more reactive and less positive attitude towards the job. There appears to be some support for the hypothesis that those who are working harder are also more likely to report positive improvements in their jobs. A total of 79 per cent of respondents who scored on three or four dimensions indicating increased work effort also indicated that their work was more satisfying on at least one dimension, compared to 56 per cent of respondents who reported no change in their effort levels. Both the perceptions of increased effort levels and improvements in work satisfaction appear to provide some support for a new realism in industrial relations.

EMPLOYEE ATTITUDES TOWARDS MANAGEMENT

Finally, we examine employee attitudes toward management and whether there is a blurring of the traditional conflict of interests between management and labour. A common approach to evaluating the extent of a "them-and-us" attitude among employees and management is to ask whether management and employees are on opposite sides or the same side (see Mann, 1973; Ramsay, 1975; Ramsay et al., 1990). In the present survey, two separate questions were used to measure the prevalence and strength of a them-and-us attitude between employees and management (see Table 3.11). A third question dealt with how fairly employees believed that they were treated by their management. All the questions were phrased in a positive way, with the possibility that answers might be biased slightly towards agreement rather than disagreement with the questions.

Table 3.11(a): Employee Perceptions of Management, 1979

	Full teamwork is possible because workers and management are on the same side				
Response	*Professionals*	*White Collar*	*Skilled*	*Unskilled*	*All*
Agree	49%	41%	32%	34%	39%
Disagree	38%	46%	52%	49%	47%
No Opinion	14%	13%	16%	18%	15%

*   The original question was phrased negatively as follows: "Full teamwork agree is impossible because workers and management are on opposite sides".
Source: Employee Survey and Whelan, 1982: 39–40.

Table 3.11(b): Employee Perceptions of Management, 1994

	Management and workers are on the same side				
Response	*Professionals*	*White Collar*	*Skilled*	*Unskilled*	*All*
Agree	52%	25%	29%	29%	30%
Disagree	36%	62%	58%	57%	56%
No Opinion	13%	14%	13%	14%	14%
	Full Teamwork is possible in this company				
Response	*Professionals*	*White Collar*	*Skilled*	*Unskilled*	*All*
Agree	69%	54%	54%	56%	56%
Disagree	28%	36%	30%	35%	34%
No Opinion	3%	11%	16%	10%	11%
	Management behave fairly towards employees				
Response	*Professionals*	*White Collar*	*Skilled*	*Unskilled*	*All*
Agree	81%	48%	42%	54%	53%
Disagree	13%	40%	43%	34%	35%
No Opinion	6%	13%	15%	13%	13%

Source: Employee Survey.

Whelan's (1982) survey of workers in the Dublin region allows some measurement and comparison of the degree of change in

employee attitudes between 1980 (the actual survey was carried
out in 1979) and the early 1990s. The question used to measure
them-and-us attitudes in the earlier survey was separated into
two distinct question in the present survey. Whelan (1982) concluded that Irish workers displayed extremely high levels of distrust in management generally. Overall, only 39 per cent of the
workers surveyed believed that workers and management were
on the same side. This compared quite unfavourably with survey
findings in Britain. In Goldthorp et al.'s (1968) study of affluent
care workers in Luton, the majority of workers (73 per cent) believed that they were on the same side as management. Similarly,
Wedderburn and Crampton (1972) reported 80 per cent of the
sampled workers agreeing with the statement, and Cotgrove and
Vamplew (1972), in their survey of process workers in high-
technology areas such as chemicals and oil-processing plants, recorded a positive response of 70 per cent.

The present survey indicates little change in this area. Indeed,
an even smaller proportion of employees — 30 per cent compared
to 39 per cent — believed that management and workers were on
the same side. More surprisingly, the percentage of white-collar
workers agreeing with the statement has declined quite dramatically from 41 per cent in Whelan's (1982) survey to 25 per cent in
the present survey. A majority of employees, excluding professional workers, perceived that there was a conflict of interests
in the employment relationship. However, a majority of employees
(56 per cent) also believed that full teamwork was possible in
their company. Many employees were apparently making a distinction between the conflict of interest inherent in the employment relationship and the possibility of co-operation with
management. While 57 per cent of manual workers (160) believed
that management and workers were not on the same side, 64 (39
per cent) of this group nevertheless believed that full teamwork
was possible. A majority of respondents also believed that
management in their companies behaved fairly towards employees. It is particularly notable that almost 54 per cent of unskilled manual workers agreed with this statement. Finally, 60
per cent of all respondents agreed with the statement that employees and management co-operated in their company in order to

compete against other companies with similar products. Only 22 per cent disagreed with the statement. Surprisingly, the highest positive response rate was among the unskilled manual workers, and the lowest among the clerical/technical administrative employees. Some caution is necessary in interpreting these responses since they are at variance with normally expected trends. Given the intermediate position between management and workers of these employees there may be a tendency to answer this question in terms of their evaluation of manager and worker cooperation rather than their own actual attitudes towards management and the issue of competing with other companies.

Some of the evidence from the employee survey of nine companies appears to support the view that a new realism has emerged in these companies. A large proportion of employees across all occupations believed that they were working harder now than in previous years. The majority of employees indicated that full teamwork was possible and also that employees and management co-operated in order to compete against other companies.

Table 3.12: Occupational Status and Competition in the Market

Compete*	Professional	White Collar	Skilled	Unskilled	All
Agree	65%	44%	62%	65%	60%
Disagree	16%	33%	19%	20%	22%
No Opinion	19%	23%	19%	15%	18%
	100% (31)	100%(86)	100%(68)	100%(209)	100%(394)

Chisq: 12.6
SIG: 0.05
*   Question: Employees and management co-operate in order to compete against other companies with the same product as this company.
Source: Employee Survey.

However, there was no evidence of an ideological crisis for unions. Excluding professional workers, a majority of employees believed that there was a conflict of interest between management and workers. However, as we have seen, this attitude does not appear to affect attitudes towards co-operative behaviour or the awareness of competition from other companies with similar products. Both of these areas showed considerable variation across the companies. In Table 3.13, companies are ranked in terms of their overall mean score on trust in management and competitive awareness.

Table 3.13: Company Scores on Trust* and Competitive Awareness

Compete means (range: 1=low to 5=high)		Trust means (range: 1=low to 5=high)	
Mineral Ltd.	2.95	Mineral Ltd.	2.19
Clothing Ltd.	3.27	Senchem	2.51
Mitch	3.37	Mitch	2.94
Senchem	3.44	Dairyfoods	3.01
Micro Engineering	3.49	Clothing Ltd.	3.07
Dairyfoods	3.63	Micro Engineering	3.19
Chemton	3.7	Burchocks	3.3
Burchocks	4.0	Electro Engineering	3.35
Electro Engineering	4.17	Chemton	3.39
Overall Respondent Mean	3.49		2.96

*   In order to develop a comprehensive measure of trust the three questions from Table 3.11 have been combined into one factor (reliability score (α) = 0.77).
Source: Employee Survey.

There were significance differences across the companies, with employees in those companies having more favourable attitudes towards management also more likely to be aware of product-market competition. Companies with low scores on trust were more likely to have a low score on awareness of the market. The concept of trust as a measure of the attitude held by employees about the company's management is a central factor relating to a variety of industrial relations aspects already discussed. As such, the development of trust between employees and management is a significant factor in determining the overall climate of industrial relations in an organisation. Using the employee survey it is possible to assess the internal company factors which affect the level of trust between the parties (see Appendix 2 for a detailed description of the results). Chapter 4 focuses on the external factors affecting industrial relations.

Overall, the level of trust in management varied positively with satisfaction with grievance procedures, satisfaction with non-monetary benefits, high job-satisfaction levels and whether work had improved in recent years. Surprisingly, satisfaction with gross salary or take-home pay had no significant impact on employee attitudes towards management. It could plausibly be argued that average wages in the manufacturing sector have increased to such an extent that they are not at present an issue of conflict. Cost per worker, which is roughly equivalent to gross pay per worker, continued to increase in real terms in the 1980s, although at a slower rate than previously (see Table 1.3). Similarly in the companies surveyed, employees' real wages have, at the least, kept pace with the rate of inflation, and in most cases have achieved increases above the inflation rate. Alternatively, it may also be the case that the operation of some form of national wage agreement, where pay increases are set centrally since 1987, has partly deflected employee concerns with pay away from company-level grievances towards those parties which negotiate the central wage agreements and wider socioeconomic considerations, especially rates of taxation and pay-related social insurance premiums. It is difficult to establish the precise reasons for this relationship. However, it is clear from the results of the employee survey that industrial relations factors, non-monetary benefits and the nature of work are critical elements in determining employee attitudes towards management. An explanation of these factors can only occur in relation to the shifting patterns of industrial relations over time (see Chapters 4 and 5). An understanding of such patterns is only possible in the context of each company's market position, economic performance and union–management relations.

CONCLUSION

A majority of companies reported that work practices had become less restrictive in recent years. Changes in the way that work is organised and carried out are a result of the introduction of new technology, increased emphasis on quality standards and team-work. Evidence from the employee survey shows that many of the changes have been beneficial for employees: almost 60 per cent indicated that their job was now more interesting; 41 per cent believed that they were less tightly supervised; and 50 per cent maintained that they had more freedom and discretion in their work. A related trend is the reduction in the number of manual grades. However, the evidence on occupational mobility indicates that the majority of manual employees do not receive a promotion of any type during their working lives. Not surprisingly, a majority of these employees were dissatisfied with this situation. A substantial minority of manual employees — 46 per cent and 36 per cent respectively — were also dissatisfied with the sick-pay and pension schemes available.

While 60 per cent of employees agreed with the statement that employees in their company were in competition with companies that had similar products, this market awareness does not necessarily herald a new realism in industrial relations. Although a majority of employees indicated that they were working harder, there was no clear relationship between increasing work effort and market awareness. More significantly, a comparison of employee attitudes towards management between 1979 and the present survey reveals little change in employee perception of a "them and us" divide. At any rate there is scant evidence of an ideological crisis for trade unions in the companies surveyed.

Finally, employee attitudes towards management emerge as a critical factor relating to the climate of industrial relations in a company. Positive attitudes toward management are linked with increased awareness of competitive realities; higher levels of satisfaction with industrial relations procedures; satisfaction with non-monetary benefits; and having more interesting work.

Chapter 4

CHANGING PATTERNS OF
INDUSTRIAL RELATIONS

There have been several attempts to categorise patterns of labour–management relations — that is, to develop a taxonomy of industrial relations types (Purcell, 1981). Generally these types have been located along a continuum ranging from confrontational or adversarial relations to co-operative relations between management and labour. Walton (1985) distinguishes between a control and a commitment approach to the management of employees. The control strategy is based on the principle that an organisation must impose control in order to extract effort from its employees. Control is achieved through building technical constraints into the production process, ensuring low levels of employee discretion, and the close monitoring and supervision of employees. Employee effort is elicited through a combination of cash inducements and strict discipline. Alternatively, the commitment strategy focuses on motivating employees through consent and self control, rather than external control. The emphasis is on high-trust relations between management and employees, allowing more discretion in direct job-related decisions, with greater flexibility in the way that work is organised, and a commitment by the organisation to the development of employees.

However, Walton's (1985) description of the commitment strategy is essentially prescriptive in intent and is difficult to verify empirically. Many commentators argue that a crucial factor in the shift from an adversarial to a commitment approach to labour–management relations is the degree of trust between labour and management (Purcell, 1981; Dastmalchian et al., 1991). Surveying the entrenched nature of industrial relations in the United Kingdom in the 1960s, Fox (1974) argued that organisations have been structured in such a way as to minimise managerial dependence on employees by reducing their discretion and control of work tasks. Three types of social relations exist in the workplace related to different structures of control: relations of low trust, medium trust and high trust. Low-trust relations are typical of jobs that are tightly bound by rules, closely supervised and have a low level of discretion (i.e. allowing employees little initiative). High-trust relations are accompanied by high levels of discretion and individual initiative, allowing scope for personal judgments and decisions. Medium-trust relations occupy a position between the two.

This division of social relations mirrors the stratification of organisations into Managerial, White-Collar and Manual Employees. While managerial and white-collar occupations are governed by bureaucratic principles where social relations are based on trust, responsibility and the internalisation of organisational rules, manual employees are governed by the principles of scientific management, which fosters relationships of minimum interaction and distrust (Hill, 1981: 29).

An important aspect of the distinction between high-trust and low-trust relations is that social interaction within a high-trust situation involves unspecified obligations, readiness to do the other party a favour and the expectation that others will also discharge their obligations in the long run. Conversely, social interaction in a low-trust situation involves the exchange of specific services for rigidly specified material rewards within an instrumental-type relationship which has no value beyond the cash nexus. In a low-trust environment, management attempts to restrict the scope of bargaining, information is often distorted, and the recognition and extent of mutual dependency on both sides are kept to a minimum and agreements are often broken. Unions often threaten industrial action and there is frequent raising of formal issues in the disputes procedure. As Fox (1974: 102) observes, low trust is accompanied by an "extreme win-lose" or "zero sum" approach to the bargaining process; a tendency to perceive the policies or values of the other side as being antipathetic to ones own interests and concerns; and gives rise to "such forms of behaviour as indifferent performance, clock-watching, high absence, sickness, and turnover rates". On the other hand, in the high-trust relationship there is a willing acceptance of each side's mutual dependence, which extends beyond the familiar matters of wages, hours and working conditions. Productive efficiency, the survival of the company and technological change, for example, are treated as matters of common interest (Walton and McKersie, 1965).

In this chapter a framework for identifying a set of typical industrial relations patterns is outlined. Secondly, industrial relations, both past and present, in each company are categorised in terms of these patterns. Finally, an attempt is made to provide an explanation of the change and stability in industrial relations over time, in terms of a company's product market and its financial performance. The question posed is whether there is a new pattern of industrial relations emerging in these companies. If there is an acceptance of the logic of the enterprise by employees (although the evidence in Chapter 3 of a new realism was slight), then it should manifest itself in a shift to more co-operative labour–management relations.

INDUSTRIAL RELATIONS CATEGORIES

Purcell (1981) argues that an overemphasis on the structural formalisation of rules and rule-making institutions as the key company-level components of industrial relations (i.e. procedures and agreements) ignores the problems in making the structures work. Both the commission of inquiry on industrial relations in Ireland and the Donovan commission in Britain equated good orderly industrial relations with well-developed formal procedures and agreements, as a means to bring consistency and order to workplace industrial relations. However Purcell (1981) points out that there is no reason why high-trust relations should not develop even where there is no formalised structure. Conversely, it is possible that low-trust relations can exist where there is a formalised system of workplace bargaining. Purcell concludes that there is no one style of good industrial relations, and proposes four ideal typical models of industrial relations by relating the maximum and minimum degree of trust with the extremes of low and high formalisation (see Figure 4.1). Two different patterns of industrial relations associated with high-trust relations are possible. Where high trust exists within a highly formalised setting, the pattern is labelled as co-operative constitutionalism. High trust and low formalisation (expressed through strong personal contacts where agreements rarely need to be recorded) is termed adaptive co-operation. In low-trust relations, there may also be developed formal structures, yet the relationship is marked by antagonism and distrust and is labelled antagonistic constitutionalism. The remaining pattern is characterised by low trust and low formalisation — no agreed rules or negotiation forum — and is termed uninhibited antagonism.

Figure 4.1: Four Patterns of Industrial Relations

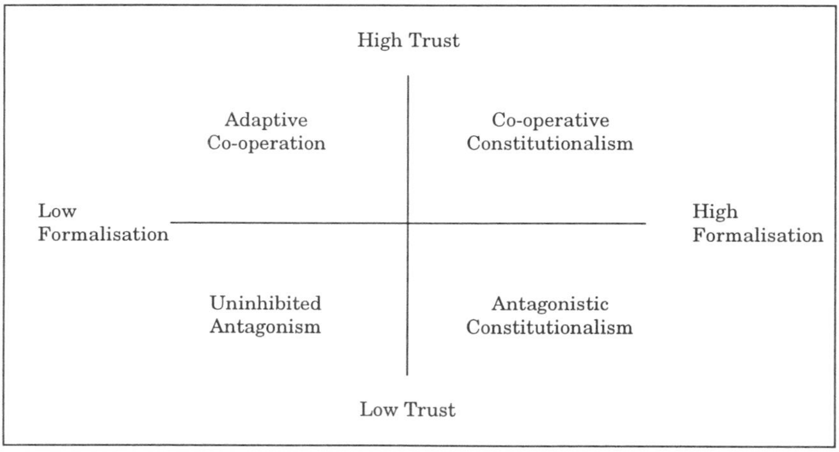

Source: Purcell 1981: 61.

According to Purcell (1981), these four patterns are ideal typical styles and unlikely to correspond completely to real situations, but are a useful heuristic device allowing comparison between companies and also within a company over time. Each pattern can be briefly summarised in terms of specific aspects of the labour management relation. In the *uninhibited antagonism* pattern, industrial relations is conducted in an ad hoc, conflict-based manner, with bargaining advantages frequently exploited by both sides when circumstances permit. The relationship is marked by mutual suspicion and distrust. The behaviour of one party is often seen by the other as irrational and unpredictable. There are few agreed rules of conduct between the parties. Custom and practice, or the "non-negotiated processes of collective bargaining", predominate. Management in industrial relations tends to be reactive and concerned with coping with short-term crises. In the event of an industrial dispute, reliance is often placed on third-party intervention.

Antagonistic constitutionalism prevails where the agreed procedures and institutions are used as a means of expressing the distrust and aggression that exist between both parties. Each party will often complain about the conduct of the other or the failure to abide by promises. Informal conduct between the parties is at a minimum and there is heavy reliance on formal procedures, especially for dispute and grievance handling. Numerous claims are pursued through the procedure by the union. Management tends to adopt an inflexible and bureaucratic stance in grievance negotiations and formal plant-wide industrial relations procedures are seen as its best defence against the unions whom it distrusts but is forced to deal with.

Co-operative constitutionalism is characterised by high trust and co-operation between the parties, which takes place within the framework of comprehensive agreements. A particular effort is made to abide by the constitution, which is seen to establish mutual rights and obligations which should not be breached. The procedure agreements are seen more as a flexible arrangement than a rigid framework. In particular, while all agreements are formally reached and recorded in the minutes, much informal activity takes place between the leading personnel of each side. "Corridor meetings" or informal chats are seen as essential if the formal machinery is to work effectively, allowing compromises to be reached or positions explained. The reliance on personal contact and informality means that leadership-type stewards are required within the union organisation.[1] The number of claims

---

[1] Batstone et al. (1977) identified two main steward types from their research: "leader" stewards who view union policy and their fellow stewards as their main source of reference in tackling workplace problems, and "populist" stewards who view their constituency as their major referent

contd.

processed through the disputes procedure tends to be relatively small, but the success rate for the union is fairly high. There will be concern to show that all grievances receive proper attention from management even if a negative outcome is known in advance, for it is felt important by both sides to encourage the use of the procedures, and to give support to senior shop stewards in handling claims raised by their constituents. Negotiators on either side are attuned to the political processes which take place in their counterpart organisations, and by subtle support, judicious bargaining tactics and communications exercises are able to support each other and help to structure favourable attitudes. The union is accepted as a necessary partner in the plant by most managers, and conversely the union officers see the company and its management as generally trustworthy. In this sense, trust is extended beyond the personal relationships of the negotiators to incorporate the union-management relationship as a whole.

The dominant characteristic in the *adaptive co-operation* pattern is a high level of trust and co-operation between negotiators, which extends to institutional trust, but is embodied in the personal relationship between a few key people on either side, supported by their advisers. There are few, if any, formal written agreements, especially of a procedural nature, or if there are, they are largely ignored, being replaced by the informal, adaptive relationship between the negotiators. Meetings occur when required, usually on an informal basis. This pattern tends to develop either through crisis and the emergence of a dominant personality or more slowly over a period of time, during which industrial relations is increasingly seen in terms of the personal interaction of the people involved. Management must channel most negotiations and consultations through the chief shop steward. This further

---

group. Leader stewards according to these authors, tend to be proactive in initiating demands and seek to develop strategies in support of claims which are congruent with wider trade union values and principles. Populist stewards tend to respond to the demands made by their work group in preference to initiating demands themselves. Thus their perspective is more sectional in orientation. Leader stewards tended to have proportionally more contact with other stewards than populists.

emphasises extreme centralisation and a personalised approach to handling industrial relations matters. Although grievances and disputes are raised at shop-floor level, and some are resolved there without the intervention of the chief negotiators, any contentious issue is quickly passed to the centre, or the steward and departmental manager asks for advice. The co-operative, yet personal and largely private, relationship between the two negotiators sets the tone of industrial relations in the plant by prescribing what constitutes acceptable behaviour. Problems tend to be "sorted out" between the chief negotiators, often with reference to precedent or earlier experiences which, while unrecorded, are readily recalled in conversation. Consultation and information disclosure are undertaken, again largely through the personal contact between the key people on either side. In particular, the shop steward will expect to be kept informed of all major developments within the company, probably receiving private briefings from the personnel manager.

In order to evaluate these patterns of industrial relations, in his empirical work, Purcell (1981) developed a measure for a number of industrial relations areas. Each of these areas can be assessed in terms of the ideal typical patterns described above. In the following section, four areas of industrial relations are assessed: the bargaining arrangements in each company; the extent of formalisation in union–management relationships; the manner in which issues are regulated; and lastly, union-related processes. Case material on these areas was obtained through interviews with the personnel manager in each company, with shop stewards and line-manager interviews providing a supportive source of information. Personnel managers were provided with a four-point scale for each industrial relations area and asked to indicate the appropriate position of their company. Each position corresponded to one of the four industrial relations patterns, though this was not disclosed to the interviewee. Where possible, respondents were also asked to indicate the companies position approximately 10 years previously, in order to measure the extent of change or shift in the pattern of industrial relations over time.

Pattern of Bargaining Arrangements at Company Level

The essential distinction in bargaining arrangements is between
a distributive and integrative approach to bargaining — that is,
between arrangements where there are winners and losers, and
those where there is mutual gain for both parties. Three aspects
of bargaining are assessed: bargaining style, use of tactical advantage and the degree of informal contact between negotiators.
Bargaining style ranges from the extremely distributive, coercive
and defensive behaviour associated with the uninhibited antagonistic pattern to the highly informal, integrative and co-operative
style characteristic of adaptive co-operation. Tactical advantages
are part of the struggle for control in the uninhibited pattern, and
union and management only meet when there are conflicts to be
resolved. In contrast, short-term tactical advantages are rarely
used in the adaptive pattern, the emphasis is on the need to preserve trust and confidence, and the bargaining relationship is
based on regular informal contact between the parties. The two
remaining patterns — antagonistic and co-operative constitutionalism fall between these extremes. In Table 4.1 the majority of
respondents indicated an integrative approach to bargaining,
related to a co-operative constitutionalist pattern of industrial relations at present.

Similarly, a majority of the companies conformed to this
pattern in the use of tactics and the degree of informal contact.
Nevertheless, a number of respondents indicated an antagonistic
or adversarial pattern in their bargaining arrangements. A total
of six companies retained a similar pattern over time, four with
an antagonistic pattern and a further two with a more co-
operative pattern. There was a distinctive shift in bargaining
arrangements in the remaining seven companies towards a more
co-operative relationship. This is more clearly evident when the
overall patterns of bargaining arrangements are considered
together. Only three companies in the past were recorded as
having co-operative-style bargaining arrangements, whereas at
present eight companies can be classified in this category.

Table 4.1: Bargaining Arrangements and Industrial Relations Patterns

Uninhibited Antagonism	*Antagonistic Constitutionalism*	*Co-operative Constitutionalism*	*Adaptive Co-operation*
1. Bargaining Styles			
Exclusively distributive and coercive, reflecting institutional distrust and defensive behaviour.	Distributive and often conducted with acrimony, reflecting institutional distrust. Tending to be defensive.	A marked tendency towards integrative bargaining, maximising co-operative tendencies inherent in institutional trust.	*Highly informal.* Tendency towards integrative bargaining, maximising co-operative tendencies inherent in institutional trust.
Past: 1	10	2	0
Present: 0	5	7	1
2. Use of Tactical Advantage			
Tactical advantage seen as a positive requirement in the never-ending battle for control.	Tactical advantage often used by both sides, but in the context of negotiations and disputes.	Rarely done. Emphasis on "rules of the game" and need to preserve the long-term bargaining relationship.	Rarely done. Emphasis on need *to preserve trust and confidence* of the negotiators on the other side.
Past: 5	3	3	2
Present: 2	1	6	4
3. Formality of Contact			
The parties only meet ad hoc when there are conflicts to be resolved — a reflection of mutual distrust and dislike.	Very little — a reflection of mutual distrust and often dislike.	High. Informal pre-meetings and corridor meetings in adjournments seen as vital and reflect and reinforce high trust.	Very frequent. The whole bargaining relationship is based on informal contact built around and through high trust.
Past: 7	2	3	1
Present: 5	0	6	2

Summary (Three factors combined)		*Bargaining Arrangements*	
Uninhibited Antagonism	*Antagonistic Constitutionalism*	*Co-operative Constitutionalism*	*Adaptive Co-operation*
Past: 5	5	2	1
Present: 2	3	7	1

N = 13 companies.
Source: Personnel/senior management interviews (structured questionnaire).

Formalisation of Industrial Relations

The extent of formalisation is evaluated by measuring the process of recording agreements and the procedures for discipline and dismissals. Although agreements are rarely recorded in both the uninhibited pattern and the adaptive pattern, the reasons for using either pattern differ dramatically. In the latter case there is an informal consensus on matters and verbal agreements are sufficient, while in the former case both parties are reluctant to forego possible tactical advantages by committing an agreement to writing. Agreements are recorded in both the constitutional patterns. The regulation of workplace procedures tends to be on unilateral management action in the two antagonistic patterns, whereas joint agreement, tending towards informal settlement of

Table 4.2: Formalisation of Industrial Relations Agreements and Regulation of Procedures

Uninhibited Antagonism	*Antagonistic Constitutionalism*	*Co-operative Constitutionalism*	*Adaptive Co-operation*
1. Recording Agreements			
Not done, or "scraps of paper stuffed in overall pockets".	Seen as essential by both sides as neither can trust the other to keep its word.	Seen as important both to indicate the solemn and binding nature of joint agreements and to ensure proper implementation.	Rarely done, informal consensus and agreement sufficient — except where required in law or contract
Past: 3	4	4	1
Present: 0	5	6	1
2. Dismissal and Discipline Procedures			
Unilateral management procedure based on Code of Practice.	Often unilateral management document as the union refuses to become responsible for disciplining employees.	Joint agreement, sometimes with union officers sitting in judgment on a joint panel with managers.	No formal procedures used but practice clearly understood. *Informal discussion* of case often precedes formal appeal hearings etc.
Past: 3	3	3	3
Present: 3	2	4	3

N = 13 companies.
Source: Personnel/senior management interviews (structured
          questionnaire).

problems, occurs in the two co-operative patterns. Regarding the present formalisation of agreements, seven companies can be defined in the co-operative category and five in the antagonistic category. Only one company can be defined in the adaptive co-operation category. Not surprisingly, given the high density of unionisation in the case-study companies, the majority of companies fall in the two constitutional categories where agreements are carefully recorded to ensure their implementation (Table 4.2).

Overall change has been minor in both of these areas particularly in the handling of discipline and dismissals cases.

Scope and Regulation of Issues

An important aspect of labour–management relations is the extent to which custom and practice are relied upon as a procedure in determining industrial relations issues. In the antagonistic patterns, the policing of established customs and practices is of keen interest to both parties. Management attempts to preserve existing rules and precedents in its favour while labour regards custom and practice drift as a tactical means by which procedural and substantive gains are achieved. Conversely co-operative relations are mainly characterised by disapproval of custom and practice, although some precedent is acknowledged as inevitable. Along with custom and practice, the wider scope of subjects covered in collective bargaining is associated with a co-operative climate of industrial relations. Despite the dramatic shift in the approach to custom and practice, there is still a majority of companies (eight) in the antagonistic constitutional category.

By contrast only two companies remain in this category regarding the scope of issues covered, with six companies shifting toward a co-operative pattern. Both of these areas indicate a significant shift toward a more co-operative stance. The extent of the shift is clearer when both factors are combined together. At present, 11 companies exhibit co-operative relations in these areas while only two companies remain in the adversarial category.

Table 4.3: Regulation and Scope of Issues in Collective Bargaining

Uninhibited Antagonism	Antagonistic Constitutionalism	Co-operative Constitutionalism	Adaptive Co-operation
1. Custom and Practice			
Both sides rely on precedent as a means of defence in maintaining the frontier of control. Non-negotiated agreements and custom and practice drift are chief means by which procedural and substantive gain is achieved.	Attempts by management to preserve existing custom and practice rules in its favour, and to restrict development of new custom and practice rules by means of tight control system.	Largely disapproved of by both sides but recognised as being inevitable to a degree. Management control systems used to inhibit development and monitor growth, with information shared with union.	Largely dis-approved of at section level by the negotiators on both sides *as it tends to weaken their authority*, but recognised as inevitable to a degree.
Past: 4	8	1	0
Present: 1	7	4	1
2. Scope of Issues			
Restricted to general trends or specific issues pertinent to the dispute in question.	Very limited. General trends or company perform-ance. Tendency to be restricted to "tea and toilets".	Wide-ranging, often with special reports by various func-tional directors on future prospects and plans and past performance.	Wide-ranging, often with *informal briefings* by various functional directors on future prospects and plans and past performance.
Past: 5	3	4	1
Present: 1	1	8	3

Summary (Two factors combined)		*Scope/Regulation of Issues*	
Uninhibited Antagonism	Antagonistic Constitutionalism	Co-operative Constitutionalism	Adaptive Co-operation
Past: 2	6	5	0
Present: 0	2	9	2

N = 13 companies.
Source: Personnel/senior management interviews (structured questionnaire).

Union Processes

Three key aspects of workplace unionism are explored: the extent to which union members are defended; the extent of inter-union co-operation; and the attitude of management towards the union(s) in the company. The defence of union members is a core principle of trade unionism, and can range from the defence of union members in all circumstances to a situation where certain behaviours are considered unacceptable and indefensible. Respondents in seven companies indicated that union members were defended in all circumstances. Even so, this represented a shift from past practices where members were defended in all circumstances in 10 companies. At present, the union operates a policy in six companies where certain unacceptable behaviours are not defended. Turning to inter-union co-operation, the extent of co-operation between unions (this refers chiefly to relations between general and craft unions) in negotiations has remained unchanged. There was a high degree of union sectionalism in negotiating collective agreements. In four companies there appeared to be a close relationship between unions which extended into the negotiation of agreements and a common stance on important workplace issues (Table 4.4).

A critical aspect of union–management relations is management's perception of the union. Three possible relations between the company and trade unions were provided in the questionnaire ranging from extreme distrust and marginalisation of the union to an acceptance of the union as a legitimate and trusted bargaining partner. Unions in nine companies were perceived as organisations that needed to be kept at arm's length, while the union was regarded as a trusted bargaining partner in four companies. This represents a significant shift in three companies in recent years. Even so, compared to the industrial relations areas discussed above, the union processes touched on here have changed least during the 1980s, which further confirms the findings on union organisational characteristics in Chapter 2. It may also indicate a conservatism in management approaches to the trade unions, as only two of the companies had initiated any forms of worker participation. Finally, the combined scores in the four

Table 4.4: Union Processes, Past and Present

Uninhibited Antagonism	*Antagonistic Constitutionalism*	*Co-operative Constitutionalism*	*Adaptive Co-operation*
1. Defence of Union Members			
Every member must be defended irrespective of alleged misdemeanour. Reliance on precedent.	Every member must be defended irrespective of alleged misdemeanour. Reliance on *recorded* precedent.	Clear notion of what constitutes unacceptable behaviour which cannot be tolerated. Reliance on *recorded* precedent in handling other cases.	Clear notion of what constitutes unacceptable behaviour which cannot be tolerated. Reliance on precedent in handling other cases.
Past: 4	6	2	1
Present: 3	4	4	2
2. Inter-union Co-operation			
Sectionalism in negotiations. Often membership competition, demarcation disputes and arguments over differentials.	Sometimes close, with emphasis on collective strength; but subject to strain, with arguments about representation of various unions among office holders.	Likely to be close, particularly between the leaders of the various unions.	Likely to be close, with the various unions uniting under the dominant personality of a senior shop steward.
Past: 7	1	3	1
Present: 7	1	3	1
3. Management Attitudes			
Distrust and resentment at unwarranted interference. *Avoid contact with or reliance on union* e.g. attempt to bypass union and communicate direct to workers.	Distrust and resentment. Feeling that union cannot be relied on to keep agreements, co-operate in problem-solving or keep information confidential. *To be kept under control at arm's length.*	Accepted as legitimate, even necessary organisations in representing employee interest and organising employees into a coherent interest group. *A trusted bargaining partner within the plant.*	
Past: 4	8	1	
Present: 2	7	4	

N = 13 companies.

Source: Personnel/senior management interviews (structured
        questionnaire).

industrial relations processes are added together to give one overall score for each company. Admittedly, this is a rather artificial
exercise. However, it does facilitate inter-company comparisons
and, we would argue, is a reasonably accurate measure of a company's overall pattern of industrial relations.

Table 4.5: Change in Industrial Relations Patterns

Uninhibited Antagonism	Antagonistic Constitutionalism	Co-operative Constitutionalism	Adaptive Co-operation
Past: 5	4	3	0
Present: 1	5	6	0

N = 13 companies.
Source: Personnel/senior management interviews (structured
        questionnaire).

Although no company can be classified in the adaptive co-
operation category there is a distinctive shift from extreme
antagonistic relations towards less antagonistic and more co-
operative relations (Table 4.5). At present six companies have a
co-operative constitutional pattern of industrial relations, compared to three in the past. More significantly, only one company
remains with an extremely antagonistic pattern. *Five companies*
experienced a substantial positive shift in their industrial relations pattern during the 1980s (Table 4.6). Three of these companies changed from antagonistic to co-operative relations, one
company had a co-operative pattern in the past, and the remaining company changed from inhibited to constitutional antagonism. *Eight companies* experienced little or no change in their
industrial relations. However, two of these companies have
always had co-operative relations between management and
labour and one company, although still in the antagonistic
category, is shifting towards a co-operative pattern.

  There are, therefore, *five companies* which exhibit an antagonistic pattern and have experienced little or no change over time
and *five companies* which have undergone substantial shifts in
their industrial relations, towards a more co-operative pattern.
The remaining part of this study attempts to provide an explanation of why the former group of companies is characterised by

adversarial-type relations while the latter group has experienced a substantial shift towards a more co-operative pattern of industrial relations. Two critical areas commonly linked to explanations about industrial relations phenomena are a company's product market and its financial performance, and the actual dynamics of the relationship between management and labour in specific situations and over a period of time.

Table 4.6: Overall Pattern of Industrial Relations*

Company	Past	Present	Change[†]
Dairyfoods	**15**	**29**	**positive shift (high)**
Mineral Ltd.	19	21	little change(low)
Textile	24	24	no change (moderate)
Park Foods	15	15	no change (low)
Senchem	19	19	no change (low)
Burchocks	**16**	**26**	**positive shift (high)**
Tirown Sweets	**22**	**30**	**positive change (high)**
Lola Drinks	28	28	no change (high)
Micro Engineering	32	32	no change (high)
Electro Engineering	**15**	**23**	**positive shift (moderate)**
Chemton	**26**	**32**	**positive shift (high)**
Processchems	17	19	little change (low)
Clothing Ltd.**	n/a	25/6	

* Scores across all the factors are added together for each company to give the overall total. Companies experiencing substantial shifts are highlighted[2].
† high = co-operative relations; low = antagonistic relations; moderate = either moderate antagonism or co-operation.
** Some data on Clothing Ltd. are missing. The pattern score for the present is evaluated using pattern scores and wider interview information.
Source: Personnel/senior management interviews (structured questionnaire).

[2] The overall patterns are scored as follows:
  1. Uninhibited Antagonism: Range 10 to 18.
  2. Antagonistic constitutionalism: Range 19 to 25.
  3. Co-operative Constitutionalism: Range 26 to 32.
  4. Adaptive Co-operation : Range 33 to 39.

MARKETS, FIRM PERFORMANCE AND INDUSTRIAL RELATIONS

In recent years, a growing body of literature has emphasised the link between a firm's product market and its approach to employee relations (Edwards, 1987; Purcell, 1981). While there is no overall consensus regarding the exact nature of the relationship, there is broad agreement on the central importance of the market in determining strategies for the management of labour. A simple summary of the relationship is that a firm's business strategy is determined in large part by the characteristics of its product market and its position in that market. In turn, this influences the industrial relations strategy adopted, which results in a particular industrial relations pattern over time. Although many industrial relations academics have pointed to the link between the market environment, business strategy and industrial relations strategy (Purcell, 1981; Thurley and Wood, 1983; Kochan et al., 1986), few have provided a conceptual framework which allows for comparisons of market pressures between organisations (Marchington, 1990). Three distinct approaches are examined below, one which emphasises the market position of the company, a second which uses a more comprehensive measure of market pressure exerted on a company, and a third perspective which relates a firm's industrial relations pattern to its economic performance. When a firm's economic performance is high (compared to similar organisations), it will have extra cash resources to invest in human resource management policies which encourage co-operative-type labour–management relations. There is bound to be some congruence between firms that experience a low level of market pressure and high economic performance. However, over time, high profitability in an industry encourages other firms to enter the market, which depresses average profitability for all firms (Oster, 1990). In the long run, most firms move through a number of distinct product-market positions, which have important consequences for a firm's labour–management relations.

Industrial Relations Patterns and Market Position

A common framework used to define a company's market position is the growth-share matrix developed by the Boston consultancy group (see Porter, 1985). Both Schuler (1988) and Thomason (1984) have adapted this matrix to link product market characteristics and appropriate patterns of employee relations. A company's market position is determined by two criteria — its share of the relevant market and whether this market is growing or declining. Four distinct positions have been identified as follows:

A. Low share of a rising market, demand for the product is just starting. Companies in the position are known as *Wildcat* undertakings.

B. High share of an expanding market, demand is growing rapidly. Companies here are labelled *Star* undertakings.

C. High share of a declining market, demand is stable. Companies become *Cash Cows*.

D. Low share of a falling market, demand is declining. Companies are labelled as *Dogs*.

These distinct market positions correspond to a product life cycle in which the product moves through four phases (Schuler, 1988). At the introductory phase primary demand for the product is just starting to grow, while at the growth phase demand is growing rapidly (at 10 per cent or more annually) with the technology and competitive structure still changing. In the maturity phase, growth of the product is either stable or increasing/decreasing by a small margin, and technological and competitive structures are reasonably stable. Finally, in the decline phase, real growth is negative, and weak competitors are forced out of the market.

Each group of these market positions requires different product and marketing strategies to survive and, according to Thomason (1984), business strategies are likely to be constrained, though not determined, by the undertaking's current market position. However, there is a presumption that organisations should adopt the appropriate strategy for their position (Thomason, 1984). In choosing business and industrial relations strategies, a dog cannot emulate a star without encountering serious problems, and conversely, a star should not emulate a dog as it would forego the most profitable option available. Thomason

(1984) views a company's market position as the dominant defining characteristic, influencing business strategy and industrial relations strategy. As a result, appropriate or congruent industrial relations strategies are linked with a company's market position (Table 4.7).

Table 4.7: Market Position, Business Strategy and Patterns of Industrial Relations

Market Position	Business Strategy	Industrial Relations Strategy	Industrial Relations Pattern
Wild Cat — Low share of growing market — New & Dynamic — In need of flexibility & versatility	Cost Leader	Autocratic and largely unregulated control of labour. Where union organisation occurs, chronic conflict may become an inherent feature.	Could either be one of uninhibited antagonism or antagonistic constitutionalism since it needs co-operation or at least acquiescence of labour in order to generate the market.
Star — Surplus of Cash — There is a production imperative	Dynamic Growth	Directed towards maintaining ordered relationships which may be purchased through the provision of incentives (e.g. overtime).	Likely to take the form of either co-operative or constitutional antagonism.
Cash Cow — Has moved from a star into a mature market — Relatively high cash resources	Extract Profit	Directed towards maintaining order which it may still be able to "afford". If employment has declined, with unions weaker management may have an opportunity to mould the industrial relations patterns to a greater extent than before.	Pattern could shift to adaptive or co-operative constitutionalism from an antagonistic pattern.
Dog — Little cash available.	Turnaround strategy	Emphasis on achieving control by direct coercive methods. Possibilities of buying co-operation will slowly diminish.	Uninhibited antagonism or antagonistic constitutionalism.

Source: Adapted from Thomason, 1984.

Thus, for example, a company with relatively high cash resources (cash cow) can afford to pursue a high investment strategy toward its human resources, providing extensive training for employees, harmonised working conditions and some degree of job security. As a consequence, the appropriate pattern of industrial relations will be either adaptive or constitutional co-operation. Despite the general acceptance of Thomason's (1984) framework, there is a dearth of empirical work verifying it. This is not surprising, since testing the model requires extensive information on a company's pattern of industrial relations, which can only be established from case-study work. The 13 medium/large companies in the present study provide a rich source of data on industrial relations patterns, which can be tested against the predictions in the model. Using this model, the pattern of industrial relations is correctly or approximately predicted in nine of the companies. However, three of the five companies with antagonistic relations and one company with co-operative relations are incorrectly predicted. While this may appear to be moderate confirmation of the model, this conclusion needs to be treated with some caution. Firstly, the majority of companies appear to occupy the same market position, 10 companies are defined as cash cows giving almost no variation in the market position of the companies studied. Secondly, if the model is applied to the industrial relations patterns existing during the early 1980s, the prediction rate decreases dramatically. Thirdly, as noted, the pattern of industrial relations is incorrectly predicted in four of the companies.

Industrial Relations and Market Pressure

The predictive weakness of the growth/share matrix results, according to Marchington and Parker (1990), from the broad generality of the loosely defined market positions. They argue that dividing companies into four broad market positions is not precise enough to allow for comparisons of different product-market circumstances and suggests an alternative framework to analyse "the extent to which the product markets in which companies compete appear to allow managers room for manoeuvre in their choice of how to handle employee relations" (120). The product market is divided into two separate components: the *competitive pressure* on a firm and *customer pressure*, both of which determine the overall power or pressure of the market on the firm. The principal objective is to categorise product markets according to their potential power to determine the union–management relationship. Where demand is growing, competitive pressures are likely to be less because the company's share is likely to be on the increase, and where competitors find it difficult to establish a presence in the market, management should have more room to manoeuvre in responding to market pressures and changes.

The second component of customer pressure measures the extent to which companies come under pressure from customers. Firstly, pressure arises from unpredictability in the demand for a company's product. Demand may either be stable or vary over time, but the critical factor is whether the variations are predictable in the future. A regular and predictable level of demand affords more room for manoeuvre than one that is subject to variability and unpredictability. Secondly, customer profile structures can also vary. Companies that rely on a single or small number of customers are more vulnerable to market pressures than companies whose products are bought by an unco-ordinated group of consumers and will have less room to manoeuvre. Figure 4.2 summarises Marchington's (1990) framework.

Figure 4.2: Product Market Characteristics

	Competitive Pressure	Consumer Pressure
High	Declining Demand Declining Market Share Entry of Competitors	Irregular Demand Low Predictability Reliance on Single/Few Customers
Low	Growing Demand High Market Share Barrier to Entry	Regular Demand Predictability Many Customers

Source: Marchington 1990.

The opportunity for choice is related to senior-management perception of market pressures. Using four case studies with

Table 4.8: Market Pressure and Industrial Relations*

Company	Market Pressure	Predicted Pattern	Actual Pattern
Positive IR Shift			
Dairyfoods	moderate	Co-operation	SAME
Burchocks	low	Constitutional/Adaptive co-operation	SAME
Tirown Sweets	low	Constitutional/Adaptive co-operation	SAME
Electro Engineering	moderate	Co-operation	SAME
Antagonistic IR			
Mineral Ltd.	**low**	**Constitutional/Adaptive co-operation**	**Constitutional antagonism**
Park Foods	**low**	**Constitutional/Adaptive co-operation**	**Constitutional antagonism**
Senchem	**moderate**	**Constitutional co-operation**	**Uninhibited/ Constitutional antagonism**
Processchems	high	Uninhibited/Constitutional antagonism	SAME
Textile	high	Uninhibited/Constitutional antagonism	SAME
No Change, Co-operative IR			
Lola Drinks	moderate	Constitutional co-operation	SAME
Micro Engineering	low	Constitutional/Adaptive co-operation	SAME
Chemton	moderate	Constitutional co-operation	SAME
Clothing Ltd.	n/a	Constitutional co-operation	SAME

* Market pressure is measured here using the combined score of three questions:
  1. Is the market you sell into: growing (scored 1); remains the same (scored 2); declining (scored 3)?
  2. Is the market share of the company: growing, same or declining?
  3. Do you sell/supply your products chiefly to: a large number of customers (scored 1); a small number (scored 2); one customer (scored 3)?
  The combined score gives a range from 9 — high pressure — to 3 — low pressure. The companies are divided into high, moderate and low categories.
Source: Interviews with senior/financial managers (structured questionnaire).

different market pressures, it appeared that where these were extreme, "management may see its primary task as engineering the best fit with external contingencies" (Marchington, 1990: 120), and may perceive little room for manoeuvre in how they conduct employee relations, regarding their actions as contingent on a market that appears to be beyond their control. As a consequence, management in the company experiencing the highest pressure from the market adopted an adversarial stance towards labour. This appeared to supervisors and line managers in this company to be the appropriate approach to employee relations, given the unpredictability of the market. In contrast, another case-study company experienced a favourable market environment and had the opportunity to introduce a range of polices which enhanced the status and security of employment and created a climate for a more co-operative style of industrial relations. According to this analysis, companies with a low market pressure are more likely to have a co-operative industrial relations pattern, with the opposite holding for companies with a high level of market pressure.

As Table 4.8 indicates, the market pressure approach is slightly better at predicting the actual pattern of industrial relations. Three companies are incorrectly predicted (marked in bold) compared to four in the previous model. However, the same three companies are incorrectly predicted in both cases. The market pressure model fails to explain satisfactorily why some companies, albeit a small but important group, have exhibited an antagonistic pattern of industrial relations despite a market environment which should, ceteris paribus, be conducive to co-operative labour–management relations. An alternative, if related, approach is to focus on the relationship between a firm's industrial relations and its economic performance (for overviews see Freeman and Medoff, 1984; Becker and Olson, 1987; Metcalf, 1989; Kleiner, 1990).

ECONOMIC PERFORMANCE AND INDUSTRIAL RELATIONS PATTERNS

A number of studies have shown that a firms economic performance is affected by its industrial relations climate. Katz et al. (1983) using data from 18 plants (all unionised) within a division of General Motors for 1970–79 examined the relationship between industrial relations, quality-of-work-life programmes and economic performance. The industrial relations measures used included attitudinal questions on the climate of the union–management relationship; grievance and discipline rates; intensity of contract negotiations; and levels of absenteeism. Controlling for volume of production in the various plants and plant-specific effects, the industrial relations measures appeared to be systematically related both to each other and to economic performance (as measured by direct labour efficiency and product quality). Katz et al. (1985) reported broadly similar results in a study of 25 manufacturing plants of one company. There was strong evidence of an association between measures of the performance of industrial relations systems and economic performance (see also Katz et al., 1988). Industrial relations measures used were grievance rates, discipline rates, absentee rates, attitudinal climate between union and management and participation in suggestion programmes.

In an study of 25 work areas of a large unionised manufacturing facility in the period 1984–87, Gershenfield (1991) examined how a transformation in patterns of conflict and co-operation affected economic performance. The results showed that work areas with "traditional" labour–management relations rooted in adversarial assumptions had higher cost, more scrap, lower productivity than work areas with "transformational" relations, characterised by increased co-operation and improved dispute resolutions. When industrial relations are poor, it is also unlikely that the efficiency strategies adopted by management in response to market pressures will be successful. Such strategies as improved standards, higher quality, better work organisation and work study generally are apt to increase resistance and ultimately to become costly to implement.

It has been argued, however, that the relationship between the pattern of industrial relations and economic performance may in fact be in the opposite direction — that is, high economic performance enables co-operative relations between management and labour to develop (see Hirsch and Addison, 1986; Becker and Olson, 1987). In any event, whichever way causality runs is immaterial to our present purpose, which is to establish whether there is a relationship between a firm's industrial relations and its economic performance. Economic performance is evaluated using two measures: financial performance and productivity efficiency. Financial performance is gauged as the relationship between revenue and costs (see note to Table 4.9), productive efficiency is a combination of production costs per unit of labour and level of productivity per worker. Companies are divided into high, moderate and low-financial performers and high, average and low levels of productive efficiency.

As expected, there is a close relationship between profit levels and productive efficiency. However, there are three notable exceptions — two companies, Burchocks and Lola Drinks, have high profit levels but a low level of productive efficiency, while the remaining company scores high on productive efficiency and low on financial performance. In the case of the former two companies, the level of market pressure is quite low (see Table 4.9) permitting less productive practices to survive, though, Lola Drinks is beginning to come under pressure from comparisons with other subsidiaries in this multinational. Those companies in the antagonistic industrial relations category are characterised by low or average to low performance in productive efficiency and moderate to low profit levels. Alternatively, companies that have more co-operative industrial relations or have experienced a positive shift towards such a pattern are characterised by either high profits or high levels of productive efficiency. Again, there are exceptions — Electro Engineering and Chemton have both a moderate profit level and average productivity, which is the general prevailing combination for companies with antagonistic labour–management relations. A possible explanation for these exceptions is that these companies are able, despite their present economic performance, to provide a high level of monetary and non-monetary benefits to their employees. Manual employees in Chemton enjoy the highest rates of pay compared to the rest of the companies, while Electro Engineering is ranked fourth. This raises the critical issue of employee goals and expectations in the employment relationship, as financial and productivity indicators are mainly of importance to managers and shareholders.

Table 4.9: Economic Performance and Industrial Relations

Company	Financial Performance*	Productivity Efficiency†	Industrial Relations Pattern
Positive IR Shift			
Dairyfoods	moderate/low	high	Constitutional co-operation
Burchocks	high	low/average	Constitutional co-operation
Tirown Sweets	high	high	Constitutional/ Adaptive co-operation
Electro Engineering	moderate	average	Constitutional co-operation
Antagonistic IR			
Mineral Ltd.	moderate	low	Constitutional antagonism
Park Foods	moderate	average	Constitutional antagonism
Senchem	moderate	average/low	Uninhibited/Constitutional antagonism
Processchems	low	average/low	Uninhibited/Constitutional antagonism
Textile	moderate	average/low	Constitutional antagonism
No Change: Co-operative IR			
Lola Drinks	high	low	Constitutional co-operation
Micro Engineering	high	high	Adaptive/Constitutional co-operation
Chemton	moderate	average	Adaptive/Constitutional co-operation
Clothing Ltd.	n/a	n/a	Constitutional co-operation

*   Financial performance is estimated using the following question: In assessing the overall performance of this establishment would you say the gross revenue earned over the past two years has been:
well in excess of costs = scored high
sufficient to make a small profit = scored moderate
enough to break even = scored moderate to low
insufficient to cover costs/so low as to produce large losses = scored low.

†   Productive efficiency is composed of three questions:
1. How would you compare wage costs per unit of output at this establishment with the rest of the competition in the industry — scored on a range from 1 = well above average to 5 = well below average?
2. How would you compare the average level of production at this establishment with the rest of the competition in the industry — scored as above?
3. Compared with foreign competitors, how would you rate your labour productivity — scored on a range from: much better (scored 1) to much worse (scored 5)?
The answers to the three questions are added together and categorised as high, average or low in productive efficiency.

Source: Interviews with senior/financial managers (structured questionnaire).

Two important employee goals are earnings and security of employment. Table 4.10 outlines the relationship between gross salary levels for unskilled manual employees, changes in employment, effort levels and the availability of overtime. Employment and overtime levels are classified as increasing, decreasing or remaining the same and the symbol (+) indicates a substantial change. Salary levels are graded as at the norm, above the norm and below the norm, with the norm being defined as a wage of approximately £10,500. There appears to be no discernible relationship between levels of pay and industrial relations patterns. Among those companies which have experienced a positive shift in their industrial relations, two have above-the-norm pay levels and two are at the norm. In the antagonistic category three companies have above-the-norm levels, one is below the norm and one is at the norm. However, a serious problem related to using the industrial average wage is that it fails to take into account sectional pay norms. In general, for example, chemical firms tend to pay above the norm, while textile firms tend to be at the norm or below it. Both Senchem and Processchems are chemical plants with antagonistic relations and above-the-norm pay levels. Compared to other chemical plants, however, these companies may not be classed as having above-the-norm pay levels. Therefore, some caution needs to be exercised in interpreting wage norms, particularly when, as is the case here, companies are from different industrial sectors.

An alternative and perhaps more accurate measure is manual employees' satisfaction with gross pay (scored 1 = satisfied to 3 = not satisfied). Surprisingly, there is no relationship between actual gross pay and perceived level of satisfaction with pay (Pearson correlation is a low R = 0.1 and is not statistically significant). Manual employee responses for Burchocks score the highest mean aggregate level of satisfaction with pay while Burchocks' actual gross pay barely reaches the industrial average. Conversely, Mineral Ltd. has above-the-norm pay levels, but employee satisfaction is extremely low. Making sense of these results requires concentrating not just on levels of actual gross pay or even perceived levels of satisfaction, but on the change or

Table 4.10: Employee Goals and Industrial Relations

Company	Salary Level *	Satisfaction with Salary**	Employment	Effort Levels***	Overtime	Change in Earnings
Positive IR Shift						
Dairyfoods	norm	2.26	decreased	2.2	same	slight decrease
Burchocks	norm	1.18	increased	1.81	increased	same/ increased
Tirown Sweets	above norm	n/a	decrease+	n/a	decrease+	same/slight decrease
Electro En-gineering	above norm	1.94	decreased	2.35	decreased	same/slight decrease
Antagonistic IR						
Mineral Ltd.	above norm	2.43	decrease+	2.21	decrease+	decreased
Park Foods	below norm	1.62	decreased	2.12	decreased	slight decrease
Senchem	above norm	2.0	same	2.63	same	decreased
Process-chems	above norm	n/a	decrease+	n/a	decrease+	decreased
Textile	norm	n/a	decreased	n/a	n/a	same
No Change, Co-operative IR						
Lola Drinks	above norm	n/a	increased	n/a	same	same
Micro Engi-neering	norm	1.7	increased	2.36	n/a	same
Chemton	above norm	1.41	decreased	2.53	decrease+	slight decrease
Clothing Ltd.	below norm	2.43	increased	2.2	same	same

*   The company aggregate mean gross salary level for unskilled manual workers is obtained by: (a) employee survey in nine companies; (b) information provided by the personnel manager in the remaining four companies.

**   Respondents were asked whether they were satisfied with their gross wages — scored 1 = satisfied; 2 = neither satisfied nor dissatisfied; 3 = dissatisfied.

***   Respondents were asked a number of questions concerning increased effort levels over recent years. See page 64, Chapter 3, for a description of the composite factor. The mean aggregate score for all manual workers in each company is reported here. The composite factor effort levels is scored from 0 = no change in effort levels to 4 = high levels of change.

Source: Interviews with senior/financial managers (structured questionnaire).

variation in pay and working conditions. In particular, it is the direction and impact of this change on the expectations of employees concerning appropriate pay norms and effort levels for their work which in turn affects the nature of the relationship between management and labour.

Three measures in Table 4.10 allow some evaluation of the impact of changes in employment levels, effort levels and the use of overtime. Once again, there is no apparent relationship between changes in employment or increased effort levels and the type of industrial relations pattern. In all, only four companies had increased employment numbers in the previous three years. It may be significant that no increase in employment numbers occurred in companies with adversarial industrial relations. Alternatively, three of the companies which recorded positive shifts in their industrial relations also showed a decrease in employment numbers. Similarly, there is no relationship between changes in effort levels and the industrial relations climate. No significant difference emerged in the mean score for changes in effort levels across the companies. The only notable result is that manual employees in Burchocks perceived least change in effort levels and were also the most satisfied with their gross pay.

However, there is a discernible relationship between changes in the availability of overtime and a company's industrial relations. All of the companies with adversarial industrial relations recorded a decrease in the use of overtime in the previous three years. Two of the companies — Mineral Ltd. and Processchems — recorded substantial decreases. Interestingly, employees in both of these companies had the most negative attitudes towards management (see Table 3.13). With the exception of two companies, those in the co-operative industrial relations category recorded either increases in overtime or similar levels of overtime in the previous three years. These exceptions have unique circumstances which may explain their aberrant position. Chemton has practically eliminated all overtime since 1992 when it came under severe pressure to cut production costs. But manual employees have a high rate of basic pay (the highest in the companies surveyed, ranging from £20,000 to £25,000) which is substantially more than comparable manual employees earn.

In the case of Tirown Sweets, the sharp decrease in over-time since the mid-1980s occurred against a background of more fundamental changes in the company. These changes are considered in detail in the case-study section in Chapter 5.

The argument here is that a sudden and sharp decrease in overtime levels had a depressing effect on earnings, which resulted in a poor labour–management relations climate. Where employees experience a decrease in their earnings, there is a greater likelihood that industrial relations will become more adversarial. Avoiding these negative outcomes presents a difficult challenge for firms. A possible strategy is to make explicit the link between jobs and overtime and to induce employees to accept lower earnings in return for more jobs or greater employment security. Employees' acceptance of changes in overtime availability and, more generally, changes in work effort and job content, is a function of their expectations regarding the employment relationship. Management strategy can also be designed to shift the focus away from overtime work. Overtime work is often used by management because it creates the flexibility which allows a company to meet increased market demands without the complication of hiring new workers. Moreover, management may even evaluate employees on their willingness to work overtime with a view to promotions and even retention in the present employment (Fottler and Schaller, 1975). One obvious industrial relations management strategy is to shift the focus away from the need for overtime by ensuring higher levels of basic pay.

CONCLUSION

The evidence from our analysis of the shift in industrial relations patterns is insufficient to support (or reject) the thesis that there is a distinctly new industrial relations emerging in the companies surveyed. Undoubtedly, there is an overall shift towards better relations between management and labour. Only one company is at present classed as being in the uninhibited antagonistic category, compared to five companies in the past. On the other hand, only four companies experienced substantial and positive changes in their industrial relations, and five companies could still be classed as having adversarial industrial relations. Nor is there clear evidence that declining employment numbers or increased market pressure leads to increased co-operation between management and labour, as might be predicted if a new logic of market awareness guided employee behaviour.

Attempts to locate the causes which determine a specific pattern of industrial relations showed that a company's market position, financial performance, productive efficiency and variation in employee earnings over time operate as considerable pressures on the pattern of industrial relations at the establishment level. However, any framework that attempts to relate these factors together causally is bound to be incomplete, reducing labour–management relations to a static and passive role in the face of external changes. The manner in which these factors influence and are influenced by a company's industrial relations can only be understood in the dynamic context of management and labour's responses to such pressures. A critical factor affecting such responses is the direction of change in a company's market and financial performance.

Companies experiencing increasing market pressure and poorer financial performance are under more pressure to reduce labour costs (usually through redundancies and reduced overtime), improve productivity and increase worker effort and flexibility. At such a time, it is difficult for employees and management to shift towards more co-operative industrial relations Salaries may still be above the norm but with a decline in earnings, satisfaction levels with pay will be low. Paradoxically, companies that have avoided the need to implement drastic changes in work organisation or earnings tend to have more co-operative industrial relations, even if employee salaries are at or below the industrial average. Changes in a company's market environment and economic performance impinge on a range of issues, such as overtime earnings, effort levels and work arrangements, concerning which management and particularly employees often have fixed and long-standing expectations. Undoubtedly, even within the generalised relationships linking markets, economic performance and industrial relations, the way in which these expectations are handled will vary across companies. The history of the relationship between unions and management can be expected to influence this process strongly, as well as forming the company's present climate of industrial relations. Where industrial relations are more adversarial, there is a marked tendency to perceive trade unions, flexibility and over-manning as the source of poor plant performance (Table 4.11). Conversely, managers of companies with more co-operative industrial relations are more likely to emphasise problems such as plant maintenance, quality of management and production costs.

Table 4.11: Organisational and Technical Obstacles to Plant Performance*

Company	Union Restriction	Worker Flexibility	Over-manning	Technical Problems	Quality of Mgt.	Plant Maintenance
Positive IR						
Dairyfoods	2			3		1
Burchocks	2			3		1
Tirown Sweets		3		2		1
Electro Engineering	3		1	2		
Antagonistic IR						
Mineral Ltd.	1	2				3
Park Foods	1	2	3			
Senchem	2	1				
Processchems	1	2	3			
Textile*		1				2
No Change, Co-operative IR						
Lola Drinks	1				2	
Micro Engineering				1	3	2
Chemton	3		1	2		
Clothing Ltd.	n/a					

* Respondents were asked the following question: Which of the following influences have you found to be detrimental to plant performance? A list of factors was provided and respondents asked to rank these in order of priority. Only the first three rankings are used in the table.

Source: Interviews with senior/financial managers (structured questionnaire).

The dynamic of union–management relations, although constrained by the various pressures outlined above cannot be read
off solely from external market and economic pressures, important though these may be, but is also related to a set of historical conditions, which are specific to each company. In particular, the pattern of industrial relations and the unique institutional aspects of a company's collective bargaining system, such
as its bargaining arrangements, procedural and substantive rules
and the extent of union–management co-operation, reflect long-
term implicit or explicit managerial strategies in this area. In
Chapter 5, using the descriptive case approach, we focus on the
unique set of conditions and labour–management relations in two
companies that have undergone significant change and two companies where relations have remained essentially adversarial.

Chapter 5

MANAGEMENT STRATEGIES AND INDUSTRIAL PARTNERSHIP

The pattern of industrial relations is, we have argued, clearly influenced by the firm's market position, economic performance and business strategy chosen, but is not solely determined by these factors. For example, it is not axiomatic that a firm experiencing a favourable market in terms of its market share will adopt a co-operative stance with its employees. Kochan et al. (1986) emphasise the degree of choice, particularly managerial choice, regarding both the choosing of a specific business strategy and the effect on industrial relations in the organisation. Strategic decisions are defined as those that alter the role of management or unions, or their relationship with other actors in the industrial relations system. It is acknowledged that strategic decisions can only occur where the parties have discretion over their decisions. For example, there is little room for discretion in a perfectly competitive market in terms of product pricing or labour compensation. In general, most organisations have some room for manoeuvre, and managerial responses to the business environment take into consideration the current state of industrial relations among other factors (see Table 2.19 in Chapter 2).

Industrial relations processes and outcomes are driven by a continuously evolving interaction of environmental or product pressures and organisational responses (Kochan and Cappelli, 1984). The major strategic decision/choice for firms that remain in an increasingly competitive market is whether to compete on the basis of low prices and high volume or to seek out specialised market niches where a price premium can be supported. Evolution from a growth market to a mature market usually forces firms to be more competitive with respect to prices. According to

Kochan (1984), the aims in industrial relations range from maintaining labour peace in order to maximise production, to controlling labour costs, streamlining work rules and increasing productivity in order to meet growing price competition. Whichever competitive strategy is chosen, it will have a major impact on industrial relations at the workplace and collective bargaining level.

Kochan's (1984) research has shown that there is a variety of different approaches to labour management undertaken by companies in similar product markets and facing similar external environments. Along with the empirical literature, there is a burgeoning prescriptive literature advocating appropriate human resource strategies for business success. Despite the emphasis on organisational development and change in both the academic and popular literature, few texts or articles have explicitly addressed change in unionised settings as a distinctive topic. This chapter begins with a discussion and review of the circumstances in which management and unions are more likely to co-operate. This is followed by a detailed historical analysis of the unique set of conditions and labour–management relations in four companies. Two of the companies have experienced a positive shift in their industrial relations and two continue to have adversarial relations. These four companies were chosen because of their representativeness and to reduce repetition in the narrative.

INDUSTRIAL RELATIONS REFORM IN UNIONISED SETTINGS

Kochan and Dyers' (1979) model of change in a unionised setting remains the most comprehensive and useful approach to analysing change in unionised companies. Unionised environments are considered to be distinctly different from non-union environments, in terms of a number of characteristics. The assumptions underlying the model (and also differentiating it from non-union settings) are that unions and management often have different goals and interests within the organisation, power is distributed across both parties, and as a consequence of these factors conflict is a natural phenomenon in the relationship. The employment relationship is viewed as a mixed-motive game situation. Mixed-motive situations start from the proposition that where there is a principal (manager) and an agent (employee), interests will not be identical and the nature of the relations between manager and employee will depend on how this difference will be resolved (Barbash, 1964; 1980). In a unionised setting, this partial conflict of interests is institutionalised in the formal collective bargaining system. The presence of a union implies that employees have formed within the organisation a permanent and independent structure for pursuing their interests, which is protected by law. Thus, a unionised organisation is characterised by pluralism — that is, a legitimate sharing of some degree of power, which is exercised in situations where there is a conflict of interests. As a result of the partially incompatible goals of management and workers, structurally-based conflict is seen as a natural and inevitable occurrence. Since Kochan and Dyer (1979) were concerned with joint union–management programmes of change, they argued that the effectiveness of a joint programme must be defined as the extent to which the programme contributed to the attainment of the goals/interests valued by the interest groups involved. Although Kochan and Dyer's primary focus is on union–management joint co-operative ventures external to the collective bargaining process, the model developed is applicable to all industrial relations changes in a unionised organisation.

The actual model of the change process proposed by Kochan and Dyer (1979) consists of three stages: first, the stimuli for union–management change; secondly, the initial decision to participate or commit the respective organisations to a specific change programme; and thirdly, the problem of maintaining commitment to the change programme, or institutionalising it over time. In many instances, managements and unions are reluctant both to embark on initiatives outside the formal collective bargaining process and to depart from the traditional bargaining issues of wages and working conditions. Relations between management and unions only change when there is great pressure for them to do so. A number of pressures can be identified, which are potential stimuli for change in union–management co-operation. An increase in foreign and domestic competition can initiate a search for increased productivity requiring comprehensive changes in work organisation. New technology can lead to a greater requirement for flexibility and teamwork, and improved quality standards require more committed and involved workers. New employment and labour laws may also stimulate co-operation beyond the collective bargaining process — for example, the requirement for health and safety committees, works councils and more comprehensive financial information for employees. However, it is only when the parties believe that the formal bargaining process is not capable of effectively responding to the pressures that they will be motivated to consider the formation of a joint change programme.

The second stage of the change process entails reaching an initial joint decision to embark on a specific programme of organisational change. Since management and union interests and goals are not identical, commitment to embark on a specific change effort will only be forthcoming when both perceive the change as instrumental to the attainment of their goals. Furthermore, the long-run success of the programme requires that the parties do not get co-opted into displacing the goals of their organisations and constituents for some higher goals.

The third stage — maintaining commitment over time to change the programme — depends on the extent to which the goals that both parties value are achieved by the programme, and even then internal or external pressures may change, bringing about a change in priorities in either party's goals, lessening the grounds for co-operation.

Kochan and Dyers' three-stage model is premised on the parties involved exhibiting a high level of instrumental rationalism when participating in programmes of organisational change, in that each party seeks to attain its valued goals. The creation of a high level of mutual trust among the parties is not necessarily a precondition for organisational change — rather, low-trust relations are consistent with the objective circumstances of union–management relationships which involve both compatible and incompatible interests. In such circumstances, argue Kochan and Dyer, it would be irrational for either party to exhibit totally trusting attitudes. On the other hand, an acceptance of an objective conflict of interests does not preclude both parties from cooperating. This is evident from the results of Table 3.11(b) in Chapter 3, where only a small proportion of employees, particularly manual employees, believed that management and employees were on the same side, whereas a majority of employees believed that full teamwork was possible in their company. A high degree of social integration, as indicated by positive employee perceptions of management, is most likely a result of how well employees perceive that management has delivered in terms of their interests. Solutions to pressing economic and industrial relations problems in the companies surveyed by Purcell (1981) were only considered when the conflict escalated into a crisis. The case-study work of Cutcher-Gershenfeld and Verma (1994), Schuster (1985) and Purcell (1981) provides some confirmation of the Kochan and Dyer model of change in union settings.

The common elements affecting the initiation and development of co-operation programmes were the degree of crisis (referred to as the "Trauma Principle" by Purcell, 1981) in a company and the inadequacy of the collective bargaining process to address and solve the crisis. According to Schuster (1985), the stimulus for co-operation and the manner in which it is initially addressed are based upon pragmatic concerns, such as the need to improve productivity, increase employee wages and strengthen the economic well-being of the company. Schuster (1985) argues that the first step in the Kochan and Dyer model makes no provision for instances in which a significant stimulus for change is present but the parties ignore or do not act upon it. In a number of the companies in his study, a deteriorating business environment failed to shift the traditional adversarial industrial relations pattern of union, management and employee behaviour. Nor were these companies classed as having a poor labour relations climate as measured by grievance rates, arbitration, strike activity or shop-floor conflict. In one company, serious business problems led to the union and management meeting 18 times over a two-year period, but the parties were unable to address the problems, and continued to blame each other for their difficulties. A consequence of this failure was a drastic reduction in the number employed. Purcell (1981) refers to such a process as a regressive spiral in which:

1. Financial and market problems are frequently experienced.

2. Changes in the management team occur.

3. Design and productivity changes are often made as a means of recapturing or maintaining market position causing disruption on the shop floor.

4. These changes place pressure on existing industrial relations practices and agreements.

In such circumstances, according to Purcell (1981), the prospects for a mutually-agreed, planned reform of industrial relations practices are minimal. A critical question is why some companies fail to shift towards a more co-operative process despite powerful environmental stimuli to do so. Schuster (1985) draws on Pfeffer's (1982) work on organisations as paradigms as a possible explanation. A paradigm in an organisation constitutes both the formal and informal way that behaviour is enacted in the organisation. It includes the norms guiding behaviour and, in the context of labour–management relations, the development of expectations regarding industrial relations practices and agreements. Once a paradigm has evolved and is in place the organisation tends to perform as a closed system – that is, established agreements and custom and practice provide the tools to sort out present and future problems.

In several of the sites studied by Schuster (1985), a regressive cycle occurred in which, despite a powerful external stimulus for change, the parties were paralysed by past events and a lack of mutual trust. The parties' interpretation of what is occurring is mainly influenced by the existing paradigm and not by actual environmental factors. Divisions between management and employees — the "them and us" syndrome — can distort perceptions about the motives of actors on both sides. Consequently, the system becomes further closed to potential change, and it becomes extremely difficult to arrest what may be a terminal process for the organisation. The low-trust syndrome extant in many organisations (see the earlier discussion of Fox's (1974) work and the survey results in Chapter 3) is an example of how a particular paradigm emerges and becomes a closed system. In such a closed system, aspects of work organisation and conditions — such as the rules governing job demarcations, internal transfers, seniority arrangements regarding lay-offs and promotions, and effort levels and rewards — can assume a moral force for employees, which affects their response to external events. Moral force as it is used here draws on Thompson's (1991) notion of a moral economy, which reflected and informed people's notions of what were legitimate practices in the marketplace regarding the pricing and supply of bread in peasant and early-industrial communities. In these communities, many economic relations were regulated according to non-economic norms. The term "moral" is used not in an evaluative or judgmental way, but in order to discriminate between two different sets of assumptions. The moral economy assumes (by its adherents) a set of imperatives guided by precedents and practices which override market imperatives. The alternative assumption is to treat the economy as nothing more than an intricate mechanism, allowing impersonal economic exchanges where price is determined by supply and demand. Adherence by the poor to the notion of a moral economy had little to do with the notion of an Arcadian past, but was rooted in a pragmatic necessity to overcome times of dearth when free-market principles dictated that prices should go up in times of scarcity. According to Reddy (1984) the concept of such a moral economy is bound to occur in modern industrial economies, though in a less dramatic fashion, where established values and moral standards about working conditions, effort levels and re-wards are often confronted and violated by technical and commercial change in the marketplace.

The principle of seniority in unionised settings is an example of a moral economy in modern organisations (see Gersuny and Kaufman, 1985). In these organisations (particularly those that are not exposed to severe competition) workers often develop notions of a fair wage, reasonable effort levels and fair compensation for their skills — in short, a moral economy of their organisation. A crisis which dramatically alters these notions is unlikely to provide the grounds for co-operation between the parties and a solution to the crisis, since commitment to accept change will only be forthcoming when both union and management perceive the change as instrumental to the attainment of their goals. In the following two sections, case studies are examined of two companies that have shifted towards a more co-operative pattern of industrial relations, and two companies that can still be categorised as having an antagonistic pattern of industrial relations. The industrial relations history in these companies is generally typical of the trends experienced in the remaining case-study companies, and by limiting these histories to four companies an inevitable repetition is avoided.

CASE STUDIES (A): FROM CONFLICT TO CO-OPERATION

Case Study 1: Tirown Sweets

Tirown Sweets was established in Ireland as a subsidiary of a British company in the 1930s. It manufactures confectionery products and employs approximately 198 people. In 1991, it was taken over by a Swiss multinational. The existing plant will eventually be merged with a larger subsidiary located some miles away. Tirown Sweets is one example of the import-substitution companies set up in Ireland in the 1930s (see the discussion in Chapter 2).

Financial Performance

Financial performance has gradually improved since 1986, and at present is considered to be very positive. Gross revenue is well in excess of costs and wage costs per unit of output are perceived as comparatively low, while productivity is comparatively high. Conversely, market pressure is perceived as low — the product market remains the same size but the company's market share has grown and products are sold to a large number of customers. Employment has decreased substantially during the 1980s from 785 in 1976 to 198 in 1994.

Industrial Relations, Past and Present

Union–management relations were described (company interviews) as extremely adversarial in the 1970s and early 1980s. The industrial relations pattern at the time can be defined as one of constitutional antagonism. Management's approach to the unions was to keep them under control and at arm's length. According to a union official interviewed, management avoided contact with the union representatives as much as possible. The union in the company was described as strongly militant with strong political overtones. Tirown Sweets was relatively strike-free until the 1960s. From 1960 to 1985, however, there were frequent and bitter official and unofficial strikes. The company was a frequent user of the labour court. Prior to 1960, there had been few strikes. The company's approach to its employees could be described as paternalistic. The lifting of trade barriers during the 1960s, and entry into the European Economic Community in 1973 undermined the company's competitive position. As a result, management had to reduce labour costs and improve productive efficiency. The traditional paternalistic relationship came under strain because of these changes.

The decade of the 1970s was particularly disruptive, with strikes (mainly unofficial) occurring frequently. A further factor which ensured a strong reaction from employees was the strength of the trade unions generally during the 1970s. According to shop stewards interviewed, there were more activists in the union during this period. There was a core group of active members. At the same time, there was very tight supervision, and management was waiting for people to make mistakes. Management went in for confrontation rather than conciliation. Many of the benefits, such as sick pay, medical facilities and pensions were secured by the union in the 1970s.

Despite the economic problems experienced by this company, the overall business environment was buoyant. Unemployment, a good barometer of union strength, averaged less than 10 per cent during the decade. Relations between union and management have become more orderly since the mid-1980s. No strikes have occurred since 1984, and there is less frequent use of the Labour Court and other third-party mechanisms. The present pattern of industrial relations can be defined as constitutional/adaptive co-operation. Unions are perceived as a trusted bargaining partner. A high level of trust and informality exists between the union official, shop stewards and management.

Pressures and Triggers for Change

There is a high level of consensus among those interviewed in the company that the last strike experienced in the company in 1984 was a pivotal point of change in union–management relations. After a nine-week strike, management threatened to close down the factory (a threat taken seriously by the union official involved) unless each employee signed an agreement registered with the Labour Court, in which they pledged not to resort to strikes unless all procedures had been exhausted. The registered agreement ensured that workers had to adhere to grievance and disputes procedures.

The solution to the financial and organisational problems of low profitability and low productivity were overcome during the 1980s through (a) re-orienting commercial strategy, (b) a new investment programme, and (c) shedding employees. Product changes included reducing the range of products manufactured and producing only a small range of products. At present, most of the products sold through the company are imported from UK plants. The company now manufactures only 7 per cent of sales in Ireland, compared to 45 per cent of sales in the old factory in 1986. A new, but lower capacity production unit, was built in 1986 and the old factory closed. As one interviewee observed, the company had by 1987 become more a commercial organisation than a production one. The switch from the old factory to the small production unit with its automated processes obviously required fewer employees. A major redundancy programme occurred at the end of 1986 and 400 of the 600 employees were made redundant. This was a voluntary package and there were, in fact, more applications for redundancy than the required number, allowing management to weed out those they wished to dispense with. The numbers seeking redundancy were partly a result of the demographic structure of the work force. For example, the present average age of a male manual worker in the company is 50. The switch to a mainly warehousing/commercial organisation has dramatically shifted the structure of the work force, which is predominantly white collar, with only 50 manual workers remaining. Not surprisingly, perhaps, there is a low level of involvement in union activities among the remaining union membership.

The shift to a more co-operative pattern must be viewed in the context of the changes outlined above. The construction of a new production unit and the closing down of the old factory effectively removed the traditional restrictive customs and practices associated with the old factory. More importantly, the number of employees remaining in the unionised manual category represented only a fraction of the pre-1987 work force. As in the Kochan and Dyer (1979) model, improved relations between management and employees did arise from a crisis situation in the 1980s, but it can hardly be seen as any kind of deliberate recognition by union and management of a need to co-operate in a constructive manner. Nor did either party attempt to develop any approach outside the collective bargaining system to confront the crisis in competitiveness in order to remain as a substantial manufacturing company. The essential strategy chosen was to switch from production to a warehousing operation.

According to a long-serving shop steward, the company was never able to develop a business strategy separate from the parent company: "While senior management blamed the industrial relations environment for the lack of investment, they did little to change their confrontational stance and take a different approach".

Summary

Overall financial performance has been improving in recent years, but numbers employed have decreased. While industrial relations in the past were extremely adversarial, they are currently much more co-operative, with the unions being treated as a trusted bargaining partner. Business and financial reorganisation in the 1980s provided the context for increased co-operation.

Case Study 2: Electro Engineering

Electro Engineering manufactures small motors and capacitors and, although classed as an engineering firm, there is a considerable electronic input into its products. The company was established in Ireland in 1966 as a subsidiary of a multinational. In 1989, it was taken over by an American multinational. At present, approximately 300 are employed at the establishment.

Financial Performance

Financial performance improved greatly over the three years, 1991–93. Gross revenue earned over the years 1991–93, according to the financial manager, was sufficient to make a small profit. Wage costs per unit of output are average for the industry, and production per worker is also average compared to Irish competitors, but is perceived to be worse than foreign competitors. Market pressure is perceived as moderate: products are sold to a small number of customers. The market share of the company remains the same, though the market for its products is growing. Employment decreased dramatically from 930 in 1980, to 300 in 1993.

Industrial Relations, Past and Present

Industrial relations in the past were extremely antagonistic (circa 1985). The extent of the antagonism between employees and management at this time is only equalled by two other companies in the study (see Table 4.8). Management's attitude towards the trade union was that it should be kept under control and at arm's length. In 1978, according to the personnel manager, there were few full weeks worked. This culminated in the 1982 strike. At this time, the skilled craft workers would not adhere to procedures. The company threatened to close. A radical shift in industrial relations has occurred over the past five years to a position between constitutional antagonism and constitutional co-operation. This shift can be partly explained by a reduction in the size of the organisation. The larger the firm, the more difficult and complex it is to manage industrial relations, and the greater the likelihood of conflict occurring.

A more important factor, however, was the take-over of the company in 1989. Despite the non-union stance of the Electro Engineering corporation (the Irish subsidiary is the only unionised plant), management has accepted the legitimacy of the union presence. Relations between union and management have developed to the point where a number of workplace initiatives are possible. Despite the non-unionism of the parent corporation, management has taken a pluralist approach to the union. Trade union organisation and commitment remain strong among

company employees. There is a well-supported shop-steward committee comprising seven stewards and a convenor. Out of 215 permanent and part-time manual workers, it is estimated (steward
interview) that there are 20 core active trade unionists and a
further 50 interested members. In general, there is a high level of
participation in expressing views and voicing concerns at general
union meetings. There are approximately 30 craft workers who
negotiate separately, and there is a set differential between operatives and craft workers which is vigorously defended. The craft
workers are perceived (by some general union members) as defensive towards change and even hostile to the company. In the most
recent case of major redundancies in October 1991, there was no
unified or concerted approach by the general and craft unions to
the redundancy situation.

Although unions are still not viewed by management as a
trusted bargaining partner, there are initiatives which may indicate a move towards greater union–management co-operation (see
discussion below). Third-party intervention in disputes has declined from four in 1986 to zero in 1993. The number of Labour
Court recommendations on disputes in the company has also
declined.

Pressures and Triggers for Change

Declining profits, increasing competition and a reduction in numbers employed occurred in the first half of the 1980s. Between
1980 and 1985, employment declined from 930 to 402. There were
several attempts during the 1980s to improve productivity, reduce
costs and become more competitive. In 1989, the company was
taken over by an American multinational and, though further
redundancies have occurred, most notably in 1991, management
believes that the company is now more cost effective and efficient.
Indeed, within the new corporation, Electro Engineering is now
rated as having above-average performance on a number of criteria, compared to other plants in the corporation. Since the take-
over several additional developments have occurred, which indicate a more constructive industrial relations environment. Employees surveyed in Electro Engineering scored the second highest level of trust in management and were also ranked second in

their satisfaction with grievance procedures. However, prior to the take-over in 1989 a number of important changes occurred. In 1985 a flexibility agreement was concluded with the operatives (giving almost total flexibility), which reduced the number of job grades from 5 to 1. This was a prelude to an agreement in 1986 on teamwork. The shop steward is supplied with financial and some strategic information. Employees are given financial information. It is interesting to note that the employees surveyed in Electro Engineering (N = 18 operatives) had the highest score as regards awareness of other competitors.

The initial teamwork programme has been developed beyond simple groups of employees based on distinctive work areas. There are now improvement teams spanning natural work units, which meet once a week to solve problems and suggest improvements in areas such as quality, machine efficiency and materials. While team leaders are usually supervisors or engineers, the intention of management is to develop operators to direct and lead their own teams. How well the teams work in practice is difficult to assess, but from interviews conducted with employee representatives there are differing opinions among employees on their impact. While some employees appear to welcome new workplace initiatives because they allow more direct participation in their work, there are others who have reservations about the long-term implications of these initiatives. The improvement teams are now part of an overall strategy on total quality management (TQM), which has implications for union–management relations external to the collective bargaining system. In 1992, the company launched a TQM programme which required greater employee participation in all aspects of the production system. It required management and particularly supervisors to share responsibility for production and quality with the operatives. Within a few months of implementation, the union refused to work the new system. A summary of the convenor's concerns are:

- Fear that flexibility and work changes were now being dictated by the TQM process, that is, by management

- Lack of official union input into the TQM process

- Disagreement with the strong overtones of unitarism in TQM

- Fear of displacement of the conventional bargaining process

- Lack of democracy — need to acknowledge the place of the unions as partners

- Need to share the benefits of TQM (e.g. share options).

Shortly afterwards, the union and management agreed to work together to develop structures that included union representation, in order to implement the TQM programme fully. The union agreed to implement the programme for the duration of the extant national wage agreement (Programme for Economic and Social Progress), after which the union would review its position. Management accepted that many aspects of the programme required the consensus of employees to work effectively. Union representatives and members wished to have some control over the process and to ensure a fair return for employees' participation and flexibility. This approach initiated a series of meetings between the management (principally the personnel manager and production manager) and the convenor and shop stewards. From these meetings a number of documents were drawn up. A general agreement on the content of the TQM programme, separating it from the conventional negotiation process setting out the joint aspirations of both management and the union was established. The last phase of discussions centred on the type of structures required to monitor the TQM process. The proposed structure was a steering committee composed of senior management and union representatives. At the time the present research was being carried out, the structures and agreements were reaching the final stages before being presented to employees. This participatory process and the extent of union–management co-operation are by far the most developed initiatives in the companies surveyed. In effect, they are an example of union–management co-operation going beyond the traditional collective bargaining process in an attempt to establish an area of joint governance.

More recent developments in the company, however, also highlight the pitfalls and cyclical nature of such attempts. Follow-up calls to Electro Engineering revealed that a new convenor and almost new committee of shop stewards were elected in recent union elections. It appears that many union activists were concerned about the direction taken by the old convenor and committee and were more cautious about the TQM initiative. A number of reasons were advanced for the turn in events. These can be summarised as problems with the structure and outcomes of the TQM process. The newly-elected convenor is critical of the proposed steering committee structure, on the grounds that it lacks any real power to make and implement policies. It is viewed as merely an advisory committee, which would be geared towards management concerns. The outcomes of the TQM programme — that is, the costs and benefits of the system for shop-floor employees — are a second area of concern for many union members. There is a fear that the successful implementation of TQM could lead to job losses and to changes in work organisation, which are no longer negotiable through the conventional collective bargaining process. Employees are also concerned with sharing the economic benefits accruing from the implementation of TQM. A share of the benefits has assumed increasing importance as the company has shifted from losses to profit over the past few years.

Overall, the new convenor and committee appear to be adopting a more defensive stance, which it is claimed is more representative of the median union member. This in turn may change management's approach to the union–management co-operation process, with management less willing to give as much as before. It is difficult to know whether this is merely a temporary hiccup in the process of union–management co-operation. What is clear is the difficulty in Irish industrial relations of developing structures (even with union representation) which are external to the conventional collective bargaining process. It also confirms Kochan and Dyer's conclusion that union management co-operation initiatives can only persist where both parties perceive that it is serving their interests. The convenor and shop stewards are looking for a long-term policy on TQM which will deal with all the issues. It is difficult to be optimistic that such a policy will emerge unless unions and management can agree on a joint union–management governance structure which has the power to decide on policy and how it is to be implemented. Such a structure should not only encompass the areas of mutual interest between unions and management, but should also be capable of resolving the inevitable conflicts and stresses which accompany organisational changes.

Summary

Overall, the firm has experienced an improvement in financial performance, and currently has an above-average performance on key dimensions compared to sister plants. Concomitantly, a shift from antagonistic to a more constitutional/co-operative type of industrial relations has also occurred. Recent years have also witnessed the development of process-improvement teams and a TQM programme as part of a broader co-operative effort. However, there are some difficulties with current co-operative initiatives as both parties do not agree that they are serving their ultimate interests.

Conclusion

Both companies have shifted in varying degrees from confrontation to more orderly and co-operative industrial relations. The triggers and the process of change differed according to each company's unique circumstances. Despite similar manufacturing facilities, products and markets, Burchocks and Tirown Sweets have experienced contrasting routes to their present pattern of industrial relations. A notable feature of the companies is their positive financial performance in recent years. This is a general feature of companies experiencing an improvement in their industrial relations, though Dairyfoods is an exception to this pattern. However, the enterprise, of which Dairyfoods is a subsidiary, has grown steadily in terms of turnover and profits in the past 10 years. During the economic recession of the 1980s, there was a general downward trend in the numbers employed in the manufacturing sector. In both companies, the shedding of employees was a key strategy in reducing costs in the search for competitiveness. Both reacted to the employment crisis through the conventional collective bargaining process. There was no evidence at the time of any attempt to cope with the crisis beyond the traditional process. The shedding of employees during the 1980s did not provoke a sufficient crisis to unravel the tried and trusted approach by unions and management to the competitive crisis of the recession. As we pointed out in the introduction, despite the reduced numbers working in manufacturing from 1980 to 1989, real wages more than kept pace with inflation. The concerns of union and management were not sufficient to bring about a new alignment of union–management co-operation in the face of the employment crisis. Electro Engineering is now in the process of putting in place a TQM programme which is a result of the change in ownership rather than a company crisis.

CASE STUDIES (B): CONTINUING ADVERSARIAL RELATIONS

Case Study 1: Parkfoods

Background

Parkfoods is a manufacturer of food products, principally for the Irish market. Organisation-wide, employment as a whole has decreased by approximately 500 in recent years as a result of rationalisation. Present employment at this location is approximately 1,500.

Financial Performance

Competition in the marketplace is severe and it has been increasing over the past five years. The organisation supplies to a large number of customers. In assessing the overall performance of the establishment, the gross revenue earned over the past two years has been sufficient to make a small profit. The market for some products continues to grow, while for others it remains the same. The costs of production at the plant are approximately the same as those of competition generally, but could potentially be improved given that the obstacles to plant performance are perceived to be internal. Those influences which have been detrimental to performance relate to trade union restrictions, a general lack of worker flexibility in some areas, and over-manning which is set to grow as an issue given the current investment in new advanced technologies. On the issue of workforce performance generally, wage costs per unit of output, when compared with the competition, are about average, and the average level of production per worker is also average. When compared with foreign competitors, labour productivity is "neither better nor worse".

Trends in Industrial Relations

Industrial relations is by far the overriding concern of the personnel function, and as a concern it has intensified in recent years. However, the human resources manager is of the opinion that the time spent on industrial relations matters is well justified given the "magnitude of the job to be done". Current relations between the parties at the plant can best be described as "antagonistic". However there are mismatched perceptions among the parties concerning the extent to which things have changed.

Senior management believes that the trend in recent times has been towards a less adversarial relationship between management and employees. The human resources manager maintains that some years back, before a merger, relations in the plant were extremely poor. As a response to this and an ongoing problem with unofficial action, management introduced a 4 per cent bonus. The consequence of this was that should employees take any form of unofficial action, they would forfeit the bonus. This 4 per cent was taken as a percentage of gross earnings. The adversarial relationship between management and labour during this period is epitomised by two actions, according to the human resources manager. Firstly, employees went outside the gate over a trivial issue (the provision of boots for a worker), and secondly, in the early 1980s, the shareholders came in in person and ran the plant in an attempt to "frighten" the unions.

The reduced level of antagonism between management and employees in recent years, the human resources manager argues, has been precipitated by three key facts: firstly, there has been a change in personnel in the unions — there is a less militant union committee although it does remain strong within the organisation; secondly, there is an increased awareness on the part of employees of the increasingly competitive circumstances facing the organisation, and as a result the need to agree costs and control expenditure; thirdly, the action taken by the owners may have illustrated that the union position is not invulnerable.

However, the unions are of a different opinion. According to one shop steward, the union is "tolerated at most" on a good day. In normal circumstances, the union is treated with contempt, principally by management putting off issues all the time. From his perspective, the attitude among management is "ignore it and it will go away". A second shop steward elaborated further on the nature of the relationship between the union and management. He suggests that there is a low-trust environment, arising principally from management's superior status attitude — "These are old managers who look down on all the others". He compares these managers to the old rural Irish village doctor or priest who, regardless of character, was regarded in high esteem. He maintains that there "is a gap and it is widening rather than narrowing". Relations in his eyes, have taken a turn for the worse. The union is tolerated by management because it has to tolerate it, but there is "no compromise". Communications are very poor and rumour tends to fuel a great deal of employee behaviour.

The human resources manager agrees on the point concerning poor communication, and indeed he expressed the need to communicate more frequently. However, this desire to communicate more frequently with the union does not appear to stem from the recognition that such a mechanism is successful, but rather from the fact that the union represents an organised employee voice in the present circumstances. The human resources manager expressed a desire to see a reduced role for stewards in the dissemination of information and in the communications process more generally, because in his eyes some of the information is being distorted and diluted as it is being passed on, and also some of the stewards are not as effective as others because, according to management, they lack direction and are populist in orientation.

From the union perspective, it "is not seen as being a legitimate group". This low-trust adversarial relationship, according to all the shop stewards interviewed, has always existed. When asked what improvements were planned, there were none that they were aware of. According to the human resources manager, a number of improvements are planned, but no specific concrete programme is apparent other than a general desire to secure greater employee involvement. In any case, past involvement initiatives have been attempted with relatively limited success. The site manager has attempted to meet employees for discussions, but found it difficult to break down barriers. This he attributes to a small inflexible core of workers.

The Necessity for Change

As a result of stiff competition, a necessity to innovate in product and process terms and a necessity to deploy staff because of the large element of seasonality in the business, the plant has undergone changes in the recent past, and from a business perspective has a number of others in the pipeline.

Employee transfer and the deployment of labour more generally is an important mechanism within the plant. During peak season, employees are taken on to cover demand. When the season draws to a close, the staff numbers are once again cut. While voluntary lay-off alleviates the problem to some extent (this benefit will only accrue if unemployment is not taxed) such reductions do cause problems. Lay-offs that are compulsory are made on the basis of seniority. When vacancies do arise, more senior members of staff can transfer to other areas within the plant. Seniority allows them to move back into a job, even if they are not trained to perform this job. In the process, they are usually displacing a more junior member of staff who has been trained to perform that particular job. Thus, the deployment of labour is an area of considerable concern which management is currently endeavouring to address in the organisation. Furthermore, over the past five years there have been some tenuous attempts at multi-skilling, which to date have failed. However, this continues to be a central area of concern in an attempt to improve the plant's overall competitive position.

The grading system has been a significant issue over the past number of years. The previous job classification/occupational structure was developed in 1978 in response to technological change and a desire among the unions for a new system. The human resources manager believed that in developing that system they had "created a monster". The present grading system, which replaced the 1978 system, was opposed vigorously by the unions, which felt that the system lacked transparency. During its implementation, management initially provided the unions with a minimum of information. However, despite its reticence, management was forced to disclose the information to the union in an attempt to get the system approved. This resulted in the unions being concerned about the increases in responsibilities that were being allocated to the new grades. The plant now has an internal grading committee to which individuals can appeal if they are unhappy with the grade awarded to them.

Employee communication is a third area of concern, and attempts to improve it have met with some difficulties. An employee newsletter was available in the past. However, it ran into some difficulties simply because those appointed to look after it continuously failed to meet deadlines. It was produced for approximately 12 months and then abandoned.

Attempts were also made in the past to communicate directly with employees through notices in their pay packets. While this was a relatively infrequent occurrence, it was generally opposed. Finally, a system of twice-yearly meetings operated for a time. In such meetings the yearly and interim accounts were explained to employees. However, the process was often used as a bargaining tactic on the part of the unions who would boycott the meetings if they were in dispute with management. A key area of contention in this process concerned payroll costs. While employees were given overall payroll costs, management was not willing to give a breakdown detailing how much of these costs were contributed by managerial employees.

Overall, change initiatives in the plant have been met with some opposition, confirming once again that resistance will rarely be overcome unless all the parties to the process perceive that initiatives of this kind are serving their interests. Management has failed to develop an agenda which employees perceive as integrating their interests with management's goals, and the lack of trust between the parties continues to result in very calculated defensive behaviour.

Summary

There is a tendency to retain centralised management prerogatives and a relatively traditional approach to maintaining occupational status in the company. Management has failed to gain employees' trust, and there are some negative management attitudes towards the union. Overall, this has resulted in an inflexibility and a preference for the maintenance of the status quo, at least until some mutually acceptable alternative is worked out.

Case Study 2: Senchem

Background

Established in 1974, the plant currently has 177 employees. Employment decreased during the 1980s but lately has stabilised and even increased slightly. There has in recent years been significant capital investment in plant and equipment. Currently, plans exist to build new plant, but this is subject to planning permission and final board approval.

There are three unions represented at the plant, one general and two craft unions. Currently, general operatives are divided into two distinct groups, one unionised and the other made up of former union members who have resigned from the union. This has generated considerable tension in the company's industrial relations.

Financial Performance

The product is supplied to a large number of customers. Competition in the marketplace is severe, particularly in an international context. Over the past five years this competition has increased dramatically, both in terms of rival competitors and between subsidiary plants of this parent company throughout the world. In assessing the overall performance of the establishment, the gross revenue earned over the past two years has been sufficient to make a small profit. It is substantially smaller than prior to 1987 when the plant returned very large profits. When comparing the costs of production at the plant with the rest of the competition in the country, it is about average. The obstacles to improving plant performance in this respect are both internal and external, mainly concerning lack of worker flexibility, trade union restrictions and, given the recent large scale investments in new technology, over-manning. The major external factor concerns the product patent, which runs out after a specified period, forcing the plant to cut product prices and improve production volumes.

With respect to wage costs per unit of output relative to the rest of the competition in the industry, these are average in a national context, but well above average relative to other subsidiary sister plants and foreign competitors. Similarly, the average level of production per worker at the plant is about average relative to the rest of the competition in the industry.

Trends in Industrial Relations

Industrial relations are of primary importance in the plant and play a central role when consideration is being given to fixed capital investment. When asked to articulate the organisation's philosophy towards its employees, the human resources manager responded that "in exchange for committed competent employees, the organisation will ensure that in their jobs, employees are given the maximum opportunity for company benefits". It is industrial relations considerations which occupy most time and effort, though it is anticipated that the human resource function's involvement in industrial relations issues will decline in the future as it adopts more of a facilitative-type role. However, industrial relations issues are currently a priority, simply "in an attempt to get the right climate".

At present, as in the past, industrial relations at the plant are regarded by both parties as poor. There are numerous reasons for the emergence of this poor relationship, but central among them is the fact that historically the plant was highly successful and constantly "paid for peace given that production was paramount". This led to a perception among employees and their representatives that their interests were different from those of the organisation and could best be served by pursuing "an adversarial approach to industrial relations in an organisation that seemingly has limitless resources". Present relations remain very poor with, according to management "the historical adversarial relations in the plant proving to be somewhat of a nightmare with a core of individuals insisting that we live in the past". One manager interviewed observed that "it would be so much easier to function without the interference of the trade unions but the fulfilment of this aspiration is not feasible in light of the present circumstances in which the organisation finds itself".

Relations in the past were poor but, given the profits being made, they were sustainable. The decline in economic performance has disturbed the status quo, giving rise to greater friction between management and labour. The period 1974–82, according to one line manager, was a "milk cow period" for the trade union in the plant. For corporate-wide reasons, the plant could not afford to have a stoppage, and thus the idea was to "keep everybody sweet". From 1982 to 1987, a new personnel manager was appointed to turn things around. During this period there were five stoppages. Despite this, the plant continued to be highly successful as it was the sole world manufacturer of a particular product. Procedures were ignored on both sides when issues and disputes arose. Often the procedures were used to block any proposed change as the status quo must prevail during the stages of the grievance procedure. Furthermore, because of the shift system in operation, if an issue arises on a Saturday, the next time that that individual is working is nine days later. Consequently, issues constantly tend to drag on without being solved.

While there have been few disciplinary issues over the years, one line manager believed that there were more disciplinary breaches than recorded. He maintains that it is difficult for those working in the front line to kick the discipline procedure into action "as one has to work with these individuals in the future". Furthermore, in the past when the discipline procedure has been invoked, people have simply tended to react by registering a grievance. This situation came to a head in 1987 when, because of employee dissatisfaction with the union, and enticements from the company, half of the general union members decided to leave the union and enter into individual contracts with the company. The company championed this move in an attempt to reduce the power of the union. Individuals who made the move to individual contracts were re-employed on a merit performance basis, and significant pay differences have emerged between this group and those remaining union members. It was envisaged by management that over time, the remaining union members would leave the union and join this merit group but this failed to occur and positions are currently so polarised that individuals are well and truly entrenched in their respective positions.

The company has a history of regularly resorting to third-party intervention. Management believes that this was the case simply because the plant was so successful. However, the shop stewards believe that it was because of poor management. Since 1987, there have been fewer interventions because those on individual contracts operate an internal company grievance system. If an issue arises among the non-union merit group, their last resort, after supervisor and middle management failure to resolve the grievance, is an appeal to the general manager, thus forcing an internal settlement on issues which previously would have proceeded to an external third party.

Relations between the shop stewards and the union official are described as "average", and management generally feels that the stewards have by and large had an inordinate impact on the role of the union official. The official's job has also been made increasingly difficult by the fact that the union no longer represents all manual employees. One shop steward interviewed believes that the organisation is attempting to "pull a fast one" — that there is a hidden agenda, with management intent on breaking the union.

With respect to information-sharing, management maintains that the organisation tries to have an "open policy" and tell things as they are. Several communication initiatives are in place. These include monthly briefings, briefings through the supervisors on any new relevant issues, and currently, as part of the company's world class manufacturing initiative, employee meetings and team briefings.

Management's intention is, where possible, to decrease the role of shop stewards and the union official and to marginalise the role of the union generally, because, in its eyes, the union is seen as a key factor in preventing changes in working practices that could make the plant more competitive, particularly when compared to other subsidiaries in the corporation.

Change Initiatives

The major change initiative within the plant, which has been ongoing since 1986, relates to the deployment of labour and the general improvement of functional flexibility. Prior to 1986, there were four different production units within the plant. These units were serviced by a system of fixed-station rostering, which dictated that once an individual had been assigned to a particular job as part of a specific shift, they could not be moved from that shift. In 1986, without any key structural changes, the plant underwent an automation process and introduced a new production control room. At this juncture, there was a protracted dispute over manning levels as a result of the introduction of the new advanced manufacturing technology.

Currently, the intention is to move to a stage where the focus internally is not on any one of the four units within the plant, but rather on the plant as a whole. This would have the added advantage of allowing individuals to move between units and cells, and would give the plant the functional flexibility it seeks. Furthermore, the intention is to push as much responsibility as possible to the point of action. This is likely to be resisted by the union on a number of fronts. Firstly, the increased automation that will inevitably occur as part of this process may lead to lower manning levels. Secondly, while this new organisation scenario will result in greater transfers between units in the organisation, concomitantly there will be fewer promotions in the future.

Summary

The economic context of the firm is one of reduced profits compared to an earlier period of good economic performance. At present, the workforce is divided between employees who are members of the union and those who have left the union. This division has both polarised and defined industrial relations issues in recent years. Thus, while there are negative attitudes towards the union in some management quarters, equally there has been strong union resistance to any change in the status of the union and the existing collective agreement.

Conclusion

Both companies continue to have confrontational antagonistic industrial relations. While the contextual factors vary for each company, there are some common elements which can be viewed as key determinants of the current patterns of industrial relations. Firstly, these companies are characterised by relatively poor economic performance; secondly, they are experiencing severe market competition; thirdly, there is a distant arm's length relationship with the trade unions (reinforced in one company by a divided union organisation). Currently, as historically, there are low-trust relations between the parties, and this tends to create severe tensions during periods of rapid change.

Although there have been crises (sudden and large reductions in employment numbers, for example) in both the co-operative and antagonistic groups of case studies, no successful attempt to go outside the formal collective bargaining process has occurred. The first step in the Kochan and Dyer model, the initiation of a joint management union initiative in response to a crisis, did not occur, indicating a preference by both parties to handle crises within the conventional collective bargaining machinery. This tends to confirm Schuster's (1985) argument that in many instances, despite a powerful external stimulus for change, management and unions can be paralysed by past events and low-trust relations. Senchem and Parkfoods illustrate this position. In Senchem the interpretation of what is occurring is influenced by the past responses of both management and labour, and it is difficult for either side to escape this closed paradigm which is also characterised by elements of a moral economy. Similarly, Parkfoods is characterised by low-trust relations and a paradigm characterised by management suspicion and distrust of the union.

If crisis and trauma are insufficient to explain the instances where labour–management relations have shifted toward more co-operative relations, what then are the factors common to these companies? It is difficult to extrapolate a complete and comprehensive set of clear and relevant explanatory factors from the unique histories of the case studies. Undoubtedly, as the previous chapter showed, the economic context and performance of a company are critical factors influencing industrial relations. The case studies confirmed that persistent poor economic performance is often associated with poor industrial relations. A second factor is the attitude of management towards the trade unions, which was uniformly negative in the antagonistic group. Lastly, in this group of companies (particularly Senchem), the union organisation was divided in its approach to management, which further exacerbated industrial relations tensions.

Beyond these few common factors it is not possible to draw any confident conclusions about the triggers and inhibitors of a good union–management relationship. Industrial relations are influenced by such internal organisational items as the dominant management and union personalities involved; the role and legitimacy accorded to the personnel function; the union's organisational structure, the calibre of union activists and the union approach to collective bargaining; and the ownership structure of the company (whether public or private limited company). External factors such as the company's product market and its unique market strategy and, in the case of multinational subsidiaries, the parent company's level of involvement in its affairs, also influence labour management relations. It is difficult, therefore, to include all of the factors which define a company's industrial relations climate over time, particularly as many of the factors are idiosyncratic to each company.

Chapter 6

THE PERSONNEL FUNCTION — CHANGE OR CONTINUITY?

Kieran Foley
Patrick Gunnigle

Increasing political, social and industrial change has prompted a re-evaluation of the role of the personnel function and manager. Fahey (1989) suggests that many practitioners have reacted by setting aside the more "traditional activities" and immersing themselves in strategic human resource management. The shape of the personnel role is being redefined in the light of such pressures. In this chapter we focus on the nature and activities of the personnel function, in an attempt to assess its strategic role of in the companies surveyed. In particular, we assess the extent to which the personnel function acts as a strategic lever for affecting industrial relations change.

THE STRATEGIC ROLE OF THE PERSONNEL FUNCTION

In recent years, a number of attempts have been undertaken to categorise the activities of the personnel function. Tyson and Fell (1986) developed a three-tier categorisation of the role of personnel, based on the level of discretion afforded to the personnel function. The *Clerk of Works* category designates a low-level administrative model where personnel matters are not seen as an integral part of business planning. The *Contracts Manager* model emphasises well-established personnel policies, deriving, in the main, from traditional industrial relations practices. Personnel staff are specialists and are often custodians of existing procedures, agreements and contracts. Finally, the *Architect Model*, suggests that managers are involved in taking business decisions and are often represented at board level. Corporate plans embody human resources considerations, with personnel expected to quantify reactions of employees to any subsequent change. One of the key implicit arguments underlying Tyson and Fell's (1986) framework is that the architect model is a more sophisticated approach to the management of human resources (Storey, 1992), and that recessionary pressures will initiate polarisation of personnel practice towards the clerk of works and architect models (Tyson, 1987). Indeed, Baird and Meshoulan (1987) suggest that the role of the personnel function should not remain static but rather should develop and be supportive of changes in the organisation.

Research in Irish companies, however, has failed to verify any substantial adoption of such a role in more than a small number of isolated cases. Monks (1992) found no indication of an abandonment of traditional industrial relations approaches to personnel practice. Where change did occur in the personnel function, it was usually a result of environmental imperatives such as declining product markets and cost-cutting measures generally. As a consequence, the personnel function reacted by becoming increasingly professional and expert, and by adopting either a "macho management" or "collaborative approach" to the management of its human resources. Storey (1992) developed a two-dimensional model which categorises the personnel function in terms of strategic to tactical and interventionist to non-interventionist continuums. Functions are differentiated on the basis of the degree to which they pursue a strategic role and also the extent of direct hands-on activity by the personnel function.

The overlapping of the two dimensions gives a four-fold categorisation of personnel

(a) **Advisors:** The role of personnel in this case is one of providing support to line and general managers. While this function is carried out at a strategic level, it is reactive and non-interventionist, providing expertise and specialist skills in a consultancy capacity.

(b) **Handmaidens:** Handmaidens represent the position of lowest status within this model. Practitioners operating within this context function in a low-level and non-interventionist capacity, reacting to the needs of line managers in response to day-to-day operational problems.

(c) **Regulators:** Personnel is decidedly interventionist but rarely at the level of strategy formulation. This role encompasses that of the contracts manager, devising and negotiating policies and procedures and ensuring the smooth operation of the organisation.

(d) **Changemakers:** Personnel makes a strategic contribution to the formulation of corporate strategy in a proactive and interventionist way. This represents the highest level of the operation of the personnel function in this model and bears marked similarities to Tyson and Fell's architect typology.

Figure 6.1: Strategic Role of the Personnel Function

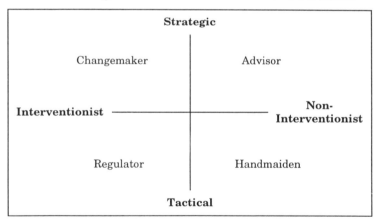

Source: Storey, 1992.

THE PERSONNEL FUNCTION: STATUS AND ACTIVITIES

All of the case companies indicated that they had a personnel function and that the top personnel practitioner was a member of the top team. In excess of 85 per cent of respondents report to the managing director or equivalent (see Table 6.1 below), and in one case the top personnel practitioner was also the managing director. Such findings support recent research conducted in Ireland on the status of the personnel manager (Monks, 1992; Shivanath, 1987) and confirm the continuing strength of the personnel function in Irish companies. Indeed, Hacket (1990) suggests that Irish companies in general place a high regard on the personnel function, with the majority having personnel represented at main board level. This view is echoed in the responses of the practitioners in the case companies to questions concerning their perception of their power and influence in their respective organisations. Almost without exception, practitioners indicated that they felt that they wielded enough power and influence to achieve functional objectives.

Table 6.1: Reporting Level of Top Personnel Practitioner

	N	%
General Manager	2	16.6
Managing Director	5	60.2
Chief Executive Officer	1	8.3
Director of Personnel	1	8.3
Group Personnel Manager	1	8.3
Operations Director	1	8.3

Source: Company Interviews.

The position in relation to board-level representation is particularly encouraging when viewed in the light of the survey results in Gunnigle et al. (1994) and Shivanath (1987). While the practitioner in these surveys was represented at board level in 30.5 per cent and 9.1 per cent of cases respectively, this compares with 50 per cent of the case organisations. While evidence cited above seems to verify the strong hierarchical position of the personnel function, it gives little indication of its power in an organisational sense. This is of particular interest in the light of Storey's (1992) findings concerning the propensity of the personnel functions in some organisations to have a non-interventionist role while represented at the highest levels within their respective organisations. The case evidence, however, does not substantiate such arguments, with all but two practitioners feeling that they had sufficient power to undertake their role effectively.

Responses from personnel managers in the case companies suggest that not only are they adequately placed in their organisations to undertake a strong role, but also that they wield sufficient power for this to be the case. Such responses suggesting a strong personnel function reject the "personnel in crisis" stereotype which is often associated with modern-day personnel. In the next section, the activities in which the function are involved are examined. Such analysis is important as it gives some indication of the prominence of the personnel function in respondent organisations, and the extent to which this has resulted in the adoption of a proactive and sophisticated role in personnel activities.

Activities in the Personnel Function

In recent years, the literature has emphasised the changing nature of the personnel function and the need for it to develop and grow in response to changing environmental and organisational demands (Baird and Meshoulan, 1987). While the need for change has been the subject of little disagreement, the likely or required direction of such change has been strongly contested. In an effort to quantify the magnitude and direction of such change, practitioners were asked in what manner the personnel function in their organisation had changed in recent years. Below, a cross-section of the responses to the above question is reported, which indicates the degree to which change processes in respondent organisations differ.

In a number of organisations, the practitioner indicated that there had been relatively little change, the personnel specialist in Parkfoods suggesting that the "role has not changed ... [we're] doing the same as traditionally has been done — even more intensively". In this organisation, such emphasis refers to a preoccupation with industrial relations. In recent years, mergers and rationalisations have heightened this concern. Lola Drinks also indicated that the role of the personnel function was unchanged in recent years. In a greater number of organisations, however, change had occurred. This change in general appeared to be away from the traditional preoccupation with industrial relations to a more developmental long-term focus. An example of such change was Dairyfoods where the top practitioner felt that the function had moved through the phase of "strategic planning, then HRM and PR and now to internal consultancy".

In Burchocks, the personnel function "has become more strategic and integrated into the business objectives — more concerned with overall organisational goals"; and in Chemton, "the personnel function is seen as the key to developing the organisation, and the personnel function has become more central to the organisation. Personnel has driven the change".

In contrast to much of the literature, which suggests that personnel is in crisis, interviews with practitioners in respondent organisations suggest that personnel is deeply involved in the strengthening of the role of the function. As seen above, practitioners in case organisations by and large indicated a great deal of change in the role of their function. However, prima facie reference to the activities of the function fails to substantiate such movement. Industrial relations, typically the key concern of personnel practitioners in organisations in Ireland (Shivanath, 1987), continues to be the major concern for the case organisations. Eight of the 11 companies indicated that industrial/employee relations were a significant concern for them. Initially, such a finding points to the continuing dominance of the reactive "contracts manger" typology in Ireland. Such a finding seems a little hard to equate with the views expressed above but may be better understood by reference to the fact that the personnel function in many of the companies is at present in a stage of evolution, and industrial relations concerns are unlikely to be completely shed in the short to medium term in favour of other concerns. There can be little doubt, however, that the shift in emphasis is increasingly towards strategic planning and organisational development. While industrial relations remains a key concern, responses from five of the organisations suggest that they are attempting to move away from the reactive role to adopt a longer-term focus involving strategic planning processes. Five of the 11 organisations indicated that strategic planning was a key activity. Other critical issues include recruitment, organisational development, training and personnel administration (Tables 6.2a and b).

Table 6.2(a): Key Activities Undertaken by Personnel*

	Cyc	St Pl	Pen	Rec	PR	Ins	IR	TQM
Dairyfoods	✓	✓	✓	✓	✓	✓		
Burchocks	✓	✓					✓	
Electro Engineering		✓						✓
Chemton		✓					✓	
Park Foods			✓	✓			✓	
Micro Engineering	✓	✓						
Clothing				✓	✓	✓	✓	
Senchem	✓			✓			✓	
Tirown Sweets				✓			✓	
Lola Drinks								
Mineral Drinks							✓	

* Respondents were asked to indicate the activities that took a large proportion of their time and effort.
Cyc = Cyclical; St Pl = Strategic Planning; Pen = Pension Funds; Rec = Recruitment; PR = Public Relations; Ins = Insurance; IR = Industrial Relations; TQM = Total Quality Management.
Source: Company Interviews.

Table 6.2(b): Key Activities Undertaken by Personnel

	Org Dev	Job Eval	Per Ad	T&D	Env	Cost Imp	Emp Rel	Emp Ser	Saf
Dairyfoods	✓								
Burchocks									
Electro Engineering									
Chemton	✓								
Park Foods		✓							
Micro Engineering									✓
Clothing			✓	✓	✓				
Senchem				✓					
Tirown Sweets			✓					✓	
Lola Drinks						✓	✓		
Mineral Drinks	✓		✓	✓					

Org Dev = Organisation Development; Job Eval = Job Evaluation; Per Ad = Personnel Administration; T&D = Training and Development; Env = Environmental Issues; Cost = Cost Improvements; Emp Rel = Employee Relations; Emp Ser = Employee Services; Saf = Safety.
Source: Company Interviews.

While the above represents the actual activities taking up the majority of practitioners' time, they were also asked to indicate which activities they felt should have their priority (Tables 6.3a and b). Only two of the 11 organisations felt that their emphasis on industrial relations was desirable. Six respondent organisations indicated that strategic planning should be a major concern. This, coupled with the increasing emphasis on long-term development is further confirmation of movement towards a more strategic role. In view of these responses, the time accorded to industrial relations must be viewed as driven by pragmatic concerns rather than deliberate choice. Of course, such trends are not universal, with two organisations indicating a desire to spend more time on day-to-day reactive issues.

In general, the evidence suggests that the change of emphasis has shifted away from the traditional reactive role to a more strategic planning role. The key conclusion that can be drawn from the interviews is that there has been a significant change in emphasis in recent years, away from day-to-day industrial

Table 6.3(a): Activities that Should Take Most of Personnel's Time

	St Pl	Rec	IR	OD	PA	D to D	PIMs	Comm
Dairyfoods	✓	✓			✓		✓	
Burchocks	✓					✓		
Electro Engineering	✓							
Chemton								
Park Foods			✓	✓				
Micro Engineering	✓							
Clothing	✓							
Senchem	✓	✓		✓				
Tirown Sweets						✓		✓
Lola Drinks								
Mineral Drinks			✓	✓				

St Pl = Strategic Planning; Rec = Recruitment; IR = Industrial Relations; OD = Organisational Development; PA = Performance Appraisal; D to D = Day-to-Day Issues; PIMs = Profit Impact on Marketing Strategy; Comm = Communications.
Source: Company Interviews.

Table 6.3(b): Activities that Should Take Most of Personnel's Time

	TQM	BPE	PS	Wel	Con	Line Dev	T&D	Saf	Per Ad
Dairyfoods									
Burchocks									
Electro Engineering									
Chemton									
Park Foods									
Micro Engineering	✓	✓							
Clothing			✓	✓					
Senchem									
Tirown Sweets									
Lola Drinks					✓	✓			
Mineral Drinks							✓	✓	✓

TQM = Total Quality Management; BPE = Business Process Engineering; PS = Problem Solution; Wel = Welfare; Con = Consultancy Role; Line Dev = Line Management Development; T & D = Training and Development; Saf = Safety; Per Ad = Personnel Administration.
Source: Company Interviews.

relations administration to more long-term issues. However, it appears that this shift away from industrial relations will remain incomplete since, as the personnel manager from Dairyfoods observed, "the emphasis [on industrial relations] depends on the particular issues at hand", and the importance of industrial relations tends to be cyclical in nature. While strategic planning and long-term organisational development are increasingly being seen as those issues that should take up most of the practitioners' time, it is also clear that emphasis on industrial relations will fluctuate over time. Industrial relations issues by their nature may erupt at any stage — the potential implications of ignoring such issues (industrial action, loss of production, strike and closure of plant) will ensure that industrial relations issues will remain relevant. In Clothing Ltd., for example, negotiation of the craft deal still absorbed most of personnel's time and effort.

While the shift in emphasis has not been total, it remains significant and heralds a desire to adopt a longer-term focus on

the part of practitioners in case companies. Perhaps the most concrete manifestation of such a change of emphasis is the initiatives
that have been introduced by, or in co-operation with, the personnel function to facilitate the move away from ad hoc reactive
management towards a more integrated strategic approach
(Tables 6.4a and b).

The most frequently mentioned initiative was that of performance appraisal, with seven of the 11 organisations indicating
that they had introduced or had moved some way towards
introducing a performance appraisal programme. McMahon and
Rowan (1992) found that 60 per cent of companies in their survey
had some form of appraisal system. While performance appraisal
has traditionally been confined to the evaluation of management,
the trend is towards its extension to increasingly wider cohorts of
employees (Foley, 1992). Increasingly, such appraisals are being
linked to the individual performance of the employee. In Chemton, key issues have been work redesign, the initialisation of performance appraisal and also ongoing improvements in communications (new house magazine, for example). In Burchocks, the key
initiative has been a culture change from a control to commitment
orientation. The emphasis has been on a partnership approach
and the long-term aim is the integration of all the workforce into
a performance appraisal system and, if the circumstances are
right, the dismantling of the tight control system in operation. In
Dairyfoods, the personnel function has adopted a central role in
the introduction of an appraisal system and variable pay systems
for managers (senior managers' salaries fluctuating by up to 25
per cent). The underlying rational behind the introduction of such
schemes is the desire to tie individuals to the performance of the
organisation and their contribution to that performance.

Communication initiatives have been introduced in almost half
of the companies and take a number of forms. As may be seen
from the examples below the amount type and frequency of
information dissemination varied from company to company.
Dairyfoods disseminates financial information through arranged
meetings with (small) groups of employees. Electro Engineering
gives information on production, financial information and

Table 6.4(a): HRM Initiatives Introduced

	WR	PA	Comm	TQM	Del	Shares
Dairyfoods		✓	✓			
Burchocks		✓				
Electro Engineering		✓	✓	✓	✓	✓
Chemton	✓	✓	✓			
Park Foods		✓				
Micro Engineering		✓		✓		
Clothing						
Senchem				✓		
Tirown Sweets		✓				
Lola Drinks			✓			
Mineral Drinks			✓			

WR = Work Redesign; PA = Performance Appraisal; Comm = Communications; TQM = Total Quality Management; Del = Authority Delegation; Shares = Employee Shareholding.
Source: Company Interviews.

Table 6.4(b): HRM Initiatives Introduced

	ICC	PRP	Per Ap	Aut Gr	PB	None
Dairyfoods		✓				
Burchocks			✓			
Electro Engineering	✓					
Chemton						
Park Foods				✓		
Micro Engineering				✓		
Clothing						✓
Senchem					✓	
Tirown Sweets						
Lola Drinks						
Mineral Drinks						

ICC = Internal Customer Criticism; PRP = Performance Related Pay; Par Ap = Partnership Approach; Aut Gr = Autonomous Groups; PB = Pay Banding.
Source: Company Interviews.

strategic information, particularly to the union committee. At present, the functional manager talks to all employees each month, but the intention is to devolve this function to supervisors.

Despite increased emphasis on direct employer–employee communications, respondents indicated that unions continued to have a key role in information dissemination. Other key initiatives included TQM and Autonomous Workgroups. Often the introduction of HR initiatives is associated with the reduction in the power of trade unions, frequently borne of the perception that trade unions undermine the profit potential of firms (Belcher and Olson, 1992). No company had an explicit policy to reduce the role of trade unions. This, however, does not mean that all initiatives were introduced with the support of the unions. Indeed, in one particular organisation, the union committee or "war council" was felt to be an inhibiting factor preventing organisational change. As may be seen from Table 6.5 below, the impact of the initiatives on trade unions has been mixed. While one third of case respondents indicated that the initiatives had strengthened the role of the trade union in their organisations, this is matched by five organisations which felt that such initiatives had marginalised

Table 6.5: Impact of Initiatives on the Trade Union

	Relations Improved	Union Marginalised	Union Forced to Adapt	Union Strengthened	Same
Dairyfoods	✓				
Burchocks		✓	✓		
Electro Engineering					
Chemton	✓				
Park Foods	n/a				
Micro Engineering				✓	
Clothing					✓
Senchem		✓			
Tirown Sweets				✓	
Lola Drinks					
Mineral Drinks		✓			

Source: Company Interviews.

the role of unions or at least forced adaptation on their part. Such marginalisation seems to be a by-product of the introduction of the initiatives, rather than the aim behind their introduction.

THE ROLE OF NON-PERSONNEL SPECIALISTS IN PERSONNEL

The personnel department has increasingly used the expertise of external consultants, both internal and external to the organisation, in the introduction of employee initiatives. Here we focus on two key groups: external consultants and line managers.

One of the key features of the personnel function in recent times has been the increasing utilisation of external consultants to carry out many of the tasks traditionally considered to be within the ambit of personnel (MacKay, 1987; Clark and Clark, 1991). This, in many cases, has been an indictment of the personnel function and its inability to deliver in the face of increasing competition (Reynolds Allen, 1991). Whether or not this approach has been as a result of a conscious policy decision, a trend does currently exist towards reassessing the level of intervention that personnel departments engage in, and thus the level of intervention represents an informative measure of the role of personnel (Tables 6.6a and b). Eight respondents indicated that their use of external consultants had increased in recent years, some significantly, such as Chemton where such usage had increased by 300 per cent. Consultants, as may be seen from Tables 6.6(a) and (b), were used in a wide range of areas.

A number of practitioners indicated that in general their use of consultants had increased as the service provided by such specialists became increasingly professional. Common rationales suggested by practitioners for the increased use of consultants were that often the personnel function did not have the resources both in terms of time and specialist skills to undertake particular tasks, which could be quite easily sourced from external consultants. The personnel function, according to Guest (1987) and Storey (1992) is increasingly being integrated and shared with line management. Line managers are increasingly being called upon to carry out personnel activities with employees, and their role is no longer restricted to organising purely production activities (Lowe, 1992; Mallory and Molander, 1989).

Table 6.6(a): Consultant Usage in Case Organisations

	ISO	T&D	Grad	OD	WD	PA
Dairyfoods						✓
Burchocks						
Electro Engineering						
Chemton		✓		✓	✓	
Park Foods	✓		✓			
Micro Engineering		✓				
Clothing					✓	
Senchem		✓		✓		
Tirown Sweets						
Lola Drinks	✓					
Mineral Drinks		✓				

ISO = ISO9000; T&D = Training and Development; Grad = Job Evaluation/Grading; OD = Organisation Development; WD = Work Design; PA = Performance Appraisal.
Source: Company Interviews.

Table 6.6(b) Consultant Usage in Case Organisations

	WM	SP	BPR	WCM	Rec	Saf
Dairyfoods	✓	✓				
Burchocks						
Electro Engineering						
Chemton						
Park Foods						
Micro Engineering			✓	✓	✓	✓
Clothing					✓	✓
Senchem						
Tirown Sweets						
Lola Drinks						
Mineral Drinks						

WM = Work Methods; SP = Strategic Planning; BPR = Business Process Re-Engineering; WCM = World Class Manufacturing; Rec = Recruitment; Saf = Safety.
Source: Company Interviews.

Line Managers

Of the eleven case organisations on which information was gathered, in terms of their personnel function, only three organisations reported that the role of the line manager was being reduced (Table 6.7).

Table 6.7: Has the Role of Line Managers Changed in Recent Times?

	Increased	No Change	Decreased
Dairyfoods	✓		
Burchocks		✓	
Electro Engineering	✓		
Chemton	✓		
Park Foods			✓
Micro Engineering			✓
Clothing	✓		
Senchem			✓
Tirown Sweets		✓	
Lola Drinks	✓		
Mineral Drinks	✓		

Source: Company Interviews.

In two of these companies, this had occurred because the position of the line manager was being changed as part of a larger process of organisational restructuring. The increased participation of line managers in industrial relations takes the form of increased accountability for personnel issues within the scope of line manager's areas of responsibility. However, a practitioner from a large drinks manufacturer stated that "the role has not theoretically changed", suggesting that the management of personnel has always been a responsibility of line managers although it is in recent times that such emphasis has been pushed down. Such a view stems from the perception that "the HR Function are the consultants, the line managers are the doers" (personnel manager, American Multinational).

Evidence from case organisations seems to refute the argument that the personnel function is adopting a less inter-

ventionist role. While the role is not as interventionist as has
traditionally been the case, it still appears to have retained a
strong interventionist facet. The personnel function in most case
companies, advises and coaches line managers in their changing
role, which a practitioner from a chemical/pharmaceutical firm
describes as becoming "facilitators as opposed to their traditional
role". Case evidence seems to suggest that practitioners feel that
the role of the personnel function is increasingly becoming one of
a specialist service function. Line managers in one large textile
manufacturer are now responsible for absenteeism, transfers of
staff, health and safety, and accidents within their own departments. Their involvement is increasingly being used in the recruitment process to build commitment to the individuals hired.
Such experience appears to be relatively common in the case
companies. A number of managers also expressed the concern
that if line managers were to function successfully, it was felt that
they needed to be given more autonomy.

While the increased participation of line managers in personnel activities was common amongst case companies, two companies — one a chemical/pharmaceutical plant and the other a
large engineering plant — indicated that the role of the line
manager in employee relations had declined or was set to do so in
the future. The decline in the role of the line managers stemmed
from structural changes and the movement towards an emphasis
on team-based structures. Such changes had led to a levelling of
the hierarchical structure. In the former organisation it was envisaged that the teams would be become self-researching, team
leaders would become involved in all aspects of management
including personnel activities. It was further felt that such a
move would reduce the importance of shop stewards and line
managers and that the personnel function would adopt a more
coaching role, allowing it time to move away from the traditional
reactive approach.

The rationale for the lessening of the role of the line manager
in the latter organisation was also a move in the long term towards self-directed work systems. In the intervening period, it is
unlikely that the role of the line manager in this company will
expand, despite the increase in employment numbers in recent

years. A second reason advanced by a number of respondent practitioners for the slow decentralisation of personnel activities to line managers is the opposition and reluctance on the part of the line managers to accept increased responsibility. The response to attempts to decentralise was often one of opposition: "[Line managers] were more opposed to the changes than anyone else" (practitioner chemical/pharmaceutical firm). The reaction cited by a line manager from the textile and chemical industries — "We don't have time.... It's not our job" — would not appear to be an atypical response. While of course such a response was not universal, it is true to say that where decentralisation has occurred, it has very much been the case of responsibility being pushed down on to line managers from a centralised personnel function, rather than being elicited from line management to undertake an expanded role. A second problem highlighted by personnel practitioners, albeit a minority, was the perception that line managers did not possess the requisite skills to undertake such an expanded role.

Table 6.8: Line Managers and Personnel Skills

	Possess Needed Skills	*Do Not Possess Needed Skills*
Dairyfoods	✓	
Burchocks	✓	
Electro Engineering		✓
Chemton	✓	
Park Foods	✓	
Micro Engineering	n/a	
Clothing		✓
Senchem		✓
Tirown Sweets	✓	
Lola Drinks	✓	
Mineral Drinks	✓	

Source: Company Interviews.

In recognition of this problem and its potential deleterious consequences, a training programme had been implemented or was planned in almost all organisations to equip line managers adequately. The problem that inadequate skills could lead to was illuminated by a practitioner in the food-manufacturing industry. While the line managers in this case were not adverse to taking on increased responsibility, he felt that: "Managers, particularly those new to the organisation, having taken on new responsibilities [had] created a number of problems ... part of which was attributable to their lack of skill in personnel and related areas". As may be seen from case evidence discussed thus far, there has been a relatively widespread decentralisation of personnel activities to the shop floor, although such moves have been tempered by the opposition of line managers and their lack of appropriate skills to undertake such a role. Typically this has occurred through responsibility being pushed down by a relatively strong and centralised personnel function. However, in no case discussed thus far, has decentralisation been complete. Complete decentralisation implies the inclusion in the role of line manager all personnel activities, to the extent that the function only exists through the activities of line managers. While in no instance was this the case, Textile was moving in that direction.

STRATEGIC ROLE DEFINED

The question of how to decide whether or not the personnel function is adopting a strategic role is a complex one. Several models of strategic HRM exist (Sisson and Timperley, 1994). For the purposes of this discussion a specific definition shall be adopted. *Strategy* refers to "an *overall plan*" and *strategic* refers to *integral involvement in the development of the organisation's overall plan*. The overall plan in an organisational context refers to the organisation's corporate strategy, and thus a key test of a strategic role for personnel, in this chapter, will be integral involvement in the formulation of corporate strategy. A strategic role for personnel is not a black and white concept, however — organisations need not of necessity fall into either strategic or non-strategic categories, but rather may vary on the degree to which they have adopted a strategic role. In the succeeding section, therefore, a composite measure of a strategic role for the personnel function is developed. Such a measure helps not only to define which organisations have adopted a strategic role, but also to facilitate the categorisation of those organisations which have not.

1. Formulation of Corporate Strategy

As stated above, if an organisation is to adopt a strategic role, then it must be involved in the formulation of corporate strategy. Such strategy is the overriding organisational plan which converts the intangible values of the mission statement/philosophy into tangible objectives, which assess environmental threats, establish organisational goals and develop long-term business plans. The primary measure therefore is the extent of *participation in the formulation of corporate strategy*. While generally high, case organisations indicated differing degrees of involvement in the formulation of corporate strategy in their respective organisations. A number of respondents indicated virtually no input ,as was the case in Clothing where personnel and other functions "just signed into the policy". A particular problem was faced by those practitioners who worked in subsidiaries of foreign multinational companies based in Ireland. Strategy in the Irish plant was constrained and, to an extent, determined by parameters set by the strategy-formulation process in the parent plant. Such a sentiment was expressed by the practitioner from Tirown Sweets who indicated that in his organisation, "Nobody is involved — strategy is set in the parent company". In many such instances, there is no possibility of input into strategy for the personnel function in the subsidiary. Being excluded from such formulation may place the function in the position where it is merely reacting to the human resource problems that may result from the exclusion of personnel from the decision-making processes at the highest levels.

To infer, however, that the personnel functions in subsidiary plants merely act in a reactionary fashion is overly simplistic, particularly in light of the view expressed by the practitioner in Chemton. In this organisation it was felt that plants acted autonomously. While overriding precepts were established in the parent company, subsidiaries acted largely independently of the parent plant. In such a situation there was scope for practitioners to adopt strategic developmental roles. In eight of the case organisations, the top practitioners indicated that they were involved in the formulation of corporate strategy.

2. Board-Level Participation of the Top Personnel Practitioner

A second key indicator, and a corollary of the first is the participation of the personnel function at the highest echelons of their respective organisations. Corporate strategy represents the highest level of planning that is undertaken within organisations. If the function is to be integrally involved in the formulation of such strategy, it is axiomatic that it must be represented at the highest level within organisations. In an organisational context, such a level represents the boardroom, an area from which the personnel function has been excluded in the past. The participation of the top practitioner at board level represents a second indicator of the level of strategic input of the personnel function. The case evidence offers further evidence of the trend toward increasing representation of the top personnel practitioner at board level. Five respondents indicate that this was indeed the case. As is to be expected, given their hierarchical position all the practitioners who indicated that they were represented at board level also indicated involvement in the formulation of corporate strategy at the development stage.

The conclusion that can be drawn thus far is that the personnel function in respondent organisations is ideally placed in a number of the case organisations to adopt a high-level strategic role. While in terms of the definition outlined above such organisations are adopting a role that is strategic in nature, it is intended to refine the model further. If the intention of personnel acting at such a strategic level is to impact on the practice of personnel management throughout the organisation, it is important that decisions taken at operational and tactical levels are internally consistent with those taken at "strategic level". Indeed, Fahey (1989) asserts that strategic management may be a waste of time unless supported at lower levels of the organisation. The remaining measures, therefore, strive to ascertain to what extent the function has adopted an integrated and co-ordinated approach to personnel activities to support this strategic approach. The rationale is that functions that are truly strategic will not only be in a position to impact on top-level decision-making, but will also ensure that personnel policies adopted will be closely integrated into overall business strategy, and decisions taken at top levels will be devolved down through the organisation. The third major indicator of a strategic role for the personnel function is the adoption of an integrated and consistent approach to personnel management.

3. An Integrated Approach to Personnel Management

The existence of such an approach is identified by three sub-measures, which are outlined below. Organisations indicating that they fulfil all of these criteria are deemed to have adopted an integrated approach to personnel management. The measures are:

- The existence of a personnel strategy

- Integration of personnel and business issues

- The existence of strategic planning systems in relation to human resources.

The Existence of a Personnel Strategy

If the personnel function is to operate effectively at the highest levels within its organisation, it is imperative that the function has a strategy in relation to the organisation's human resources. The existence of a clear policy or philosophy on human resources represents a framework which guides managerial actions in dealing with employees. Development of a formalised personnel strategy not only offers the opportunity to break out of the traditional knee-jerk mould which has characterised some areas of human resource activity, but also is a prerequisite to participation in corporate strategy. The existence of such a strategy will be measured by the presence of an explicit personnel strategy in respondent organisations. A clear policy or philosophy on human resources represents a framework that guides managerial actions in dealing with employees. As such it is instrumental and acts as a cement to bind HRM policies and outcomes (Guest, 1989).

Seven of the case organisations indicated that they had a personnel strategy that was written. Of the remaining four organisations, one had a strategy that was not written, a second claimed that its personnel strategy was incorporated in the over-all strategy, the third organisation was in the process of develop-ing such a strategy, with the remaining organisation having either no plans or desires to formulate such a strategy. Evidence therefore suggests that a majority of respondents have clearly-developed strategies for achieving personnel goals. If, however, the function is to contribute in a positive way to the working of the organisation, such strategy must be vested in, and supportive of, the overall corporate strategy.

Personnel Activities and Business Strategy

The existence of both corporate and personnel strategy is no guarantee that the personnel strategy is supportive of corporate strategy, the top practitioner in Tirown Sweets indicating that: "While we have a policy in all the personnel areas ... [these poli-cies] are not integrated with the corporate or business strategy". If human resource concerns are to be truly integrated into and supportive of corporate strategy, it is imperative that such re-inforcement is not limited to the level of strategy formulation, and that personnel activities taken at lower levels of the organisation are internally consistent, supporting the personnel and conse-quently the corporate strategy. One mechanism by which con-sistency of purpose can be achieved is to draw programmes and deadlines from the strategy for lower levels of the organisation.

To ensure the integration of personnel and business strategy, it is necessary that personnel activities at each level of the orga-nisation support the business goals. With the exception of one company, those companies which have a corporate strategy also indicated that the strategy was converted into deadlines and pro-grammes. It appears that the personnel function is attempting to link personnel strategy explicitly to the achievement of organisa-tional goals as embodied in the corporate strategy. An interesting point to emerge from the case interviews was that the personnel function was not always the key driving force behind the development of a personnel strategy and its integration with business strategy. In Burchocks, for example, the process had been a reactive one on the part of personnel to initiatives put in place by top management. The top practitioner commenting on the very close integration between business and corporate strategy felt that: "the change occurred as a result of the setting up of the executive committee (13 senior managers) ... they run the business and everyone has to contribute to the business objectives". The need of personnel to contribute "integrates personnel in a practical and operational day-to-day way" and the perceived impact of such integration has been the "breaking down of narrow functionalism and petty protectionism".

A key issue to emerge in recent years is not only the need of personnel to be integrated with business strategy, but also the need to quantify in concrete terms the contribution of personnel to organisational objectives. Mercer (1989) suggests that: "everyone that works in the business world knows that the purpose of business is to make money. Unfortunately many organisations view their HR departments as being somehow removed from the process of contributing directly to the bottom line". While the above assertion is perhaps more clearly applicable to private-sector organisations (Wilson, 1988), it is obvious that a personnel department must be capable not only of facilitating the fulfilment of organisational goals but also of quantifying its contribution in terms of the financial cost-benefit ratios of personnel activities.

Driver et al. (1988) argue that the financial aspects of personnel management are growing in importance as managers become increasingly aware of the major impact that human resource costs have on operations. Evidence from the case companies, however, indicates that relatively few respondent organisations (four of the case companies) systematically review the performance of their personnel functions. Even where such evaluation takes place, it appears that it is of a low-impact nature, largely confined to measuring the role of the personnel incumbents and their ability to fulfil their objectives. Two companies indicated that the review of the personnel function was undertaken informally, with a further four companies indicating that such evaluation was not undertaken. While low-impact strategies may draw attention to personnel activities, they are not a sufficient basis for demonstrating active management (Rhodeback, 1991). One company, however, had adopted a more sophisticated mechanism for evaluating the effectiveness of the personnel function. It sought the views of those functions to which personnel provided a service, asking them for their perceptions of the effectiveness of the service and any recommendations on how this service could be improved. These views, together with the function's own perceptions of its performance and the standard performance review, provide some yardstick by which the personnel service may be quantified objectively, and improved.

Evidence from Gunnigle et al. (1994), and the case evidence in the present study, suggests that the personnel function is becoming increasingly integrated into overall business strategy. However, the personnel function in respondent organisations, as has traditionally been the case (Kossek, 1990), places little emphasis on evaluating the impact of personnel programmes. Such evaluation is becoming increasingly important given the need of organisations to respond to cost pressures and the question of what they add to the value of local operating units (Lawler, 1988).

The Use of Strategic Planning

While Gunnigle and Flood (1990) and Read (1988) suggest that high-performing companies invest heavily in planning, Ellig (1989) and Herren (1989) assert that planning is also an activity that is carried out least effectively. Personnel practitioners are not above reproach in this area (Storey, 1992), asserting notoriously that the HR planning process has been the arena of prescription, with a dearth of hard evidence that practice was in any way being affected. If the personnel function is to undertake strategic planning at corporate level, then it is important that planning of human resources is also strategic. While planning horizons fluctuate across industries and organisations, strategic planning is generally considered to be long term (Gunnigle and Flood, 1990, citing a period of 3–5 years). While the majority of respondents (seven) indicate that they carry out manpower planning, only two such organisations indicate that their planning horizons are in excess of one year. Obviously there was a great deal of difference in the systems employed, ranging from situations where it was felt that such planning was not needed, to systems where succession planning was the main emphasis, to systems which planned based on workforce profiles, sales estimates and production plans, audits of skill requirements and other contingency-planning targets. The short-termism of such planning is not in keeping with a strategic perspective (usually regarded as medium to long term) of human resource management, and only in these two organisations is manpower planning directly integrated into business planning. Table 6.9 presents the other types of planning commonly undertaken by the personnel function among the firms that participated in the research.

Table 6.9: Planning Undertaken by the Personnel Function

	T&D	Rem	Prod	PA	IR	Invest	Prob Res	WCM	None
Dairyfoods									✓
Burchocks	✓	✓	✓						
Electro Engineering			✓	✓					
Chemton									✓
Park Foods				✓	✓				
Micro Engineering									✓
Clothing		✓				✓			
Senchem								✓	
Tirown Sweets									✓
Lola Drinks									✓
Mineral Drinks									✓

T&D = Training and Development; Rem = Remuneration; Prod = Productivity; PA = Performance Appraisal; IR = Industrial Relations; Invest = Investment; Prob Res = Problem Resolution; WCM = World Class Manufacturing.
Source: Company Interviews.

EVIDENCE OF STRATEGIC INTEGRATION

Four levels measuring the strategic nature of the personnel function have been outlined above. These measures can be combined to categorise the case organisations. From a strategic perspective,

companies can range from those involved in strategy implementation only, to those involved in formulation, right through to the
adoption of a completely integrated approach to strategic human
resource management.

All organisations must fulfil the criteria of having a formalised, established personnel function. Since the measure of a strategic role is composite, each succeeding category must fulfil all
pre-existing criteria (for example, those organisations that adopt
an integrated approach must meet all the preceding criteria).
This model may be used to differentiate the personnel function in
respondent organisations.

**Table 6.10: Case Organisations and Strategic Personnel
Management**

Adopt an integrated approach to strategic HR					2
Represented at board level				5	
Integrally involved in formulation of strategy			8		
Implementation of corporate strategy		11			
Existence of personnel function	11				

Source: Company Interviews

As may be seen from Table 6.10 above, all the case organisations
report the existence of the personnel function and also a minimum of input into corporate strategy. Only eight of these organisations indicate that they are included at the outset of the
formulation of corporate strategy, five organisations fulfil the
criteria of board-level representation and integral involvement in
the formulation of corporate strategy, with only two of the 11
organisations adopting an integrated approach to the strategic
management of human resources. The development of this model
also facilitates the placing of organisations on the tactical strategist continuum. Those functions not represented at the highest
levels within their organisations (board level) may be categorised
as adopting a tactical reactive role (the assumption being that if
one is not involved in the formulation of strategy, one must react
to its implications). Organisations involved in strategy formula-

tion at the highest levels are in a position to undertake a strategic role. The degree to which such is undertaken in an integrated manner will determine the extent to which each organisation will be placed towards the right side of the continuum. The case organisations may be placed on this continuum as follows in terms of this model (Figure 6.2).

The six organisations that are not represented at board level (see Table 6.2 above) are regarded as being reactive to a greater or lesser extent. Exclusion from the key policy-making forums of organisations renders it axiomatic that the function and the top practitioner will be reacting to decisions taken at these levels. Of course, those practitioners not represented at board level are not necessarily acting at merely administrative levels. A number of practitioners indicated that, while not involved in the formulation of corporate strategy, they had a large role to play in terms of its development. Such practitioners were deemed to have a adopted a *Sophisticated Tactician Role*, those practitioners merely involved in implementation categorised as *Tacticians*. Of the six reactive organisations, three fell into the category of Tactician and three were categorised as Sophisticated Tactician. As may be seen above, only two of the case organisations fulfil all of the criteria and adopt what has been termed a *Pure Strategist Role* — that is, they act at the highest levels within their organisations and have adopted an integrated approach to personnel. The three organisations that had not quite reached the level of the pure strategist were termed *Intermediary Strategist*. The case organisations can therefore be placed along a strategist/tactical continuum.

As may be seen above, the personnel function has undergone a major change of emphasis in recent years, which has resulted in a shift of emphasis away from the reactive management of industrial relations. Industrial relations concerns are increasingly being supplanted with concerns surrounding long-term organisational planning and development issues. Companies defined as strategic (pure and intermediary) are also more likely to have shifted towards a more co-operative pattern of industrial relations. The analysis of industrial relations patterns in Chapter 4 indicated that five companies experienced a substantial positive shift in their industrial relations during the 1980s. Four of these companies (Chemton, Burchocks, Dairyfoods and Electro Engineering) are also associated with taking a pure or intermediary strategic approach to managing their human resources (Table 6.11). The remaining company defined as adopting a strategic

Figure 6.2: Tactical-Strategist Continuum

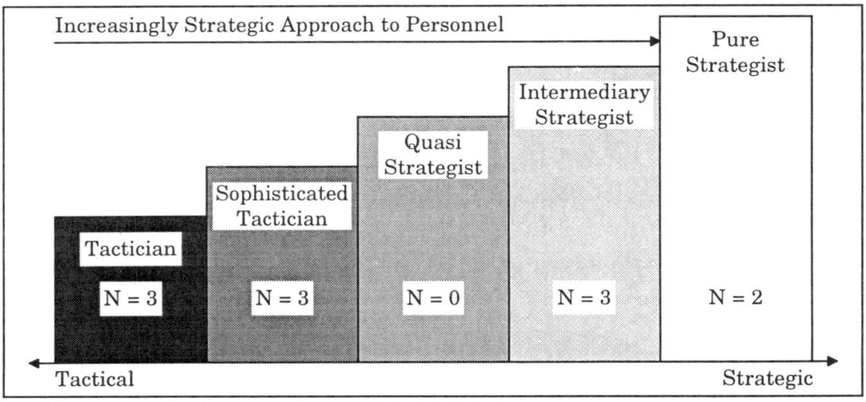

Table 6.11: Patterns of Industrial Relations and Strategic HRM

Company	Change[†]	Strategic HRM
Dairyfoods	**positive shift (high)**	**HIGH**
Mineral Ltd.	little change(low)	LOW
Textile	no change (moderate)	LOW
Park Foods	no change (low)	LOW
Senchem	no change (low)	LOW
Burchocks	**positive shift (high)**	**HIGH**
Tirown Sweets	**positive change (high)**	LOW
Lola Drinks	no change (high)	**HIGH**
Micro Engineering	no change (high)	LOW
Electro Engineering	**positive shift (moderate)**	**HIGH**
Chemton	**positive shift (high)**	**HIGH**
Processchem	little change (low)	LOW
Clothing Ltd.*	Not Available	

†   high = co-operative relations; low = antagonistic relations; moderate = either moderate antagonism or co-operation.
Source: Personnel/senior management interviews (structured questionnaire).

approach, Lola Drinks, though changing little in the 1980s, has always had a co-operative constitutional pattern of industrial relations.

With two exceptions — Tirown Sweets and Micro Engineering — there appears to be a significant relationship between a strong personnel function with the capacity to play a strategic role in the management of human resources, and the shift away from traditional-type adversarial industrial relations.

CONCLUSION

Case evidence cited in this chapter points to the continuing strength of the personnel function in the companies surveyed. Such evidence, coupled with that from Gunnigle et al. (1994) and recent evidence in the Irish context, does much to dispel the notion that there is a crisis in personnel management. The personnel function, as with all other managerial functions, has been forced to re-assess its contribution to organisational effectiveness and to ensure that the function continues to support and contribute to organisational survival and growth. A number of notable issues arose from the case evidence, which points to significant changes in the traditional personnel function. Personnel practitioners are increasingly achieving board-level status. Such achievements facilitate the integral involvement of the function in the key decision-making fora within organisations, and enable the function increasingly to move away from the fire-fighting duties which have traditionally been associated with personnel work. The case evidence also suggests that such change will be a slow evolutionary process rather than the complete rejection of the traditional personnel activities and adoption of the "new sophisticated" personnel role.

While change has been slow, the evidence here indicates that the trend is toward the adoption of a more strategic role for the personnel function. While relatively few have achieved a *Pure Strategist* level, evidence suggests that movement is in this direction. Of primary importance in this respect is the extent to which a strong personnel function acts as a strategic lever for industrial relations change. The data from the present study suggest that there is an important association here. Companies that have experienced a positive shift in industrial relations, with one exception, also rank high in terms of strategic HRM practices. Conversely, those organisations that have experienced little or no change, again with one exception, score low along strategic HRM dimensions.

Chapter 7

EMPLOYEE RELATIONS IN SMALL MANUFACTURING FIRMS

Juliet MacMahon

Storey (1990) argues that small firms are not just scaled-down versions of large firms, but have characteristics which are different in type from large firms. Although interest in the small-firm sector in Ireland as a source of economic prosperity has increased, there is as yet little research in the area. Employee relations in small firms is a particularly under-researched area in the Irish context. As research from other countries (most notably Britain, e.g. Curran and Stanworth, 1981; Curran, 1986; Storey, 1990) shows, it is not enough simply to apply large-firm employee relations theory to the small firm. This chapter attempts to redress the balance and provide an insight into the complexities of small-firm employee relations. In keeping with the theme of this book, issues of change in the small-firm sector, particularly in the area of employee relations, will also be examined. For instance, do current issues such as "new realism" apply in the arena of small-firm employee relations? For the purposes of analysis a small firm is defined as one employing 100 people or fewer.

THE CHANGING ROLE OF THE SMALL FIRM IN THE IRISH ECONOMY

The increasing importance of the small firm to the Irish economy can be estimated using a number of sources. Using data from the Industrial Development Authority (IDA), Figure 7.1 indicates that *small firms form the vast bulk of manufacturing companies in Ireland.*

According to the IDA data, there were approximately 51,111 manufacturing establishments employing fewer than 50 people in

1993. If all small companies (with fewer than 100 employees) are taken together, they account for *46 per cent of total employment* in Irish manufacturing, employing approximately 88,251 people, and this share is steadily increasing as can be seen from Figure 7.2.

Figure 7.1: Size Structure of Irish Manufacturing Industry

Number of Firms by Size
(IDA data November 1993)

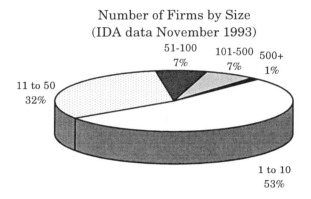

Source: IDA Annual Employment Survey, November 1993.

Figure 7.2: Employment Trends in Small Manufacturing Firms

Employment Over Time

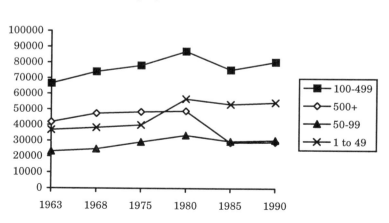

Source: Kennedy et al., 1985; and Census of Industrial Production Table 3, 1985–1990.

Small firms in Irish manufacturing have increased their employment share, especially since the mid to late 1970s. Firms employing 500+ have in general experienced a sharp decline in employment share from 48,647 in 1980 to 28,953 by 1990, and now account for a smaller proportion of total employment than firms under 50 and firms employing between 50 and 99 people. In short, the employment share of firms employing *fewer* than 100 is increasing, and the employment share of those employing *more* than 100 has been decreasing since 1975.

To evaluate employee relations in small firms four case-study companies were selected (see Table 1.6 for a summary of company characteristics). Below is a brief profile of the case-study companies.

City Engineering Ltd.

This company was founded in 1973 and is located in Dublin. In 1991, the company experienced growth which enabled it to expand its office units. City Engineering also has a branch in another Irish city. It is Irish owned and is not quoted on the stock exchange. The owner plays a dominant role and acts as managing director. There are 32 full-time employees. Of these, 30 are male and two are female. There are two senior managers and five middle managers. The production department consists of two units: fabrication and coating, with one manager in each area. Ten operators and craft workers work in each area. The total number of employees has increased in the past three years. Two new staff members were recruited in the past six months. Numbers are currently rising, but the workforce was larger three years ago, with 38 employed.

City Engineering estimates that it has about 60 per cent of the market in its main products. Most of its competitors — of which there are about 40 in the region — would be "just too small to bother us". The largest competitor in the Irish market would be a Northern-Irish-based company which is of a similar size in the Northern market, but whose turnover in the Republic is only about £400,000 a year. The company manufactures about 15 products. City Engineering normally supplies many customers, none of whom account for a significant proportion of the business.

To achieve and sustain competitive advantage, the company relies heavily on the skills and expertise of its employees, in conjunction with a well-known brand name. There is a strong commitment to cater for the specific needs of individual customers, and a strong emphasis on training employees. Most of the training carried out is on-the-job training. There is a training officer, and an annual training plan is drawn up for the company. Much of City Engineering's business is with the construction industry and it is currently experiencing increasing cost competition for job tenders from low-price tendering by the main contractors. According to the owner:

> The customer is often prepared to take the lowest-price supplier, even if the quality and expertise is not of the same calibre, if only to knock our prices. So the text book will tell you we've got 65 per cent of the market — we should be in a dominant position to force up the prices — but the reality is not that simple.

The owner-manager presides over operations; senior and middle management represent one level of hierarchy between the owner and employees. The usual span of control consists of 10 persons per supervisor. All employees, excluding management, are members of the trade union SIPTU. There has never been any overt conflict in the form of industrial action.

Innovate Engineering Ltd.

This company was established in 1973 and is run by the owner who is the managing director. There are currently 44 people employed on a full-time permanent basis. There are no part-time or temporary employees. There are eight skilled manual male employees, five clerical female employees, one clerical male employee, three female craft workers, eleven engineers, and the remaining employees are skilled male craft workers. Innovate Ltd. is mainly a supplier of general engineering products, and an assembler of compressors and generators. It is an Irish-owned firm and is not quoted on the stock exchange. The majority of staff are engineers. In 1987, in order to combat the threat of increased competition from large-scale manufacturers, the company decided to set up a research and development centre to develop new products. It drew together a team of mechanical, industrial and electronic engineers. Very high manufacturing standards are employed to produce a wide range of Diamond and CBN tools to the highest, most consistent and repeatable levels of quality, and to acknowledged international standards. The company produces four main products, has multiple customers for these products, and is constantly working on developing new products. The number of employees has increased in the past three years and apart from seasonal variations the demand for products has increased.

Innovate Ltd. has built a good reputation in sub-contract research and development work, and its future depends on continual research and development. The usual span of control of supervisors is between six and eight persons. The company has a written corporate strategy, to become a world-wide leader in the field of electronic torque measurement. It is very sensitive to changes in the external environment and is very aware of large firms poaching products that it has developed. Innovate Ltd. requires employees with a high level of technical training. At assembly level, employees are expected to have the potential for multi-skilling, as a high degree of flexibility is required. Employees are perceived as being jointly responsible for their own development. If an employee selects a training course, the owner will consider it if there is evidence of some benefit to the company. It is estimated that approximately £12,000 was spent on training during the year prior to the interview. In 1991, £50,000–£60,000 was spent on technical training needs. There is no official training manager — the owner-manager takes this responsibility. There is no formalised training function.

Yarn Ltd.

This is a textile company situated in a rural area. It has been operational under its current European owners for the past 11 years. There are 100 employees: 20 female manual, 68 male manual, two female clerical, and 10 male professional and technical staff. The managing director is a European national. There are no part-time or temporary employees. This was originally an

American-owned company that had operated in Ireland since the early 1970s, and at the time of its closure employed 600 people. The plant was bought by the European company which started manufacturing here in 1983. The decision to locate in Ireland was taken because the building and machinery were suitable and cheap and there was a surplus of the appropriate skilled workforce available. There were also generous grants available, such as export sales relief. Since the take-over, the workforce has been reduced from over 600 to 100 employees. This has been achieved mainly through a redundancy programme in 1989, and a high turnover of employees for the first six years of operation. Industrial relations problems increased up to and during the redundancy programme, including sit-ins, strikes, and dismissals.

One of the biggest problems the company has is matching the size of its workforce with cycles in the market demand for its products. There have been temporary lay-offs over the past six years when there have been lulls in the market. These have not been operated on a last-in-first-out basis (LIFO), but operate plant-wide, affecting everybody except staff and some maintenance craft workers, because maintenance has to be continuous. There has either been a complete shut down or a roster system where people are laid off on a weekly basis, depending on the situation. The company maintains that it cannot operate LIFO as there are different processes, and different people are trained for different machines.

The product is described as high-volume low-cost, but there has to be a "certain" level of quality. The main customer is a European company, which takes about 80 per cent of production. Up to two years ago this would have been 98 per cent, but the company has managed to branch out somewhat, and now has a number of "third-party" customers. However the main customer to a large extent dictates matters such as production methods, quality and costs. There are several competitors in the same size bracket outside Ireland which are difficult to compete with. These would mainly be in Turkey, Portugal and Germany. The competitive situation is said to be static at the moment, but the main problem facing the company is its ability to remain competitive, largely on the basis of cost.

Autoeng Ltd.

This company has a rural location. It was established in 1973, and is owned by a European who lives in Ireland and is also the managing director of the company. There are 34 full-time employees, mostly male. The owner is described as very much a "hands-on" manager. There is one management layer between him and the manual employees — a financial manager, a quality assurance manager and a production manager. The company also has two quality assurance technicians and one semi-skilled tool-maker. There are six females employed in the sewing department. The rest of the workforce is unskilled manual.

Autoeng's product is described as high-volume, medium-cost, "standard" quality. However, lowering the costs is becoming a major consideration. The main customer base is international — Irish markets for the products are described as "non-existent". The company acts mainly in a sub-contractor capacity, and approximately 60 per cent of its business is with a large company in Germany, which supplies the DIY market. Autoeng Ltd. buys raw materials from this larger company and sells them back the finished product. Because this large company takes so much of the business, it dictates what Autoeng does and how it does it.

Autoeng also supplies to two major car manufacturers in the UK. The manager interviewed accepts that this reliance on one major company in the automotive industry, which is "in a very bad state" in Europe at the moment, is risky. In fact, in 1982 the company nearly closed because their main customer at the time, which was taking almost 80 per cent of production, went into liquidation. Overall in the market, competition has increased. There used to be a limited range of competitors in the automotive market, but this has radically changed. The product market situation is now described as "cut-throat". Because of this, prices have become critical and, in turn, the large car manufacturers are now looking all over the world for component parts — no longer just in Europe. The end result is that Autoeng Ltd. is now in competition with companies in emerging countries such as India and Korea. According to the manager, Indian manufacturers in particular are posing a very serious threat, as they are constantly improving the quality of their goods, while maintaining "ridiculously" low prices. In fact, the company has no option at times but to buy completed goods from Indian manufacturers and to sell them on in an effort to survive. Japanese and Taiwanese companies used to pose stiff competition on the basis of quality, but are no longer a threat as they are too expensive. Thus, competition in the automotive market is growing all the time and costs are becoming as important as quality.

Autoeng Ltd. is coping better with the market situation than other small companies in the region supplying automotive parts, because of the contracts it has secured with two UK-based manufacturers, but is nevertheless feeling the effects. An expansion programme was embarked upon before the competitive situation changed and a new building was built. This should have resulted in new employment but, because of the current market situation, the company has just about managed to *maintain* employment levels and the new building is virtually unused. Autoeng has also begun to employ people on a temporary basis. Industrial relations in the company have been described by union official and management as adversarial. All manual employees are members of SIPTU. There have been two strikes in the company and there is an ongoing dispute in relation to shift allowances. There is also a system of lay-offs in operation at the moment as a result of market conditions and this are the source of considerable conflict. Table 7.1 summarises the characteristics of the four companies.

Table 7.1: Company Characteristics

	City Engineering Ltd.	Innovate Engineering Ltd.	Yarn Ltd.	Autoeng Ltd.
Ownership	Irish	Irish	European	European
Employment	32	44	100	34
Skill Level	Moderate	High	Low	Low
Competition	Moderate	Moderate to Severe	Severe	Very Severe
Customers	Many Customers	Many Customers	80% to One Customer	60% to One Customer
Business Strategy	Differentiation Strategy	Differentiation Strategy	Low Cost Strategy	Low Cost Strategy
Market	National/ International	National/ International	International	International
Industrial Relations	Co-operative	Co-operative	Adversarial	Adversarial

FACTORS AFFECTING EMPLOYEE RELATIONS IN SMALL FIRMS

Much of the early research on small-firm employee relations (such as Bolton, 1971; Ingham, 1970) has been criticised for failing to take account of the influence of factors in the external environment. However, more contemporary research emphasises the importance of variables or factors external to the small firm, which impact directly both on employee relations outcomes and also on the internal dynamics of the small firm, ultimately affecting the outcomes or practices of employee relations (see, for instance, Rainnie and Scott, 1986; Blyton and Turnbull, 1993; Curran, 1987). Previous research has shown how product markets impact both directly and indirectly on employee relations in both large and small firms (see Marchington, 1990) and cause changes in both employer and employee attitudes and approaches to work organisation (see Chapter 3 above). The question that arises is whether such factors affect employee relations to the same extent in small firms, creating a new realism in employee relations in such firms.

Indeed, factors in the external environment emerged as perhaps the most significant in relation to differentiating between employee relations practices in the different case-study companies. For companies that aimed to maintain a competitive edge through high quality, there were implications for employment practices and workforce structure. In City Engineering Ltd., there was a commitment to customise products to meet particular needs of customers, and a high degree of flexibility and multi-skilling was required, leading to a greater emphasis on training. In Innovate Engineering where competitive advantage was achieved through innovative R&D, a high degree of employee autonomy was evident and the workforce consisted largely of highly qualified professional/technical staff, and rewards were above average for small manufacturing companies. There was also considerable investment in training and development. There was a marked antipathy towards unions on the part of the manager, on the basis of flexibility. His view was that unions would reduce the flexibility of his staff by introducing demarcation rules and opposing change. The company was non-union.

To maintain a broad customer base and also to retain competitive advantage, both companies were constantly investing in product development (improving current products and developing new ones). Innovate Engineering was also very active in market penetration both in Europe and the US. City Engineering Ltd. looked to develop new markets to a lesser extent, and was largely oriented to the national market. Both companies were experiencing overall growth at the time of the study. Despite this, Innovate Engineering had recently reduced its workforce because it was no longer the market leader for one of its products and simply could not compete with new entrants on the basis of cost or quality. The general strategy in this company seemed to be one of innovation: develop or improve products and reap the benefits until other manufacturers "caught up", and then move on. This seems to support the findings of Smallbone et al. (1993) who found that high-growth small firms in the high-tech sector maintained competitive advantage through constant innovation and R&D. One of the main implications of such competitive strategies for employees in these two companies was an insistence on a high degree of flexibility and substantial investment in training, which will be discussed in more detail below.

Consequences of Large and Small Firm Linkages

Blyton and Turnbull (1993) and Rainnie (1989) argue that relationships between large and small firms can have a major bearing on the labour process in the latter. This seems to be borne out by the research. Inter-organisational relationships with larger companies did emerge as having a significant impact on small firms. For innovative small companies engaged in R&D, such as Innovate Engineering, there was a recognition of the threat of large companies "poaching" products, thus making them no longer viable for the small company, often resulting in job losses. Other small companies that have built up steady customer bases are often threatened by large firms trying to "muscle in" on them and undercut them in terms of cost. Another source of instability in the small-firm sector, according to the owner of City Engineering Ltd., occurs when a large company closes down and the redundant employees attempt to set up their own small enterprise.

These new establishments, often operating in the black economy, can afford to charge lower prices, putting established companies out of business. This leads to instability in the small-firm sector and affects job security for employees.

For small companies, becoming dependent on a single major customer can also have implications for the labour process (Rainnie, 1989). Large firms invariably dominate small firms in such relationships and dictate terms to them. The result of such relationships for large firms is very different from that for small firms. For large firms, such sub-contracting out of parts or components considerably reduces risks and overheads, can lead to greater stability, and facilitates more employee-oriented policies for their own "core employees". The result for the small company very much depends on the competitive position of the large customer within its product market. If the larger company is operating successfully, it can be to the advantage of the small supplier as it is ensured of sales. Large customers operating to quality standards can also impose these standards on their suppliers, which can be beneficial for employees in terms of increased training. However, where the competitive position of a large customer takes a downturn, the impact on the supplier can be significant, to the extent that it can precipitate the closure of the small company (as almost happened in one of the case-study companies). Less extreme, but also with significant consequences for the workforce, is the increased emphasis on cost reduction that is often forced upon the small supplier in such circumstances. This can lead to a claw-back of privileges considered too expensive in the straitened circumstances, and conflict over rewards. Job tenure can also be affected in terms of lay-offs and the introduction of temporary employment. Longer-term consequences can be a lowering of trust between employer and employees — a far cry from the harmonious. "happy family" analogy presented by earlier research.

Two of the companies (Innovate Engineering and City Engineering) actively worked to avoid becoming too dependent on one particular customer, though in City Engineering's case, one customer was accounting for 30 per cent of current business. However, the owner maintained that this was a very unusual situation and that it would not remain like this. Yarn Ltd. and Autoeng Ltd. were both in a situation where they sold mainly to one major customer in what appeared to be declining markets, and this seemed to impact on employee relations. In the case of Autoeng Ltd. which acknowledged that it was "almost totally dependent" on the automotive market, there had been a threatened closure in 1982 when its major customer at that time (accounting for over 80 per cent of total business) had gone into liquidation. The impact on employee relations was severe. There were redundancies among the manual employees, and subsequent feelings of insecurity on the part of clerical and supervisory staff caused them to join a union, the end result being a strike. There was also an inter-union dispute as the clerical/supervisory staff joined a different union from the one catering for the manual workers. Interviews with management and a trade union official revealed a low level of trust between both parties.

However, past experience did not seem to have had much effect, as the same company was now dependent on a major European automotive parts manufacturer for over 60 per cent of its business. The manager acknowledged that this had had an effect on terms and conditions for employees, in that the European company was in a declining market in Europe, and was experiencing severe problems itself in terms of cost competition from other manufacturers. Consequently, it was putting pressure on Autoeng Ltd. to keep costs to a minimum, which in turn directly impacted on pay levels in the plant, and had led to quite a substantial amount of antagonism in all issues relating to pay (for instance, the 3 per cent negotiable clause) and a shift allowance (the latter issue had given rise to a dispute which was still ongoing at the time of the interview). The situation also had an impact on numbers employed and the type of employment available. There were lay-offs on a continuous basis and the company had "no qualms" about hiring people on a temporary basis and letting them go as demand increased or decreased. There had been a number of problems with employees over the system of laying people off.

Product quality did not seem to be a major consideration. Indeed, the manager interviewed felt that the end user in the present market "couldn't care less as long as the tool was cheap and functional". Consequently, training and employee develop-ment were not perceived as relevant issues. It was pointed out that there were certain advantages to having such a close rela-tionship with a larger company, in that this single customer had helped to secure contracts with two major car manufacturers, and the resulting new business had helped the company to survive.

Yarn Ltd. was also experiencing problems because of the com-petitive position of its larger main customer, but the current com-petitive situation did not seem quite as intense as that above and there had been a slight increase in demand for some of the com-pany's products in the previous two years. The market situation had led to lay-offs in the plant at various times over the previous six years, but most of the industrial relations problems resulting from the company "becoming competitive" in its market had seemed to occur in the first six years after the take-over, when there were severe cutbacks. The situation seemed to be more stable at the time of the study, and industrial relations were said to have improved considerably. However the manager interviewed admitted that competition from other less-developed countries was a potential future threat, as their costs were lower and they were catching up in technology terms.

From the above, it would appear that product markets and competitive position have a considerable impact on employee rela-tions in small firms, just as they do in larger companies. For instance, City Engineering Ltd. and Innovate Engineering Ltd., contrary to the popular image of small companies, acted stra-tegically within their markets to remain market leaders and to remain independent of larger firms. For Innovate Engineering Ltd., remaining at the "cutting edge" of product development and placing a high emphasis on quality required a highly qualified flexible workforce, and a constant emphasis on training and development. Also, in the view of the owner, it ruled out any legitimate place for trade unions in "his" company, on the grounds of inflexibility. For City Engineering Ltd., remaining the market leader in an Irish context meant maintaining high quality, and developing new and improved products, but also competing on costs with large building contractors and new small entrants to the market. In this company there was also an emphasis on training, to meet the requirements of quality standards. Because of the wide range of products, and a commitment to meeting the particular needs of customers, flexibility of employees was also important. This had not precluded a union from being present, however, perhaps as a consequence of the high proportion of craft workers within the company and a high rate of unionisation in the surrounding area (Dublin).

Product ranges in Yarn Ltd. and Autoeng Ltd. are limited and they are dependent, for the most part, on a single major customer. Any changes in product seemed to be dictated to them by these customers. Because major customers were trying to maintain competitiveness through cost leadership, both companies had to follow suit. This resulted in tough management policies, especially in the area of rewards, though for Yarn Ltd. the worst period seemed to be over.

With regard to the idea of a "new realism", union officials and employees indicated that the so-called "new realism" had *always* been the norm for small-firm employees. One possible reason for this may be found in the subcontracting relationship that small firms have with large firms. Rainnie (1989) argues that large firms subcontract out work to cushion themselves against changes in their environments, and in doing so pass on to their small-firm suppliers the necessity to have flexible work practices. Small firms with wider customer bases are also more vulnerable to changes in their product markets than are their larger counter-parts. Therefore, in order to survive, small manufacturing firms have always had to be very flexible in responding to the market, and this has been reflected in work organisation and labour–management relations.

Legislation and Small Firms

Protective employment legislation did not seem to pose as many problems for small firms as has been claimed in previous reports (Report of Task Force on Small Firms, 1994). In relation to the Unfair Dismissals Act, 1977, owner-managers did not perceive this piece of legislation as a major problem, and it certainly did not preclude them from recruiting extra employees as the need arose (see also the findings of Williams and Whelan, 1985; and

Evans, 1986). The only changes brought about by increases in protective legislation were procedural, in that such increases seemed to affect the *process* of recruitment rather then propensity to recruit, making employers more careful in choosing candidates for employment. There was a general view that it was a factor borne in mind when considering specific candidates, in the sense that it would be undesirable to employ someone who might "cause problems", no matter what their qualifications. However, extra care in selection does not seem to be a negative consequence, especially where compatibility between employer and employee is such an important factor in the efficient operation of small companies. Such a pragmatic approach to selection seems sensible if it prevents a dismissals situation arising, which, as Scott (1989) observes, can have much deeper long-term consequences for small companies than large ones because of the more personal nature of the employment relationship.

There was some evidence among the case-study companies of a certain antipathy towards legislation pertaining to part-time employees because, it was claimed, it mitigated against employing such workers, and thus hindered company flexibility. There appeared to be a high level of ignorance among employers as to many of their obligations under the existing protective employment legislation. But legislation and directives emanating from the European Union in relation to the Social Charter and Article 119 could pose future problems. Obligations under such legislation generated considerable negative reaction, especially in relation to such things as paternity leave, holidays and working times. The main complaint was that flexibility would be reduced and labour costs increased, with a resultant loss of competitiveness.

Overall, the findings in relation to Irish legislation were that the protective legislation was not such a "burden" or disincentive to employment. The real disincentive to employment, as far as all the companies were concerned, seemed to be *taxation and social insurance costs*, a grievance they raised with the interviewer without being prompted or requested to do so. It would appear that the taxation and insurance burden directly impacts upon rewards, and indirectly it could also be said to have an effect on productivity and the employment-generation potential of small firms. Several of the case-study companies experienced diffi-culties in improving productivity as employees were wary of performance-related bonuses on the grounds that they would enter a higher PRSI/tax bracket. In relation to employment-generation potential, the case-study employers indicated that PRSI and tax costs were major disincentives to increasing em-ployment levels, much more so than protective employment legis-lation. Although such costs affect all companies, large and small, they seems to have a particularly marked effect in small firms. One of the reasons for this is that wages in small firms not only tend to be lower, but in most cases they tend to fall *just* short of the cut-off point for higher tax/PRSI payments. Therefore, a slight increase in wages, through overtime working or productivity bonuses, can actually negatively affect rewards for small-firm employees. Furthermore, such taxes are a more severe burden for small companies, as wages are generally a higher percentage of costs than for larger companies.

The External Labour Market

The idea of a *segmented labour market* in which the large firm takes the "best" of the available labour force was not supported to any significant degree by this study. The external labour market seemed to affect both large and small firms equally, in the sense that certain technical staff are in short supply and difficult to recruit for all firms (MacMahon, 1994; for similar findings in the UK see Blackburn and Hankinson, 1989). Where employees were highly skilled and scarce, not only did this have a positive effect on remuneration packages, it also seemed to affect the style of management adopted in the workplace for these categories. In brief, there was evidence that the owner-manager acted as a "first among equals" rather than as a "boss". There was evidence of such an approach in both Innovate Engineering Ltd. and, to a lesser extent, City Engineering Ltd. In general, however, it was felt that there was a ready availability of most categories in the labour market. A ready availability of unskilled workers has been shown to reduce employer dependence on employees, often result-ing in managerial styles that are less employee oriented. This was evident in Autoeng Ltd. It also affected tenure of employment, in that management placed no value on employee commitment or stability, adjusting employee numbers and employment contracts at will.

TRADE UNIONS AND SMALL FIRMS

This is another external variable which emerged from the research as having an impact on the small firm. Low levels of unionisation in small firms have mostly been attributed to tough union opposition on the part of owner-managers. But interviews with union officials and shop stewards revealed that unions often consider small firms as non-viable propositions, requiring considerable cost and resulting in few benefits, a finding in line with that of other research (Stanworth, 1991; Rainnie, 1989). This lack of interest, along with employer opposition (McGovern, 1989) has an effect on the level and influence of trade unions in small firms, which in turn impacts on the power of employees to resist managerial prerogative when it comes to wages, working conditions and the organisation of work.

On the surface, many of the external factors impacting on the small firm seem to be the same as those affecting large firms. However, as outlined above, there are differences in the external situations facing small and large companies. While protective statutory legislation does not seem to impose any greater burdens on small business or affect the propensity to hire extra employees, the increased obligations on all employers, emanating from the European Union, are perceived by small-firm employers, to a greater extent than large firms, to affect them negatively in terms of costs. New directives on paternity leave, for instance, have elicited greater opposition from the small-firm sector on the basis that small firms do not have the same resources as larger firms in human or financial terms to comply with such obligations. It is also suggested that in innovative small firms, the presence of a high proportion of highly skilled, highly flexible staff (often more highly qualified than the owner) can have a greater effect on the *management style,* resulting in a type of "fraternalistic" relationship with employees.

Internal Factors Affect Employee Relations in Small Firms

Managerial influence emerged as a particularly important factor in shaping small-firm employee relations, to a greater extent than employee relations in larger firms. The type of *organisational structure* characteristic of the case-study firms was a simple centralised power structure (see Mintzberg, 1992; Curran, 1989). Decision-making was centralised, even for relatively minor issues, and there was evidence in this study of a marked reluctance by the owner-managers to delegate. Exceptions did occur in technical areas where particular employees were more qualified to make decisions than the owner, illustrating in certain circumstances the limits and constraints on the owner's actions. However, even in such situations, it would seem that owner-managers liked to be kept informed. The effect of such a dominant owner-manager presence was reflected in different ways in each of the firms' employee-relations outcomes.

There are less constraints, it appears, on the exercise of managerial prerogative in relation to employee-relations issues in small firms than in large firms. Managerial attitudes and approaches to trade unions can be usefully categorised on a continuum ranging from unitarism to pluralism. Unitarism is a set of attitudes and beliefs which views every work organisation as an integrated and harmonious whole, existing for a common purpose. (Farnham and Plimlott, 1990). Conflicts of interest are seen as dysfunctional and there is no place for trade unions as they are perceived as competing with management for the loyalty of employees. A pluralist approach to employee relations, on the other hand, recognises the inevitability of conflicts of interest within the organisation. Consequently, structures are put in place (such as collective bargaining structures) to regulate the relationship between employer and employee. Trade unions are viewed as the legitimate representatives of employee interests and as such are accorded a role within these structures.

Establishing the presence of a unitarist or pluralist frame of reference in a firm is empirically difficult to measure and the following categorisations were decided upon on the basis of responses by the owners themselves to questions seeking opinions on specific issues, observing their reactions to questions in general, and also the opinions of shop stewards, union officials and employees. The most extreme case was Autoeng Ltd. where, although there was a union present, the owner-manager saw no legitimate role for the union in his company. Industrial relations were very antagonistic in this particular plant; the union was largely ignored; decisions were mainly taken unilaterally, often leading to conflict between the owner and his employees. Because of this manifest opposition to unions, this company, rather than the non-union company, is placed at the most extreme unitarist position on the continuum. Although the owner of Innovate Engineering Ltd.(the non-union company) spoke of his strong distaste for unions because of "past experience" of them, he never had any real confrontations with his employees over this or any other issue. Indeed, his employees also did not appear to feel the "need" for joining a union, which supports Curran and Stanworth's (1981) argument that employees are pragmatic when it comes to union affiliation. Also, the majority of the workforce were highly skilled professionals who did not have a strong tradition of unionisation, compared to craft workers or manual operatives. The other two companies had more positive relations with unions, even though, in the case of Yarn Ltd., it was very much a pragmatic acceptance of the union (that is, unions were accepted because they were seen as "a fact of life" or a "necessary evil" rather than because of any recognition of their legitimacy).

The owner-manager of City Engineering Ltd. was more favourably disposed to a trade union presence, probably as a result of his previous work experience as a craft worker and a trade union member. Overt conflict was highest in the two companies owned and run by foreign nationals. Employees and subordinate managers felt that this was an important factor in some of the problems that arose. According to the commercial manager in Yarn Ltd., the fact that the company had a European managing director might have had something to do with the initial teething problems, in that the managing director tended to follow the letter of the law as was the custom and practice in his own country and was not very familiar with Irish ways. It would seem therefore that previous history (nationality, occupation, experience of unions) impacts upon the frames of reference of employers, and this in turn impacts upon employee relations, especially in the small firm where the close proximity between employer and employee and the pervasive influence of the owner-manager are a dominant influence in the firm.

Most of the literature on small firms clearly indicates that trade union presence is marginal in small firms, often because of the influence of the owner-manager (Gunnigle and Brady, 1984; Millward et al., 1992; Sengenberger et al., 1990). Although small Irish manufacturing firms appear to be unionised to a higher degree than expected (MacMahon, 1994), the results still largely confirm the view that trade union influence is largely "diluted" and union density lower in small firms (Gunnigle, 1989). This would appear to be attributable to three factors: opposition on the part of employers; reluctance on the part of unions to organise such firms; and, in many cases, reluctance on the part of employees to join, either through fear of reprisals from management or perception that there is "nothing to be gained" from union membership.

Gunnigle (1989) argues that shop-steward structures are less well developed in small firms and there tends to be little interaction with trade unions at official level. In relation to shop stewards, Gunnigle's assertion was certainly found to be true with regard to Autoeng Ltd. There was one shop steward in the entire plant, even though there had been an agreement for three to be present. When asked about this, both management and union official replied that no one was willing to take the job. Yarn Ltd., on the other hand, had a very highly developed shop-steward structure. It must be borne in mind that this company is at the top of the size limit of small companies, at 100 employees. It had also formerly been a larger company than at present, so the shop-steward structure was probably "inherited" from that period. In this company, there were four shop stewards and they had their own private meeting room. City Engineering Ltd. had one shop steward who, according to both union and management, was consulted on all substantive issues. The union seemed to have considerable influence in this company in relation to substantive issues but, as stated above, the company was situated in Dublin where there is a strong union tradition, and the owner-manager seemed to see the union as having a legitimate role in representing employees. Level of development of shop-steward structures seems to be contingent on a number of factors, such as managerial opposition to, or acceptance of, trade unions; urban *v.* rural location; and in-company tradition. Contact with union officials appears to occur only if there is a crisis. The weakly unionised nature of small firms is important in relation to employee responses to changes in work practices and issues of flexibility, as it could be argued that one of the reasons why small-firm employees appear to be more "realistic" towards flexible work practices is that they have no real means of opposing them.

MANAGEMENT STYLES IN SMALL FIRMS

As already noted, the presence of a highly skilled workforce can influence *management style* by constraining unilateral decision-making and encouraging more employee-centred styles of management (e.g. fraternalism). Conversely, if the workforce is low skilled and readily available, this facilitates the exercise of uninhibited managerial prerogative. Supplier relationships with larger firms can also impinge on managerial style, depending on what demands are made on the small company. Demands for lower costs, for example, can result in tougher styles of management. On the other hand if the large company demands greater quality or product development, this can give rise to more employee-oriented management styles.

In an attempt to get away from the homogenous view of small-firm employee relations, Goss (1991) developed a model of managerial "modes of control" within small firms. His basic argument is that even though small-firm owner-managers might veer to a unitary frame of reference with consequent paternalistic styles of management, their freedom in this respect is often constrained through the power of employees. Goss's (1991) model has two dimensions: the dependence of the employer upon certain employees and vice versa, and/or the power of the workers individually or collectively to resist the exercise of proprietorial prerogative. It demonstrates that managerial styles reflecting the

frame of reference of the owner-manager are often constrained by
the above variables, and the result can be one of the following
typologies of style (Figure 7.3).

Figure 7.3: Management Styles in Small Firms

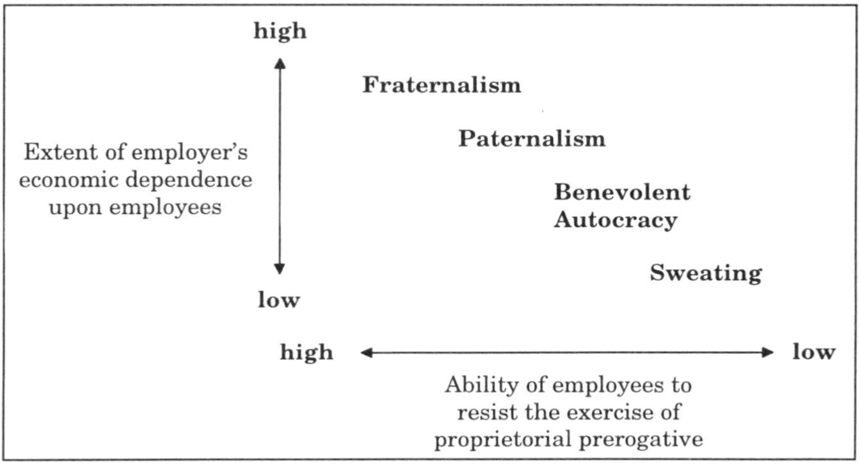

Source: Goss, 1991: 73.

Briefly, the styles are as follows:

Fraternalism reflects a high level of employer dependence upon
workers who provide labour that is both vital to the success of the
business and in short supply in the labour market. This style has
also been labelled "egalitarianism" (Goffee and Scase, 1985: 65),
where the emphasis is on the control of "key" workers in a manner which both sustains commitment and stabilises economic dependence upon their services, primarily through the granting of
considerable degrees of autonomy and discretion within work
tasks.

Paternalism arises when the employer's dependence upon
labour is less pressing and where the position of the workers is
such as to limit their power to resist proprietorial prerogative.
Unlike fraternalism which seeks to organise workers without
clearly defined hierarchical control, the differentiation of employer and employed is at the centre of paternalism. At the same

time, however, this strategy also seeks to foster the identification of subordinates with their superiors.

Benevolent Autocracy emphasises the closeness of the links between employer and employee but does not seek to cultivate the employment relationship in directions which extend beyond the workplace or which lead to expectations of employer obligations towards employees which override the exigencies of the market (Goss, 1991: 79).

Sweating exists where concessions to employees are deemed largely unnecessary by employers, as workers can be recruited and replaced readily without disrupting business activities. Here the principal factor in the employment relationship is cost rather than stability or trustworthiness.

Based on responses from owner-managers themselves, union officials, shop stewards and employees, it was decided to "test" the model — that is, to see if any of the typologies matched the style of management in any of the case-study companies. Autoeng Ltd. seemed to have many of the characteristics that would fit the *sweating* typology. This typology is said to exist where concessions to employees are deemed largely unnecessary by employers, as workers can be recruited and replaced readily without disrupting business activities. The principal factor in the employment relationship is cost rather than stability or trustworthiness. In Autoeng Ltd., the workforce was largely unskilled and readily replaceable because of high unemployment in the vicinity. Cost control appeared to be the guiding rule. There was a union present, but it did not seem to have much influence within the company. This was confirmed by the union official and by a manager within the company who observed that "in a rural areas such as this where there are so many people unemployed, employers do tend to have the upper hand". This company did not appear to be too interested in a stable or committed workforce, and management had no compunction about taking people on and letting them go as the need arose.

In Innovate Engineering Ltd., many of the characteristics relating to the *fraternalism* typology were present. This typology reflects a high level of employer dependence upon workers who provide labour that is both vital to the success of the business and in short supply in the labour market. The emphasis is on control of key workers in a manner which both sustains commitment and stabilises economic dependence upon their services, primarily through the granting of considerable degrees of autonomy and discretion within work tasks. The majority of the employees in this company were highly qualified engineers, most of them technically more competent than the owner-manager. They were also in short supply in the labour market. One qualification must be added to this typology: although employees had a large degree of autonomy within their jobs and were consulted on technical issues, that was the limit of this "fraternalism". The owner-manager was still very much in control and made all decisions concerning the direction of the firm.

To a certain extent, City Engineering Ltd. had some elements of the *fraternalism* typology for some employees, and *benevolent autocracy* for others. Characteristics of fraternalism were evident in the relationship that the owner had with professional/technical staff and some craft workers, but for the remaining employees the style of management employed seemed closer to benevolent autocracy. However, the power of employees through their union seemed greater than that illustrated on the model for this typology, thus supporting Stanworth's (1991) criticism that the benevolent autocracy typology is too broad, and also his assertion that more than one approach can exist in a company depending on the occupational category.

Yarn Ltd. was difficult to "categorise". Like the *benevolent autocracy* typology, management did not seek to cultivate the employment relationship in directions extending beyond the workplace or which led to expectations of employer obligations towards employees. Neither did management appear interested in emphasising the closeness of the links between employer and employee.

In general, these typologies of managerial styles are useful for eliminating the "all good" or "all evil" view of management styles in small firms. Paradoxically, it is the two extreme typologies that proved the most usable and appropriate.

EMPLOYMENT RELATIONS PRACTICES AND OUTCOMES IN SMALL FIRMS

In this section, the employee-relations practices of small firms are analysed and evaluated. These practices are the "outcome" or results of the interplay of the external and internal factors discussed above. The following key areas will be discussed: employment practices, conflict, procedures, rewards, recruitment practices and training.

Employment Practices in Small Firms

It has already been pointed out how workforce structure can constrain or facilitate particular styles of management. Although the literature largely reports small firms as employing mainly young people (Curran and Stanworth, 1979), the majority of employees in the case-study small firms were over 35, with long years of service. Labour turnover appears to be low among long-serving employees in established small companies. For new recruits, however, the opposite appears to be the case, with *very high* levels of turnover reported. Reasons given for this were that new people either "fitted in" or left after a short period of time.

In relation to *redundancy situations*, it would appear from the research that small firms are more reluctant to let permanent employees go, and in the case of one company, the owner usually attempted to find them alternative employment. It should be noted here that the sample consisted of companies that were approximately 20 years old, and a sizeable proportion of their employees had been with them since their establishment, which might explain the settling difficulties of new recruits. The situation might be different for "younger" small firms. However, this highlights a possible disadvantage of the "close-knit"-family type culture so often lauded as one of the best features of small firms. In times of expansion, a high turnover of recruits could lead to increased training costs. A common perception of small firms is that they employ higher proportions of part-time and temporary staff to remain competitive (Storey and Johnson, 1987). Both the case-study companies analysed here and data from a survey of 269 Irish companies in 1991 which included approximately 80 small firms (MacMahon, 1994) indicated that in the Irish context this does not seem to be the case (for manufacturing companies at any rate). In the companies surveyed, 46.5 per cent of respondents did not use part-time staff at all, and of those that did, the amount of part-time employees as a percentage of total employees was very low — less than 1 per cent in most cases (MacMahon, 1994). None of the case-study companies employed people on a part-time basis. The main reasons for this seemed to be: a perception of a lack of commitment on the part of such employees; and, in two cases, increased legislative protection afforded to such employees.

In general, larger companies seem more amenable to atypical employment forms such as temporary contracts, fixed-term contracts and part-time employment. This reluctance to utilise atypical employment forms seems to contradict the popular view of small firms as being to the forefront in making use of such employment forms. However, this particular study was confined to manufacturing, and in this respect should be treated with caution as it would not be valid to apply this finding to small firms *in general*, because of the exclusion of service-sector firms, which would appear to employ large numbers of people on part-time and temporary contracts.

Conflict and Industrial Relations Procedures

While overt "collective" conflict does appear to be low, there are indications that conflict exists in a more covert form and manifests itself at a more individual level — high levels of turnover among new recruits, for example. Many small firms are dependent on a single larger firm for business and are constantly under pressure to keep costs down. As a consequence, small firms often adopt tough management policies, which can lead to conflict and low-trust relations. A problem with much of the early research on small firms resulted from a failure to place employee-relations processes in the context of shifts in the business cycle, thereby implying that employee relations are *always* harmonious, regardless of external business and customer pressures. In relation to conflict resolution, only Yarn Ltd. and Autoeng Ltd. had utilised formal third-party mechanisms available from the Labour Relations Commission and the Labour Court. The remaining two companies had no record of industrial disputes and had never availed of third-party services. Innovate Engineering Ltd. had been due to appear before the Employment Appeals Tribunal but the plaintiff had not turned up.

Informality in the use of procedures in employee relations appears to be the norm in small companies (Gunnigle and Brady, 1984). According to Scott (1989), procedural formality is often re-garded as the antithesis of all that is worthy in small firms, and rigid application of formal procedures — especially in the area of discipline — is largely perceived as dysfunctional, in that it would destroy the "affective" focus of the employment relationship and highlight the inequalities of power that actually exist but are usually obscured. Scott (1989) argues that this lack of "personal distance" between employer and employee can result in both sides taking issues much more personally when they do arise, with longer-lasting effects on relations within the company.

Compensation, Recruitment and Training

Remuneration in small firms is usually lower than that for similar occupations in large firms (Sengenberger et al., 1990; Wallace, 1982; Kennedy et al., 1985). Wages in three of the case-study companies were lower than the average industrial wage for each category of worker. In Innovate Engineering Ltd., some of the technical research and development staff were on salaries equal to their counterparts in larger companies, because of past experiences of skilled employees being poached by larger firms. This finding is in line with that of Scott (1989), who found that the high-tech sector did not fit the image of the small firm as a low payer. He found evidence of more attractive packages being offered to professional/technical employees in small high-tech companies. But, as Scott (1989) points out, the greater career potential offered by large firms can negate the attractiveness of the benefits package offered to professional/technical staff in small companies (for example, an employee of City Engineering left because of the better career opportunities available in a local large firm). However, while City Engineering and Innovate Engi-neering had difficulty retaining highly skilled technical staff, the owners claimed that there were a lot of advantages of a more intrinsic nature in working for a small company, such as more responsibility, greater autonomy and greater job satisfaction.

Recruitment practices in small firms tend to be more informal and less sophisticated than those in larger firms, at least for lower grades of employee (MacMahon, 1994). Word of mouth seems to be the most popular method for sourcing manual employees, and advertising externally seems to be perceived as unnecessary and costly. Formal selection methods such as interviews and aptitude tests are rarely used in small firms. In relation to problems recruiting certain types of employee, both small and large companies would appear to have the same difficulties. Electronic engineers and R&D staff are both in short supply in the labour market. However, the view among small-firm owner-managers is that they do *not* feel themselves at a disadvantage when seeking to recruit these employees, on the basis that the greater intrinsic satisfaction that accrues from working in a small firm can offset the better remuneration packages that large companies can provide. The problem for small firms is the retention of skilled staff as large firms often engage in "poaching" these employees. Employer preference is a critical factor in the recruitment and selection of employees in small firms (Blackburn and Hankinson, 1989; Curran, 1986). Compatibility of candidates with the owner's values and work practices was cited by the case-study respondents as a critical factor in selection decisions, often taking precedence over qualifications. Perhaps one of the reasons why the demands of the market are accepted by employees in small firms is the emphasis placed on employing people who will "fit in" and are prepared to be flexible in their working practices.

Investment in training in small firms depends on the competitive position, customer base and nature of the product produced. Small firms that aim to retain a competitive edge through innovation will need to maintain a highly trained, flexible workforce. On the other hand, firms for which cost minimisation is the overriding factor may perceive training as an unaffordable luxury. Both City Engineering and Innovate Engineering invested substantial amounts of money in training. City Engineering actually allocated a yearly budget and employed a training manager. This company retained its leading market position in Ireland by maintaining reasonable-quality products and constantly seeking to develop new and improved products within its general area of "fencing". Innovate Engineering had no formal budget, but sent people on formal training schemes on an "as the need arises" basis and sponsored employees willing to gain relevant qualifications in nearby colleges. In 1992, £12,000 had been invested in training, while in 1991, £50,000–£60,000 was invested in technical training needs. Training in the other two companies was largely informal and mostly on the job. These two companies were not seeking to develop new products — indeed they were cutting back on product range, and most of the work required few skills. It is not possible, therefore, to generalise about training in small industry: account has to be taken of the particular industrial sector, the product, and the product market.

CONCLUSION

According to the Industrial Development Authority, small firms employing fewer than 100 people account for *92 per cent* of all manufacturing units in Ireland and are responsible for 46 per cent of total employment in the manufacturing sector. The employment share of small manufacturing units has also been found to be *increasing* over time. Employee relations in small firms is, therefore, an important area of study. One of the criticisms of the earlier research which examined the process of employee relations in small firms is that it failed to take into account the wider context of the small firm and the affect of external variables on employee-relations processes. Small firms are "open systems" and changes in the external environment can impact significantly on internal dynamics, usually to a greater degree than in large companies. As the contemporary literature suggests, it is not sufficient to view employee relations in the small manufacturing firm from a one dimensional perspective, or to offer mono-causal reasons for employee-relations practices. Employee-relations processes are complex and involve the interaction of many variables, both internal and external. In short, the simplistic "industrial harmony thesis" is not valid in the context of the small firm. Some of the external factors identified as important were legislation, product markets, inter-organisational relationships and the external labour market. Internal factors were

managerial frame of reference, organisation structure and sources
of employee power, either through trade unions or occupational
expertise. While these factors are identical to those affecting large
firms, this chapter has shown that it is the *way* in which these
factors impact on small firms that makes the situation for small
firms different from that of large firms.

There are higher levels of informality of procedures within
small firms, which arguably enhance flexibility, but can also lead
to contentious issues being viewed from a much more personal
level; reward systems tend to be less sophisticated; training in
small firms is less developed than in large firms, often as a result
of cost and time constraints. In the context of a "new realism" in
Irish industrial relations, it has been argued during the course of
this chapter that such "realism" constantly imposes itself on
employees in the small firm. Competition is intense for most
small firms and the relationship between wages, employment
security and market considerations is immediate and stark for
employees. This realism is further reinforced by recruitment practices whereby owner-managers will only employ people who "fit
in", and where recruitment fails, there is an early weeding out
and exit of undesirable employees.

Chapter 8

CONCLUSION

It is a truism to say that commercial organisations in the developed industrial societies are subject to growing external pressures from more competitive markets and growing internal challenges from changes in technologies and product standards. What is often less clear is what the long-term implications of such changes are across a range of organisational matters which include labour–management relations. In order to understand what is happening to industrial relations at the workplace level, it is necessary to examine over time both the collective bargaining structures, including the relationship between management and labour, and the economic and market context of the firm. This study of firm-level industrial relations attempted to outline the industrial relations history in a number of long-established manufacturing firms between 1970 (and earlier) and 1994. The contrast between industrial relations in the 1970s and from the mid-1980s onwards, at least in terms of overt measures of conflict, is quite dramatic. The production performance of the manufacturing sector also changed dramatically during this period. The volume of goods produced between 1953 and 1989 increased by a factor of seven and net output by a factor of ten. If the measures of co-operation between management and labour are strike frequency and man days lost, then the 1970s can be described as a decade of industrial disruption and adversarial industrial relations. By 1992, the manufacturing sector as a whole was virtually strike free. Whether these macro-level changes heralded a reorganisation of industrial relations and worker attitudes at workplace level provided the leitmotif of this study.

To facilitate an understanding of the complex processes and issues involved during this time period, we drew on a conceptual

framework relating market forces to industrial relations. The
basic argument was that increasing product-market competition
in the 1980s shifted workers' concerns from issues of distribution
to methods of production and product competitiveness, because of
the clearer and increasingly closer link between wages, employment security and the firm's market position. This new concern
with the logic of the enterprise (that is, the market demands on
the enterprise) amounted to an acceptance of the market by
workers as the essential mechanism determining employment
experiences, leading to a new realism in their attitudes towards
the enterprise's goals and more co-operative relations between
management and labour. A new realism in industrial relations is
usually seen as being reinforced by the increasing globalisation of
economic activity where capital flows to the most productive
location. Hence, labour, particularly unskilled labour, is competing in a world rather than a national labour market. Such
changes were viewed as posing major problems for existing forms
of workplace unionism, creating both an *institutional* and an
ideological crisis for the trade unions. The reorganisation of
industrial relations in the manner described above, in terms of
worker attitudes, new patterns of industrial relations and the
threat to union presence at the workplace, were at the core of this
study.

STABILITY AND CHANGE IN WORKPLACE INDUSTRIAL RELATIONS

There is no evidence of an institutional crisis for the trade unions.
Our findings indicate a clear continuity in union organisation and
management acceptance of union legitimacy in the companies
studied. Procedural rules which govern the establishment and
administration of employment appear to have remained relatively
unchanged in the period studied. The organisational factors
which allow union input into the establishment and monitoring of
such rules remain intact. Union density remains high and includes 100 per cent of manual workers in all of the companies
surveyed. Shop stewards still occupy a central role in industrial
relations and are regularly consulted by a significant portion of
the membership. Steward structures, facilities and training also

exhibit more continuity than change, and, according to the stewards interviewed, managements do not interfere with stewards carrying out union business. Union organisational factors are characterised by a stability and legitimacy which is not apparently threatened, at least from within the company.

The substantive indices or output indicators resulting from the monitoring and administration of rules are more obvious. All of the companies studied have been strike-free since 1990. However, as 73 per cent of official strikes and 61 per cent of unofficial strikes were accounted for by only two companies, the change is not as dramatic for the remaining companies. There is no evidence of a change in the use of third-party machinery since 1986. What is changing is a preference, particularly by the unions, to settle more issues at the conciliation stages and avoid recourse to the Labour Court proper. Overall, we would argue that the procedural aspects of industrial relations are characterised more by continuity than change. Finally, industrial relations matters remain a central concern for personnel managers and management generally when making decisions on such matters as capital investment, changes in production methods, wages and conditions of employment.

Turning to the substantive content of employment rules, the evidence suggests substantial change in effort levels, payment systems, job content and work organisation. A majority of respondents in the employee survey reported that their work was more difficult than before, that it required more mental effort and left them more tired at the end of the day than in the past. Work practices have generally become less restrictive in recent years and there appears to be a trend towards a reduction in the number of grades for manual employees. However, the evidence from the employee survey indicates that the majority of manual employees are unlikely to be promoted beyond their initial starting position in a company. The most common benefits offered to employees include VHI contributions, pensions and sick-pay schemes, and while there are still some differences in the level of benefit offered to various grades of employees, in a majority of organisations these differences are not substantial.

Apart from the direct substantive issues, we also considered whether the internationalisation and development of a global market and its logical corollary, a global labour market, had brought a new realism into labour–management relations — that is, a realisation among workers of the fragility of their jobs and living standards, which demands a new logic of behaviour in labour–management relations, embracing change and flexibility in occupational structures, work systems and effort levels in order to protect jobs and living standards.

Although the evidence from the employee survey indicates some shift towards a new realism, there was little change in workers' attitudes towards management. A majority of employees believed that they were working harder than previously, though this is not significantly related to a belief that employees and management co-operate in order to compete against other companies with comparable products. A majority of employees believed that management and workers were on opposite sides. Surprisingly, perhaps, this result is similar to the results of an earlier survey carried out in 1979. Despite these views, most employees still believed that they could have full teamwork in their company. Thus, the evidence of an attitudinal shift is not sufficient to confirm the existence of a new approach in labour–management relations. Nor is it apparent that there is an ideological crisis for the trade unions. Speculation about the passing away of collectivism as a method for regulating labour–management relations, and its replacement by a "human resource management" approach with its emphasis on mutual interests and the regulation of employee relations through the individualisation of the employment relationship finds little support here.

It was argued in Chapter 7 that employee relations in small firms have always been characterised by a realisation by employees of the fragility of their jobs and living standards. This realism constantly imposes itself as a result of the competitive market in which most small firms operate, but is not necessarily associated with industrial harmony between management and employees. As the case studies on small firms revealed, there is a range of possible employee-relations outcomes linked to managerial styles ranging from fraternalism to sweating. A particular pattern of employee relations is a result of a complex set of internal and external organisational factors, the extent of an employer's economic dependence on employees, and the ability of employees to resist the exercise of proprietorial prerogative.

The companies surveyed in this study have, apart from two companies, been established in Ireland for at least two decades and have always had a trade union presence. As such, it could be argued that they are representative of established medium/large firms in the Irish manufacturing sector. However, the evidence from new companies establishing in Ireland since 1987 indicates a less benign environment for trade unions (Gunnigle, 1994). Furthermore, the firms in the electronics industry (and related areas), the fastest-growing sector in manufacturing, are more likely to be non-union than those in other industries (Roche and Turner, 1994). While newly established non-union firms may in time become unionised, there is also the possibility that they represent an emerging trend in manufacturing, providing practical and visual examples of the non-union option as a viable human resource strategy for firms.

CONTINUITY AND CHANGE IN INDUSTRIAL RELATIONS PATTERNS

A core focus of this study is the nature of the relationship between labour and management, the development of this relationship and the determinants of the relationship. In order to facilitate a comparison of a company's industrial relations over time, and relations between companies, four industrial relations patterns were used, based on a company's position on a number of criteria. The four patterns ranged from uninhibited antagonism to adaptive co-operation. There is among the companies studied a distinct shift from antagonistic labour–management relations towards more co-operative relations. While five companies in the medium/large category can still be classed as having antagonistic relations (though not as extreme as previously), five companies have shifted toward a co-operative pattern, and the remaining three companies retain a co-operative pattern of industrial relations similar to in the past. This was insufficient evidence to support (or reject) the thesis that there is a distinctly new industrial relations emerging in the companies surveyed. To explain the shifting patterns observed in labour–management relations we drew on two inter-related causal factors: a firm's product market and financial performance and the unique labour–management relationship specific to each company.

Comparisons of a company's financial performance, productive efficiency and variations in employee earnings and overtime indicated the important influences of these factors in structuring a particular climate of industrial relations. However, a critical aspect of their impact depends on the direction of a company's economic and market performance. Declining performance levels are generally associated with less co-operative labour–management relations. The consequence for employees is a decline in earnings, usually through reductions in overtime. The decline is not in the absolute level of earnings, since they may still earn above the average industrial wage, but rather refers to disappointed expectations about current earnings compared to past earnings. In such a situation, the development of more co-operative relations between labour and management is apt to be difficult. The example of companies defined as having antagonistic labour–management relations tends to confirm this point.

According to the industrial relations literature, the initial stimulus for increased co-operation between management and labour is usually a crisis in the organisation. However, there was little evidence from the case studies that unions or managements confronted financial or employment crises outside the conventional collective bargaining process. Although three of the companies had substantial redundancies during the 1980s, there is no evidence to suggest any attempts by labour and management to cope with the crisis other than through the conventional bargaining process. There are, at present, indications that two of the companies are attempting to initiate developments outside the collective bargaining process. Where increased co-operation does occur, it tends to be based upon pragmatic concerns, such as the need to improve productivity, employment earnings and security, and the general economic well-being of the company.

While economic pressures are important influences, the specific and historically unique relations in each company are also important in shaping labour–management relations. Apart from economic constraints, the unique internal and external circumstances in each company influencing industrial relations make it difficult to identify a comprehensive list of explanatory factors common to all the companies. However, three factors did emerge as relevant. The case studies confirmed that continuous poor economic performance is often associated with poor industrial relations. A second factor is the attitude of management towards the trade unions, which was uniformly negative in the antagonistic group. Lastly, in this group of companies, the union organisation was often divided among itself in its approach to management, which further exacerbated industrial relations tensions. In many instances, industrial relations in these companies could appropriately be described as occurring in a closed paradigm in which the parties responded in terms of past experiences which were usually negative, giving rise to relationships based on mutual distrust.

A further important factor associated with a positive shift in industrial relations emerged from the analysis, in Chapter 6, of the personnel function. There appears to be a significant relationship between a strong personnel function with the capacity to play a strategic role in the management of human resources and the shift away from traditional-type adversarial industrial relations. Those companies that experienced a positive shift in industrial relations also ranked high in terms of strategic human resource practices, while those organisations that experienced little or no change ranked low in terms of a strategic approach to human resource management. This tends to confirm at least some of the optimistic outcomes advertised in the prescriptive human resource management literature.

BEYOND THE COLLECTIVE-BARGAINING PROCESS: PROCEDURAL INNOVATION

In the introduction, we argued that it was necessary to go beyond the traditional narrow focus on procedural concerns in order to engage the pressures and challenges being exerted on labour–management relations in the 1990s. The establishment, administration and defence of employment rules appeared to be irrelevant

at best to the substantive changes occurring in the employment
relationship, or positively restrictive in an increasingly deregu-
lated market economy. However, we would also argue that continuous substantive changes in the employment relationship
without any accompanying developments in the way that employment rules are established and administered reflects the contemporary power position of the parties, rather than any enduring mutual compromise. The establishment and administration of
workplace rules has traditionally been influenced by a contest between managerial prerogative and union strength. But if employee acceptance of change is sought through consent rather
than compulsion in a unionised setting, then the relationship
between labour and management must be based on rule-making
structures that are clearly defined and trusted by both parties.

The extant voluntary collective bargaining process is, of
course, such a rule-making process, but it does not allow workers
any *formal* input into the formulation of company policy and the
way that work is organised. This has produced an often necessary
concern on the part of unions with the policing and monitoring of
management behaviour through procedural norms and agreements. A disadvantage of this method of regulation is its tendency
to encourage low-trust relations between the parties. It often encourages defensive and reactive behaviour from employees where
the only means of protection against arbitrary management policies is a reliance on agreed procedures and custom and practice.

On the other hand, the development of joint governance structures beyond the conventional voluntary collective bargaining
process is an option that can change the basis for rule-making.
Joint governance structures, which are either voluntary (such as
union–management committees monitoring quality initiatives) or
legal (works councils, for example) are procedural developments
which create a new basis for regulating at least some areas of the
employment relationship. A key aspect of such structures is that
they institutionalise some form of power-sharing beyond the
purely consultative function. The co-determination arrangements
of German works councils are an example of such power-sharing.
Where co-determination or joint governance structures exist, workers and trade unions are more likely to accept the logic of the

enterprise and the demands of the market. Acceptance of the logic of the enterprise by employees (union and non-union) does not necessarily cause an institutional or ideological crisis for trade unions by solving all the industrial relations problems or by co-opting employees on to the management side. Issues of distribution — that is, the division of surplus value between the various contending stakeholders in the firm (shareholders, management and labour) — still remain. Tension will continue to exist over the effort levels required from employees and the rewards received, which is at the core of the employment relationship. Issues of justice, such as the fair and equal treatment of employees, will not disappear with an acceptance of the logic of the enterprise. Traditional trade union concerns are, therefore, likely to continue to be the *raison d'être* of unions in the workplace, and also their attraction for new union members. These union concerns, we argue, can be enhanced by the unions having a formal input into the firm's human resource policies and the organisation of work in a time of growing market deregulation for both capital and labour markets.

However, in order to bring about change in an organisation characterised by a closed paradigm, employee perceptions and expectations concerning effort levels, rewards and job security need to be addressed to establish an appropriate set of goals which are related to conditions in the external business environment. Changing perceptions and expectations depend critically on open and extensive communication between management and employees, which in turn depends on the degree of trust between the parties. Trust between the parties can be taken as a measure of the quality of the labour–management relationship and, according to Schuster (1990), is a precondition for long-term change in union environments. However, while improved communications and the degree of trust between the parties are important elements in the change process, they are not a sufficient condition for change and the reorientation of labour–management relations. Change must be perceived by both management and employees as meeting their expectations and goals. Crisis situations in companies usually demand changes that are inimical to employee interests. Unless employees readjust their expectations and, for example, accept a trade-off between lower wages and poorer working conditions in return for retaining their jobs and/or a promise of future gain (such as a share in the company), then any amount of changes in communication methods or exhortations for better labour–management relations will have little impact. Even where both parties do embark on a co-operative programme to improve relations, it will only be maintained as long as it can deliver on both parties' goals.

DEVELOPMENT OF JOINT UNION–MANAGEMENT INITIATIVES

Many of the above observations on the content issues and problems arising out of union–management joint initiatives are useful in alerting us to the challenges and pitfalls when embarking on such initiatives. However, there are no clear guidelines to evaluate the possible consequences of such programmes which fall outside the conventional bargaining process. A set of guidelines would enable both management and unions to estimate, even roughly, the advantages and disadvantages of a joint initiative, in terms of its effectiveness in realising their separate goals, and the overall outcomes for both parties jointly. Typical managerial goals are the preservation and strengthening of the business through increased profits and market share, and the retention of effective control of the organisation. Typical employee goals are the preservation and improvement of employment conditions, employment security and control over jobs. In both cases there is also the advancement of personal goals and ambitions, which can sometimes override the parties' formal goals. Additionally, there is the union organisational goal of preserving and strengthening the union as an institution at the workplace. Critical to understanding the substantive content of these various goals and the means used to attain them are the expectations of the parties and the extent to which they value a specific goal.

At the individual psychological level, an appropriate theory or framework that addresses these issues is the expectancy theory of work motivation. We would argue that it is possible to apply the conceptual content and linkages in expectancy theory to evaluate union–management joint initiatives and provide a *practical* method of evaluation for unions and managements. Expectancy theory developed out of the work of Vroom (1964) and subsequent additions and revisions (see Steers and Porter, 1987; for reviews see Mitchell, 1974; Connolly, 1976). The theory sets out that work motivation is determined by an individual's beliefs (i.e. expectations) regarding effort performance relationships and the desirability of various work outcomes that are associated with different performance levels. The three key terms in the theory are:

1. **Expectancy** is the probability assigned by an individual that work effort will be followed by a given level of achieved task performance.

2. **Instrumentality** is the probability assigned by the individual that a given level of achieved task performance will lead to various work outcomes.

3. **Valence** is the value attached by the individual to various work outcomes.

An individual will expend effort in order to achieve a specific task (if they believe such effort will achieve the task) and if the successful completion of the task leads to outcomes which the individual values.

Figure 8.1: Expectancy Theory Terms in a Managerial Perspective

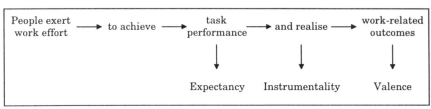

Obviously, if an individual can attain valued outcomes without having to perform a task, it is likely that a lower level of effort will be exerted in the performance of the task. If valued outcomes do not follow from successful task performance, it is also likely that the individual will expend as little effort as possible on the task in the future. The core relationships in expectancy theory are that people are only motivated by outcomes/goals that they value, and that in order to encourage effort on tasks which are not self-defined (such as organisational tasks), the individual's valued goals should only result from the achievement of the (organisational) task. Vroom (1964) argues that motivation (M), expectancy (E), instrumentality (I) and valence (V) are related to one another by the equation: $M = E * I * V$.

The implication is that employee motivation can only be high if all three factors are present. If, for example, an individual believes that their effort will lead to successful task completion and, as a result, they will attain certain outcomes, but these outcomes are not valued by the individual, then motivation will be low. Expectancy theory and motivational theories of work in general are often criticised for having a managerial bias, as they appear to be directed solely at eliciting effort from employees, with the tasks and even the outcomes being defined by the organisation (Rose, 1988). However, the adoption of an expectancy framework to evaluate union–management co-operation initiatives avoids the problem of bias since, firstly, separate motivational paths can be drawn up for union and management involvement in co-operative programmes and, secondly, each party must also take into account the other party's motivation to participate in such a programme if it is to commence and survive. The valued outcomes are self-defined rather than imposed by both parties separately.

The terms "joint governance structure" and "co-operative initiatives", although different, are used interchangeably here because the same criteria and relationships apply equally to both. Joint governance envisages a medium- to long-term co-operation programme with a well-defined structure for joint management–union interaction. A co-operative initiative includes more short-term activities or programmes in which union and management agree to co-operate on a specific item or process (for example, grading committees, introduction of new technology, and management of redundancy programmes).

Motivation to Engage in Joint Initiatives

Co-operation programmes are a means of achieving certain outcomes for unions and management. Union–management co-operation, therefore, is equivalent to the relationship between tasks and outcomes in the expectancy framework — that is, union or management will exert effort to participate in a joint initiative if they believe that certain valued outcomes will result.

Figure 8.2: Union/Management Motivation

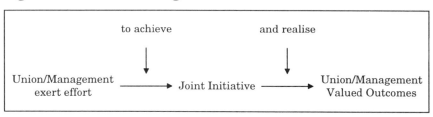

It is possible to draw up a motivational path for union and management separately, which relates efforts to participate with both sets of valued outcomes. However, participation in an initiative can have both costs and benefits. Figure 8.3 outlines possible positive outcomes for the union in becoming involved in a joint union–management initiative.

In a joint governance structure there are several possible valued outcomes for the union and its membership. It may allow greater input into management policies, which previously were management's sole prerogative — such as training and development policies, recruitment strategy and work-related productivity issues. The flow of business information to the unions is likely to increase, and hence their ability to extract an equitable share of the business profits. Conversely, there are also possible negative outcomes for the union and its membership in participating in a joint governance structure. Union members may feel that the union is taking on management concerns and interests and ignoring employee interests. This could result in a loss of members and a weakening of union organisation at the workplace. Employees may also be precluded from bargaining over issues that fall within the ambit of joint governance. The decision to participate in a governance structure is a function of a cost-benefit ratio, in which possible positive outcomes are weighted against possible negative outcomes. Prior to these considerations the union is only likely to make an effort to participate in a joint governance structure if such a structure allows for a significant input into decision and policy-making, and is capable of realising valued outcomes. Thus, for example, consultation alone is unlikely to encourage union participation.

Figure 8.3: Union Motivational Path to Enter into a Joint Initiative

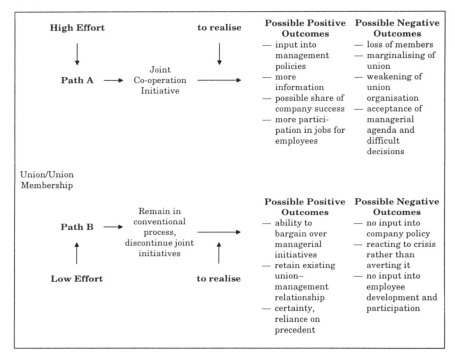

An alternative motivational path is also available to the union — that is, to rely on the conventional collective bargaining process as the means of solving workplace issues. As in the previous path, there are possible positive and negative valued outcomes. Choosing whether to embark on a joint co-operation programme or rely on the conventional industrial relations processes will depend on two considerations: first, the perceived ratio of the costs and benefits of the alternative path will decide which direction has the highest benefits; secondly, the ability of the joint initiative *or* the collective bargaining process to deliver valued outcomes is a critical consideration. Even if, for example, higher benefits on balance are possible with joint co-operation, there may be some question as to whether the joint initiative is capable of delivering the outcomes. Faced with uncertainty on this point, the union is more likely to choose the collective bargaining process.

A similar set of choices and dilemmas confronts management regarding its participation in joint co-operative initiatives (see Figure 8.4).

Figure 8.4: Management Motivational Path to Enter into a Joint Initiative

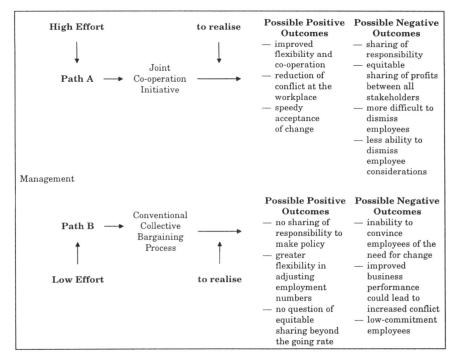

As with the unions, management's decision to initiate and participate in joint structures will depend on benefits being perceived as greater than costs. So far, we have outlined the separate motivational paths of unions and management to participation in joint governance structures, and have provided an example of the range of positive and negative outcomes possible in the various paths. However, the success of a joint governance structure depends on both union and management participation. Unless the

joint initiative can create positive outcomes which outweigh negative outcomes for *both* parties, it is unlikely to succeed. Where
there are greater benefits for one party but greater costs for the
other party, joint co-operation is also unlikely. Uncertainty about
outcomes for either party discourages co-operation outside the
collective bargaining process, and there is a preference for traditional approaches.

The framework outline here, we would argue, encourages both
parties to state their valued outcomes or goals explicitly, and also
to suggest the best means to attain them. It is a practical exercise
for both unions and management to conduct separately if co-
operation is to occur. The essential prerequisites for both parties
participating in a joint initiative are:

- Benefits must be perceived to outweigh costs for *both* parties;

- Joint initiative must realise valued outcomes for *both* parties;

- Effort on the part of unions to participate must lead to a real
  sharing of power in the joint initiative.

Whichever path is chosen, be it conventional or innovative, there
are, as we have seen, possible positive and negative outcomes.
Certainly, the development of a joint governance structure involves compromise by both parties if union–management co-
operation is to progress beyond the existing collective bargaining
approach. However, given the hierarchical nature of organisations
and the power and responsibility vested in management, the
development of new structures of co-operation and participation
rests, in the first instance, entirely with management. Joint
initiatives, if they do not entail a real sharing of power and
responsibility, are likely to collapse under the weight of their own
contradictions, where high aspirations are matched with low-
trust structures. In the companies surveyed in this study, there is
precious little evidence of a move towards the development of
joint governance structures. It may also be the case (see Electro
Engineering) that the unions are either lukewarm about, or
actively discouraging of, such initiatives.

A further possible obstacle to the development of joint

initiatives is the complex range of issues and mutual dilemmas to be resolved. Valued outcomes for both parties are dynamic goals which may alter dramatically with changes in the business cycle and related shifts in the relative strength of unions and management. It is precisely the avoidance of a cycle of confrontation in union–management relations that a joint governance structure is more likely to provide. If unions and their members are to be concerned with the logic of the enterprise — that is, with matters of production, product quality and market considerations — as well as issues of distribution, they must participate in some manner in company policy and decision-making. If managements wish to ensure that this logic of industrial relations is harnessed in a positive and constructive manner to company goals, rather than being a defensive and imposed set of behaviours, then they must share traditional areas of managerial prerogative with employees.

A central message of the contemporary literature on human resource management and organisations generally is that new technologies in the production and service industries require high levels of employee interaction and monitoring of work processes, because of the complexities of technology, more exacting product standards and greater variation in product ranges (see Piore and Sabel, 1984; Turnbull and Blyton, 1994). One measure, perhaps, of these changes is the shift in the demands of work from physical to mental effort evident in the employee survey. While 39 per cent of the employees surveyed believed that their work required more physical effort than previously, 77 per cent claimed that their work required more mental effort. Thus, in a growing range of manufacturing and service industries, the traditional business rationale for protecting managerial prerogative and maintaining tight control of employees through technical and physical means is becoming more problematic as a solution to the management and control of human resources. The new logic forming the enterprise is a consequence not only of increased competition in less regulated markets, but also the application of diverse and more complex technologies to products and services, and the increasing attention to consumer wants. Meeting the demands of business in this logic requires among other factors the commitment and participation of employees.

We would argue, therefore, that if new developments in labour management relations in unionised settings are to emerge, there must be new procedural arrangements between management and labour, which can facilitate joint initiatives. While it is impossible to predict the particular issues and problems that might arise, since each company has its own unique set of circumstances and concerns, the evaluation method outlined here attempts to provide union officials, union members and managers with the tools to engage their particular realm of reality. Ultimately, it is the interaction of these participants in particular economic and market contexts that forges their distinct pattern of labour–management relations.

Appendix 1

Summary of Company Characteristics

	Sector	Size	Ownership	No. of General Unions	Loca-tion	Estab-lished	Employment over past 5 years	No. of Employees Surveyed	Type of Survey †
Chemton	Chem	M	US	1	Rur	1970s	Dec	33	R
Senchem	Chem	M	US	1	Urb	1970s	Un	42	C
Processchem	Chem	L	Canadian	2	Rur	1980s	Dec	n/a	
Textile	Tex	M	Japanese	1	Rur	1970s	Dec	n/a	
Clothing Ltd.	Tex	M	US	1	Rur	1970s	Inc	15	C
Yarn Ltd.	Tex	S	European	1	Urb	1960s	Dec		
Burchocks	F&D	L	British	2	Urb	1930s	Inc	31	R
Tirown Sweets	F&D	M	Swiss	1	Urb	1950s	Dec	n/a	
Mineral Ltd.	F&D			1	Urb	1950s	Dec	40	C
Lola Drinks	F&D	M	US	1		1970s	Inc	n/a	
Parkfoods	F&D	L	Irish	2	Rur	*	Dec	106	R
Dairyfoods	F&D	M	Irish	1	Rur	*	Dec	41	C
Electro Engineering	Eng	M	US	1	Urb	1960s	Dec	18	R
Micro Engineering	Eng	L	US	1	Urb	1980s	Inc	76	R
Autoeng Ltd.	Eng	S	Irish	1	Rur	1973	Un	n/a	
City Engineering	Eng	S	Irish	1	Urb	1973	Inc	n/a	
Innovate Engineering	Eng	S	Irish	Non-union	Urb	1973	Inc	n/a	

Key: Chem = Chemical; Tex = Textiles; F&D = Food and Drink; Eng = Engineering; L = large; M = medium; S = small; Rur = rural; Urb = urban; Dec = decreasing; Inc = increasing; Un = unchanged; R = random; C = convenient

* These companies emerged from the earlier co-operative movement.

† Convenience sampling usually involved the distribution of questionnaires through a combination of the personnel manager and the senior shop steward. All questionnaires were provided with an addressed envelope for mailing directly to the University of Limerick.

Appendix 2

FACTORS DETERMINING EMPLOYEE ATTITUDES TOWARDS MANAGEMENT

The impact of four groups of variables on levels of employee trust in management were examined: *personal* or biographical characteristics, *organisational* details, and *intrinsic* and *extrinsic* aspects of work. Biographical characteristics such as gender, age and education may possibly effect employee perceptions of management. In particular, white-collar workers are traditionally viewed as enjoying a closer relationship with management than manual workers, and can be expected to have more positive attitudes towards management. Since low-trust jobs are associated with tight supervision, little discretion and unsatisfying work, a number of *intrinsic factors* are included in this analysis, such as measuring: (a) satisfaction with work, (b) whether jobs have improved in terms of interest and discretion levels, (c) whether work has intensified in effort and difficulty, and (d) workers' attachment to the firm in terms of other life interests.

The *extrinsic factors* can be divided into rewards, monetary and non-monetary benefits, and industrial relations matters. Monetary benefits include satisfaction with take-home pay, gross pay and the bonus system. Non-monetary benefits are work satisfaction, sick-pay scheme, pension, promotional chances and holidays and company facilities. The variables in both cases are combined into two composite factors measuring (a) monetary rewards and (b) non-monetary rewards. Industrial relations variables included are employee satisfaction with (a) grievance and (b) discipline procedures. Below are the results from regressing the composite factor measuring trust (three questions combined) on the biographical, organisational and intrinsic and extrinsic variables.

RESULTS

The only significant *personal* and *organisational* variable (see Table A2.1, equation 1) is education, which just reaches significance at the 0.05 level. Higher levels of education are actually negatively related to high trust. However, education fails to reach significance in subsequent equations, and this result must be treated with caution. It is particularly notable that the staff/manual divide has no impact on attitudes towards management. Turning to the *intrinsic* variables, there is some support for Fox's (1974) argument that intrinsic factors such as satisfying work and increased discretion in work are related to increased levels of trust between management and employees in the companies surveyed. Both of these variables are significantly related to more positive attitudes towards management, with work satisfaction having almost twice the impact as increased discretion in work. Intensification in work effort or difficulty, and worker attachment to the firm had no impact on attitudes towards management.

To assess the effect of the extrinsic variables two separate regressions are run for satisfaction with grievance and discipline procedures (they have a high correlation score, R = 0.7). Both grievance and discipline procedures are significantly related to attitudes of trust (Table A2.1, equations 2 and 3). Satisfaction with the way procedures are handled has the *strongest* impact of all the independent variables, intrinsic and extrinsic, on increasing positive attitudes towards management. Non-monetary benefits are also significantly in equations 2 and 3, with levels of satisfaction with benefits positively associated with higher levels of trust. As in equation 1, monetary benefits are not significantly related to levels of trust. To confirm the reliability of this result, satisfaction with take-home pay, gross pay and bonus pay were entered as separate variables into the equation. Also entered was the actual annual salary for each respondent. None of the variables achieved significance.

Overall the variation in levels of trust is affected by the *intrinsic* variables of (a) satisfaction with work, and (b) whether work had improved in recent years; and the *extrinsic* variables of (a) satisfaction with non-monetary benefits, and (b) industrial

Table A2.1: Determinants of Employee Attitudes Towards Management (method: stepwise regression — standardised Beta coefficients reported)

Dependent Variable	Trust	Trust	Trust	Grievances	Satisfaction
Variables	1	2	3	4	5
Personal					
Gender	N.S.			-0.21***	
Age	N.S.			N.S.	
Education	-0.1*	N.S.	N.S.	N.S.	
Organisational					
Service	N.S.			N.S.	
Staff/Manual	N.S.				
Intrinsic					
Work Satisfaction	0.27***	0.23***	0.25***	N.S.	
Work Better	0.14**	0.13**	N.S.†	N.S.	0.25***
Work Intensity	N.S.			N.S.	-0.16**
Work Importance	N.S.			-0.2**	-0.18**
Work Extrinsic					
Monetary	-0.31***			N.S.	
Non-Monetary	N.S.	-0.25***	-0.26***	-0.31***	
Grievances	-.3***	0.38***			
Discipline	N.S.†		0.37***		
R^2	0.49	0.46	0.42	0.21	0.18
f score	45***	61.2***	71***	22***	15.2***
Durban Watson Score	1.63	1.73	1.8	1.99	1.6
N	225	280	286	230	255

†   Both work better (Eq. 1) and discipline (Eq.1) just failed to reach significance, 0.052 and 0.055 respectively.
***$p < .001$
** $p < .01$
* $p < .05$
Source: Employee Survey.

relations procedures. Given that the intrinsic variable of work satisfaction and the extrinsic variable of satisfaction with griev-ance procedures have the largest impact on levels of trust, separate regressions were run to analyse the antecedents of these variables. *Work satisfaction* is related to a number of intrinsic factors. It is positively related where work is perceived to have

improved, negatively related where work has become harder, and
negatively related where an employee gives the firm a low priority in their life interests. Variations in *satisfaction with grievance
procedures* is affected by the employees gender, attachment to the
firm and satisfaction with non-monetary benefits. Women are
more likely than men to be satisfied with grievance procedures. A
higher priority accorded to the firm in terms of employees' life
interests is associated with a higher level of satisfaction with
grievance procedures. Finally, non-monetary benefits are the most
salient factor relating to satisfaction with grievance procedures.
Figure A2.1 shows the causal relationships between all the significant independent variables and levels of trust in management

Figure A2.1: Path Diagram

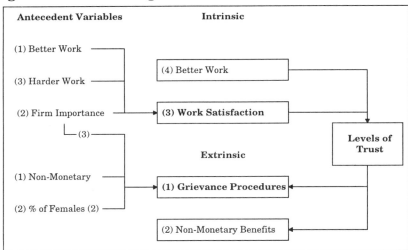

*   *Intrinsic* and *Extrinsic* variables are ranked (in brackets) in terms of their
impact on the dependent variable *Trust* using the standardised beta
coefficient: e.g. grievance procedures have the largest impact on levels of
trust followed by non-monetary benefits, work satisfaction and better
work. Antecedent variables are also ranked in terms of their impact on
Work Satisfaction and *Grievance Procedures*.

While the extrinsic variables of industrial relations procedures
and non-monetary benefits have a significant impact on levels of
trust, salary levels or satisfaction with take-home pay appear to
have no significant impact on employee attitudes towards
management.

REFERENCES

Amadieu, J. (1986): "Employment Flexibility, Unions and Companies in France", *Industrial Relations Journal*, September: 117–23.

Appelbaum, S. and Shapiro, B. (1991): "Pay for Performance: Implementation of Individual and Group Plans", *Journal Of Management Development*, 10(7): 30–41.

Atkinson, J. (1984): "Manpower Strategies for Flexible Organisations", *Personnel Management*, August: 28–31.

Atkinson, J. and Meager, N. (1986): "Is Flexibility Just a Flash in the Pan?", *Personnel Management*, September: 26–9.

Bain, G. (1983): *Industrial Relations in Britain*, London: Basil Blackwell.

Bain, G. and Clegg, H.A. (1974): "A Strategy for Industrial Relations Research in Great Britain", *British Journal of Industrial Relations,* 12(1): 93–5.

Baird, L. and Meshoulan, I. (1987): "Proactive Human Resource Management", *Human Resource Management,* 26(4), Winter.

Barbash, J. (1964): "The Elements of Industrial Relations", *British Journal of Industrial Relations,* March: 66–78.

Barbash, J. (1980): "Collective Bargaining and the Theory of Conflict", *British Journal of Industrial Relations*, 18: 86–96.

Bassett, P. (1986): *Strike Free: New Industrial Relations in Britain*, London: Macmillan.

Batstone, E. (1988): *The Reform of Workplace Industrial Relations: Theory, Myth and Evidence*, Oxford: Clarendon Press.

Batstone, E., Boraston, I. and Frenkel, S. (1977): *Shop Stewards in Action*, Oxford: Blackwell.

Beaumont P.B. (1990): *Change in Industrial Relations — The Organization and Environment*, London: Routledge.

Becker, B. and Olson, C. (1987): "Labour Relations and Firm Performance" in M. Kleiner, R. Block, M. Roomkin and S. Salsburg (eds.), *Human Resources and the Performance of the Firm*, University of Wisconsin: Industrial Relations Research Series.

Becker, B. and Olson, C. (1992): "Unions and Firm Profits" Industrial Relations, 31 (3): 394–415.

Blackburn, R. and Hankinson, A. (1989): "Training in the Smaller Business, Investment or Expense?" *Industrial and Commercial Training*, 21(2): 27–30.

Blyton, P. and Turnbull, P. (1994): *Dynamics of Employee Relations*, London: Macmillan.

Bolton, J.E. (1971): *Report of the Committee of Inquiry on Small Firms*, London: Her Majesty's Stationary Office.

Clarke, I. and Clarke, T. (1991): "Personnel Management, Defence, Retrenchment, Advance?", *Personnel Review*, 20(1): 13–19.

Clarke, P. (1989): "Payment by Results Schemes — A Review of Trends", *IRN*. 8, 23 February.

Connolly, T. (1976): "Some Conceptual and Methodological Issues in Expectancy Models of Work Performance Motivation", *Academy of Management Review*, 1: 37–47.

Cotgrove, S. and Vampley, C. (1972): "Technology, Class and Politics: The Case of Process Workers", *Sociology*, 6.

Curran, J. (1987): *Small Firms and Their Environments, A Report*, Kingston University Small Business Research Unit, Kingston-upon-Thames.

Curran, J. (1989): "Employment and Employment Relations in the Small Firm", Occasional Paper No. 6. Kingston University Small Business Research Unit, Kingston-upon-Thames.

Curran, J. and Stanworth, J. (1979): "The Social Dynamics of the Small Manufacturing Enterprise", *Journal of Management Studies*, 18 (2): 141–157.

Curson, C. (1986): *Flexible Patterns of Work*, London: Institute of Personnel Management.

Cutcher-Gershenfeld, J. and Verma, A. (1994): "Joint Governance Structures in North American Workplaces: A Glimpse of the Future or the End of an Era?" *The International Journal of Human Resource Management*, 5(3): 547–81.

Daley, A. (1989): *Pay and Benefits in Irish Industry*, Dublin: Federated Union of Employers.

Daniel, W. and Millward, N. (1983): *Workplace Industrial Relations in Britain*, Aldershot: Gower.

Dineen, D. (1988): *Employment Developments in the Irish Economy Since 1979*, Limerick: National Institute of Higher Education.

Driver, M., Coffey, R. and Bowen, D. (1988): "Where is HR Management Going?", *Personnel*, 65(1): 28–31.

Dunlop, J. (1958): *Industrial Relations Systems*, New York: Holt.

Dunn, S. (1990): "Root Metaphor in the Old and New Industrial Relations", *British Journal of Industrial Relations*, 28: 1–31.

Dunn, S. and Wright, M. (1994): "Maintaining the 'Status Quo'? An Analysis of the Contents of British Collective Agreements 1979–1990", *British Journal of Industrial Relations*, 31(1): 23–47.

Edwards, P. (1987): *Managing the Factory*, Oxford: Basil Blackwell.

Edwards, P.K. and Whitson, C. (1991): "Workers are Working Harder: Effort and Shop Floor Relations in the 1980s", *British Journal of Industrial Relations*, 29: 593–601.

Elger, T. (1991): "Flexible Futures? New Technology and the Contemporary Transformation of Work", *Work Employment and Society*, 1(4).

Ellig, B. (1989): "Improving Effectiveness through an HR Review", *Personnel*, 66(6): 56–64.

European Observatory for SMEs (1993): *First Annual Report* Co-ordinated by EIM Small Business Research and Consultancy: Zotemeer, Netherlands.

Evans, S., Goodman, J. and Hargreaves, L. (1986): *Unfair Dismissal Law and Employment Practice in the 1980s*, London: Department of Employment Research Paper No. 53.

Fahey, M. (1989): "Personnel Management, How Has it Reacted to Change?", *Industrial Relations News*(22, 8 June.

Farnham, D. and Pimlott, J. (1990): *Understanding Industrial Relations*, London: Cassell.

Fiorito, J., Louman, C. and Nelson, F. (1987): "The Impact of Human Resource Policies on Union Organising", *Industrial Relations*, 26(2): 113–26.

Flanders, A. (1965): *Industrial Relations — What's Wrong with the System?*, London: Faber.

Flinter, D. (1991): "Overseas Industry: the Future Considerations" in A. Foley and D. McAleese, *Overseas Industry in Ireland*, Dublin: Gill and Macmillan.

Flood, P. and Turner, T. (1993): "Shop Stewards in Ireland: A Profile of Union Activists in a General Union", *Irish Business and Administrative Research*, 14(2): 92–101.

Foley, A. (1991): "Interpreting Output Data in Overseas Industry" in A. Foley and D. McAleese, *Overseas Industry in Ireland*, Dublin: Gill and Macmillan.

Foley, K. (1992): *An Examination of Performance Related Pay in The Irish Context,* Unpublished BBS Thesis, University of Limerick.

Fottler, M. and Schaller, F. (1975): "Overtime Acceptance among Blue Collar Workers", *Industrial Relations*, 14(3): 327–36.

Fox, A. (1974): *Beyond Contract: Work, Power and Trust Relations*, London: Faber and Faber.

Freeman, R. and Medoff, J. (1984): *What Do Unions Do?*, New York: Basic Books.

Gershenfeld, J.C. (1991): "The Impact on Economic Performance of a Transformation in Workplace Industrial Relations", *Industrial and Labour Relations Review*, 44(2): 241–60.

Gersury, C. and Kaufman, G. (1985): "Seniority and the Moral Economy of US Automobile Workers, 1934–46", *Journal of Social History*, 18: 463–75.

Gill, D. (1973): *Performance Appraisal in Perspective: A Study of Current Techniques,* London: Institute of Personnel Management.

Gill, D. (1977): *Appraising Performance: Present Trends and the Next Decade,* London: Institute of Personnel Management.

Goldthorpe, J.H., Lockwood, P., Beckhoffer, F. and Platt, J. (1968): *The Affluent Worker: Industrial Attitudes and Behaviour*, Cambridge: Cambridge University Press.

Gorman, L., Hynes, G., McConnell, J. and Moynihan, T. (1975): *Irish Industry: How it's Managed*, Dublin: Irish Management Institute.

Goss, D. (1991): *Small Business and Society,* London: Routledge.

Guest, D. (1987): "Human Resource Management and Industrial Relations", *Journal of Management Studies*, 24(5): 503–21.

Guest, D. (1989): "Human Resource Management, Its Implications for Industrial Relations and Trade Unions" in J. Storey (ed.), *New Perspectives on Human Resource Management*, London: Routledge.

Guest, D. (1990): "Have British Workers been Working Harder in Thatcher's Britain? A Reconsideration of the Concept of Effort", *British Journal of Industrial Relations*, 28: 293–312.

Gunnigle, P. (1989): "Management Approaches to Industrial Relations in the Small Firm" in *Industrial Relations in Ireland*, Dublin: University College Dublin.

Gunnigle, P. (1992): "Human Resource Management in Ireland" *Employee Relations*, 14(5): 5–23.

Gunnigle, P. (1994): "Employee Relations in Greenfield Sites" in P. Gunnigle, P. Flood, M. Morley and T. Turner, *Continuity and Change in Irish Employee Relations*, Dublin: Oak Tree Press.

Gunnigle, P. and Brady, T. (1984): "The Management of Industrial Relations in the Small Firm", *Employee Relations*, 6(5): 21–25.

Gunnigle, P. and Daly, A. (1992): "Craft Integration and Flexible Work Practices: Training Implications", *Industrial and Commercial Training*, 24(10): 10–18.

Gunnigle, P., Flood, P., Morley, M. and Turner, T. (1994): *Continuity and Change in Irish Employee Relations*, Dublin: Oak Tree Press.

Hacket, F. (1990): "Human Resources for 1992, A KPMG Survey", *Industrial Relations News*, 45(29), November: 18–21.

Hawkins, K. (1979): *A Handbook of Industrial Relations Practice*, London: Kogan Page.

Hay Associates, (1975): *Survey of Human Resource Practices*, Dublin: Hay Associates.

Herren, L (1989): "The New Game of HR: Playing to Win", *Personnel,* 66(6): 18–22.

Hill, S. (1981): *Competition and Control at Work*, London: Heinemann.

Hirsch, B.T. and Addison, J.T. (1986): *The Economic Analysis of Unions: New Approaches and Evidence*, Boston: Allen and Unwin.

Hyman, R. (1989): "Dualism and Division in Labour Strategies" in R. Hyman (ed.), *The Political Economy of Industrial Relations*, London: Macmillan.

IDA (1984): Survey of Employee/Industrial Relations in Irish Private Sector Manufacturing Industry, Dublin: Industrial Development Authority.

Ingham, G. (1970): *Size of Industrial Organisation and Worker Behaviour*. Cambridge: University Press .

Irish Small and Medium Enterprise Association (1994): ISME Annual National Wage Survey of Small and Medium-sized Enterprises, Dublin: ISME.

Jick, T.D. (1979): "Mixed Qualitative and Quantitative Methods: Triangulations in Action", *Administrative Science Quarterly*, 24: 602–11.

Katz, H., Kochan, T. and Gobeille, K. (1983): "Industrial Relations Performance, Economic Performance and QWL Programs: An Interplant Analysis", *Industrial and Labour Relations Review*, 30(1): 3–17.

Katz, H., Kochan, T. and Weber, M. (1985): "Assessing the Effects of Industrial Relations Systems and Efforts to Improve the Quality of Working Life on Organisational Effectiveness", *Academy of Management Journal*, 28(3): 509–562.

Katz, H., Kochan, T. and Keeffe, J. (1988): "The Impact of Industrial Relations on Productivity: Evidence from the Automobile Industry", *Brooking Papers on Economic Activity*, 3: 685–715.

Keenan, J. and Thom, A. (1988): "The Future through the Key Hole: Some Thoughts on Employment Patterns", *Personnel Review*, 17(1): 20–24.

Kelly, A. and Brannick, T. (1987): "Strikes in Ireland: Measurement, Incidence and Trends" in *Industrial Relations in Ireland: Contemporary Issues and Developments*, Department of Industrial Relations, University College Dublin.

Kelly, A. and Brannick, T. (1988): "Explaining the Strike-Proneness of British Companies in Ireland", *British Journal of Industrial Relations*, 26(1): 37–55.

Kennedy, K. and Healy, T. (1985): "Small Scale Manufacturing in Ireland", Research Paper No. 125, Dublin: Economic and Social Research Institute.

Kessler, S. (1993): "Procedures and Third Parties", *British Journal of Industrial Relations*, 31(2): 211–25.

Kessler, S. and Bayliss, F. (1992): *Contemporary British Industrial Relations*, Basingstoke: Macmillan.

Kirwan, F. and McGilvray, J. (1983): *Irish Economic Statistics*, Dublin: Institute of Public Administration.

Kleiner, M. (1990): "The Role of Industrial Relations in Industrial Performance" in J. Fossum (ed.), *Employee and Labour Relations*, Washington: The Bureau of National Affairs series.

Knight, K.G. (1989): "Labour Productivity and Strike Activity in British Manufacturing Industries: Some Quantitative Evidence", *British Journal of Industrial Relations*, 27: 365–74.

Kochan, T. (1984): "Strategic Choice and Industrial Relations Theory", *Industrial Relations*, 23: 16–39.

Kochan, T. and Capelli, P. (1984): "Strategic Choice and Industrial Relations Theory", *Industrial Relations*, 23(1): 16–39.

Kochan, T. and Dyer, L. (1979): "A Model of Organisational Change in the Context of Union–Management Relations", *Journal of Applied Behavioural Science*, 12, Spring: 59–78.

Kochan, T, Katz, H.C. and McKersie, R. (1986): *The Transformation of American Industrial Relations*, New York: Basic Books.

Kossek, E. (1990): "Why So Many HR Programs Fail" *Personnel*, 67(5): 50–53.

Lawler, E. (1988): "Human Resource Management, Meeting the New Challenge", *Personnel*, 65(1): 22–7.

Locker, A. and Teel, K. (1977): "Survey of Human Resource Practices", *Personnel Practices*: 245–7.

Lowe, J. (1992): "Locating the Line: The Front Line Supervisor and Human Resource Management", in P. Blyton and P. Turnbull, *Reassessing Human Resource Management*, London: Sage Publications.

McBeath, G. and Rands, N. (1989): *Salary Administration* (fourth edition), London: Gower.

McGovern, P. (1989): "Union Recognition and Union Avoidance in the 1980s" in *Industrial Relations in Ireland: Contemporary Issues and Developments*, Dublin: University College Dublin.

McInnes, J. (1988): "The Question of Flexibility", *Personnel Review*, 17(3): 12–15.

MacKay, L. (1987): "Personnel: Changes Disguising Decline" *Personnel Review*, 16(5): 3–12.

Mac Mahon, J. (1994): *Employee Relations in Small Irish Manufacturing Firms,* Unpublished MBS Thesis, University of Limerick.

MacMahon, J. and Gunnigle P. (1994): *Performance Appraisal: How to Get it Right*, Productive Personnel Ltd. In association with IPM (Ireland).

Mallory, G. and Mollander, C. (1989): "Managing in the Front

Line: The Changing Role of Supervisors" *Journal of General Management*, 14(3): 35–46.

Mann, M. (1973): *Consciousness and Action Among the Western Working Class*, London: Macmillan.

Marchington, M. (1990): "Analysing the Links between Product Markets and the Management of Employees", *Journal of Management Studies*, 27(4): 111–30.

Marchington, M. and Parker, P. (1990): *Changing Patterns of Employee Relations*, Hemel Hempstead: Harvester Wheatsheaf.

Margerison, C.J. (1969): "What Do We Mean by Industrial Relations? A Behavioural Science Approach", *British Journal of Industrial Relations*, 8(2): 273–86.

Marsh, D. (1992): *The New Politics of British Trade Unionism: Union Power and the Thatcher Legacy*, London: Macmillan.

Marshall, R. (1992): "Work Organisation, Unions and Economic Performance" in L. Mishel and P. Voos (eds.), *Unions and Economic Competitiveness*, New York: ME Sharpe Inc.

Mercer, M. (1989): "The HR Department as a Profit Centre". *Personnel*, 66(4): 34–40.

Metcalf, P. (1989): "Trade Unions and Economic Performance: The British Evidence", *LSE Quarterly*, 3: 21–42.

Millward, N., Stevens, M., Smart, D. and Hawes, W.R. (1992): *Workplace Industrial Relations in Transition*, Aldershot: Gower.

Mitchell, J. and Saidi, M. (1991): "International Pressures on Industrial Relations: Macroeconomics and Social Concertation" in T. Treu (ed.), *Participation in Public Policy Making: The Role of Trade Unions and Employer Associations*, Berlin: De Gruyter.

Mitchell, T. (1974): "Expectancy Models of Job Satisfaction, Occupational Preference and Effort: A Theoretical, Methodological and Empirical Analysis", *Psychological Bulletin*, 81: 1053–77.

Monks, K. (1992): "Models of Personnel Management: A Means of Understanding the Diversity of Personnel Practices", *Human Resource Management Journal*, 2(2).

Mooney, P. (1992): "What's New in HRM? An A to Z of Emerging Practices", *Industrial Relations News*, 43, November: 14–21.

Murphy, T. (1981): "The Union Committee of the Workplace: A

Case Analysis of Its Role, Activities and Influence in Union Decision Making", *Irish Business and Administrative Research*, 13(2): 56–70.

O'Brien, J. (1989): "Pay Determination in Ireland", in *Industrial Relations in Ireland: Contemporary Issues and Developments*, Dublin: University College Dublin.

O'Farrell, P. (1986): *Entrepreneurs and Industrial Change*, Dublin: Irish Management Institute.

Ost, E.(1990): "Team-Based Pay: New Wave Incentives", *Sloan Management Review*, 31(3): 19–29.

Oster, S. (1990): *Modern Competitive Analysis,* London: Oxford University Press.

Pfeffer, J. (1982): *Organisations and Organisational Theory*, Boston, MA: Pitman.

Priore, M. and Sabel, C. (1984): *The Second Industrial Divide: Prospects for Prosperity*, New York: Basic Books.

Porter, M.E. (1985): *Competitive Advantage: Creating and Sustaining Superior Performance*, New York: Free Press.

Purcell, J. (1981): *Good Industrial Relations: Theory and Practice*, London: Macmillan.

Rainnie, A. (1989): *Industrial Relations in Small Firms, Small Isn't Beautiful*, London: Routledge.

Rainnie, A. and Scott, M. (1986): "Industrial Relations in Small Firms" in J. Curran (ed.), *The Survival of the Small Firm,* Vol. 2, Aldershot: Gower.

Ramsay, H. (1975): "Firms and Football Teams", *British Journal of Industrial Relations*, 13(3): 396–400.

Ramsay, H., Hyman, J., Baddon, L., Hunter, L. and Leopold, J. (1990): "Options for Workers: Owner or Employee?" in G. Jenkins and M. Poole (eds.), *New Forms of Ownership*, London: Routledge.

Reddy, W. (1984): *The Rise of Market Culture*, New York: Cambridge University Press.

Report of the Commission of Inquiry on Industrial Relations (1981): Dublin: Government Publication Office.

Report of the Royal Commission on Trade Unions and Employers' Associations (1968): London: Her Majesty's Stationary Office.

Reynolds Allen, K. (1991): How Middle Managers View the Function", *Personnel Management*, June: 40–43.

Rhodeback, M. (1991): "Embrace the Bottom Line" *Personnel Journal*, 70(5): 53–9.

Roche, W. (1986): "Systems Analysis and Industrial Relations: Double Paradox in the Development of American and British Industrial Relations Theory", *Economic and Industrial Democracy*, 7: 3–28.

Roche, W. and Turner, T. (1994): "Testing Alternative Models of Human Resource Policy Effects on Trade Union Recognition in the Republic of Ireland", *The International Journal of Human Resource Management*, 5(3): 721–55.

Roche, W. and Larraghy, J. (1990): "Cyclical and Institutional Determinants of Annual Trade Union Growth and Decline in Ireland: Evidence from the Dues Data Series", *European Sociological Review*, 6(1): 49–72.

Rose, M. (1988): *Industrial Behaviour: Research and Control*, London: Penguin Books.

Rose, M. (1993): "Trade Unions — Ruin, Retreat or Rally?" (Review Article), *Work, Employment and Society*, 7(2): 291–311.

Ruane, F. and McGibney, A. (1991): "The Performance of Overseas Industry, 1973–1989" in A. Foley and D. McAleese, *Overseas Industry in Ireland*, Dublin: Gill and Macmillan.

Rubery, J. and Wilkinson, F. (1994): "Introduction" in J. Rubery and F. Wilkinson, *Employer Strategy and the Labour Market*, Oxford: Oxford University Press.

Salamon, N. (1987): *Industrial Relations: Theory and Practice*, Englewood Cliffs, NJ: Prentice Hall.

Schuler, R. (1988): "Organisational Strategy and Organisation Level as Determinants of Human Resource Management Practices", *Human Resource Planning*, 10(3): 125–41.

Schuster (1984): "Co-operation and Change in Union Settings: Problems and Opportunities", *Human Resource Management*, 23(2): 145–60.

Schuster, M. (1985): "Models of Co-operation and Change in Union Settings", *Industrial Relations*, 24(3): 382–94.

Schuster, M. (1990): "Union Management Co-operation", in J. Fossum (ed.), *Employee and Labour Relations*, Washington: The Bureau of National Affairs series.

Scott, M., Roberts, I., Holroyd, G. and Sawbridge, D. (1989): "Management and Industrial Relations in Small Firms", London: Department of Employment, Research Paper No.70.

Sengenberger, W., Loveman, G. and Piore, M.J. (1990): *Re-emergence of Small Enterprises: Industrial Restructuring in Industrialised Countries*, Geneva: International Labour Office.

Shivanath, G. (1986): *Personnel Practitioners, Their Role and Status in Irish Industry* ,Unpublished MBS Thesis, University of Limerick.

Smith, P. and Morton, G. (1990): "A Change of Heart: Union, Exclusion in the Provincial Newspaper Sector", *Work, Employment and Society*, 4: 105–24.

Smith, P. and Morton, G. (1993): "Union Exclusion and the De-collectivisation of Industrial Relations in Great Britain", *British Journal of Industrial Relations*, 31(1): 97–114.

Smith, P. and Morton, G. (1994): "Union Exclusion in Britain — Next Steps", *Industrial Relations Journal*, 25(1): 3–14.

Stanworth, J. (ed.) (1991): *Bolton 20 Years On: The Small Firm in The 1990's* , London: Paul Chapman.

Steers, R. and Porter, L. (1987): *Motivation and Work Behaviour*, New York: McGraw-Hill.

Storey, J. (ed.) (1989): *New Perspectives on Human Resource Management*, London: Routledge.

Storey, J. (1992): *Developments in the Management of Human Resources*, Oxford: Blackwell Business.

Storey, D.J. (1990): "Firm Performance and Size" in Z.J. Acs, *The Economics of Small Firms: A European Challenge,* London: Kluwer .

Streeck, W. (1992): "Training and the New Industrial Relations: A Strategic Role for Unions?" in M. Regini (ed.), *The Future of Labour Movements*, London: Sage

Tailby, S. and Whitson, C. (1989): "Industrial Relations and Re-structuring" in S. Tailby and C. Whitson (eds.), *Manufacturing Change: Industrial Relations and Restructuring*, Oxford: Blackwell.

Task Force on Small Business (1994): *Report of the Task Force on Small Business*, Dublin: Government Stationery Office.

Terry, M. (1986): "How Do We Know if Shop Stewards are Getting Weaker?", *British Journal of Industrial Relations*, 24(2): 169–79.

Terry, M. (1989): "Recontextualising Shopfloor Industrial Relations" in S. Tailby and C. Whitson (eds.), *Manufacturing*

Change, Oxford: Basil Blackwell.

Terry, M. and Edwards, P.K. (1988): *Shop Floor Politics and Controls*, Oxford: Basil Blackwell.

Thomason, G. (1984): *A Textbook of Industrial Relations*, London: Institute of Personnel Management.

Thompson, E.P. (1991): *Customs in Common*, London: Merlin.

Thurley, K. and Wood, S. (1983): *Industrial Relations and Management Strategy*, Cambridge: Cambridge University Press.

Todd, O.J. (1979): "Mixing Qualitative and Quantitative Methods: Triangulation in Action", *Administrative Science Quarterly*, 24: 602–11.

Turner, T. (1994): "Unionisation and Human Resource Management in Irish Companies", *Industrial Relations Journal*, 25(1): 39–51.

Tyson, S. (1987): "The Management of the Personnel Function". *Journal of Management Studies,* 24(5): 523–33.

Tyson, S. and Fell, A. (1986): *Evaluating the Personnel Function*, London: Hutchinson.

Vroom, V. (1964): *Work and Motivation*, New York: John Wiley.

Wadhwani, S. (1990): "The Effects of Unions on Productivity Growth, Investment and Employment: A Report on Some Recent Work", *British Journal of Industrial Relations*, 28(3): 371–85.

Wallace, J. (1982): "Industrial Relations in Limerick City and Environs", *Employment Research Programme Final Report*, 3, University of Limerick.

Wallace, J. (1989): "Procedure Agreements and Their Place in Workforce Industrial Relations" in *Industrial Relations in Ireland: Contemporary Issues and Developments*, Dublin: University College Dublin.

Wallace, J. (1991): "Industrial Relations Act, 1990 and Other Developments in Irish Labour", Paper presented to the Institute of Personnel Management, University of Limerick.

Wallace, J. and O'Shea, F. (1987): *A Study of Unofficial Strikes in Ireland*, Limerick: College of Business, University of Limerick.

Walton, R.E. (1985): "Towards a Strategy of Eliciting Employee Commitment Based on Policies of Mutuality" in R.E. Walton, and P.R. Lawrence (eds.), *Human Resource Management:*

Trends and Challenges, Boston, MA: Harvard Business School Press.

Walton, R.E. and McKersie, R.B. (1965): *A Behavioural Theory of Labour Negotiations*, New York: McGraw-Hill.

Wedderburn, D. and Crampton, R. (1972): *Workers' Attitudes and Technology*, Cambridge: Cambridge University Press.

Whelan, C. (1982): Worker Priorities, Trust in Management and Prospects for Workers Participation, Paper No. 111, Dublin: Economic and Social Research Institute.

Williams, J. and Whelan, B. (1986): *Employers' Perceptions of the Effects of Labour Legislation*, Report commissioned by the Department of Labour, Dublin: Government Stationery Office.

Wilson, B. (1988): "Employee Relations — A Future-Oriented, Progressive Approach", *Employee Relations*, 10(4): 27–30.

Winch, G. (1981): "Shop Steward Tenure and Workplace Organisation", *Industrial Relations Journal*, 11(4): 50–62.

Woods, S., Wagner, A., Armstrong, E.G.A., Goodman, J.B.F. and Davis, J.E. (1975): "The 'Industrial Relations System' Concept as a Basis for Theory in Industrial Relations", *British Journal of Industrial Relations,* 13(3): 291–308.